Censorship:
The Search for
the Obscene

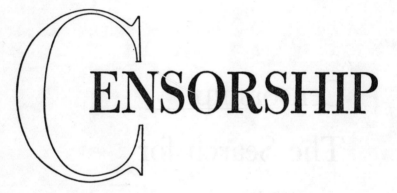

CENSORSHIP

By the Same Authors—PRIVACY: The Right to Be Let Alone

THE MACMILLAN COMPANY, NEW YORK

Some Etymological Facts and Guesses About Judicial Language

Licentious
Latin *licere,* to be permitted. Excessive assumption of liberty. Unrestrained by law, decorum, or morality. Lax, immoral. Disregarding restraints of chastity. Libertine, lascivious, lewd.

Lustful
Teutonic. Lust originally meant pleasure, delight. To long for. A lust-house was a country villa.

Obscene
Latin *obscaenus,* adverse, inauspicious, ill-omened. Later meaning: disgusting, filthy, indecent. Etymology doubtful.

Prurient
Itching: Latin *prurire,* physical itch. Later: lewd ideas, impure itch for . . .

Scurrility
Latin *scurrilis,* from *scurra,* buffoon. The quality of being scurrilous; buffoon-like jocularity; coarseness or indecency of language, especially in invective and jesting.

Margaret S. Ernst, author of *In a Word* and *More About Words.*

MILESTONES OF LAW SERIES

The Search for the Obscene

by Morris L. Ernst and Alan U. Schwartz

WITH AN INTRODUCTION BY PHILIP SCHARPER

COLLIER-MACMILLAN LIMITED, LONDON

First Printing

Printed in the United States of America

The Macmillan Company, New York
Collier-Macmillan Canada, Ltd., Toronto, Ontario

Library of Congress catalog card number: 64-17597

For Margaret and Paula

EDITORIAL NOTE

Since this volume, like the first in the series, *Privacy,* is intended primarily for nonlawyers, we have attempted to delete esoteric legalisms wherever possible and to reduce opinions to terms that are comprehensible to the layman. Judicial language is therefore often shortened and sometimes paraphrased, references to other cases have been deleted, and much of the collateral phraseology of the opinions, which lawyers call "dicta," has been removed. For the sake of clarity, all judicial opinions and legal articles have been indented and set off at the left by margin lines. The headings, where they appear, are inventions of our own.

M. L. E.
A. U. S.

Contents

PART III   THE LAW IN SEARCH OF REMEDIES

PART IV   OBSCENITY AND THE CONSTITUTION

PART V   THE SOCIAL PROBLEM

Introduction

When Plato wrote that poets should be banished from his ideal Republic, he based his magisterial action on grounds that have been repeated by the censorious ever since: the poets taught false ideas about the gods, and the poets corrupted youth. Implicit in Plato's reasoning were two premises that have also been adopted by the censorious of every subsequent age: literature of its very nature is didactic, and the youthful reader of literature is affected, all but mechanically, by what he reads.

The irony of the history of censorship in the West is this: too often those who have welcomed the censor for Plato's reasons have been forced to accept Plato's premises. Thus—to cite but one example— where a St. Augustine could express his reverence for pagan writers like Vergil and Cicero, Roman Catholic educators after the Renaissance often could not, with easy conscience, teach Milton's *Paradise Lost* because the author was a Protestant. The psychological premise beneath the pedagogical practice was that of Plato: the poet sings of error more sweetly and more suasively than the theologian can possibly proclaim the truth.

The opposite, more modern, view is equally misguided and, if anything, ultimately more corrosive, for it holds, implicitly, that literature has no effect whatsoever upon the reader. Hence it is, even at best, an idle pastime holding the mirror up, not to nature, but to the individual reader. Caliban, in such a mirror, will see only Caliban, and Miranda see only Miranda—whether the mirror be labeled *Tropic of Cancer* or *Idylls of the King*.

There is a further irony in this: that while the censor holds his post as guardian of "orthodoxy," his nay has frequently served to keep undiscovered and undisclosed the organic growth and expanding relevance of orthodox teaching. In religious terms, one can but note the irony that the writings of Thomas Aquinas were burned in his lifetime by his fellow Dominicans; in military terms, one notes the court-martial of General "Billy" Mitchell for proposing a better way to defend the very country which his judges were pledged to defend with their lives.

In short, no matter how justified it may be in principle under sharply limited circumstances, in practice censorship is no better than the censors—and censors, all too often, have betrayed their trust and thereby called the principle itself into disrepute. The policeman on the beat is rarely a moral theologian; the sheriff rarely a clinical psychologist; the censorious priest or pastor rarely a literary critic or even a devotee of the arts; the official guardian of orthodoxy's garden too often cannot distinguish between mushrooms and toadstools.

These are but some of the reflections to which the reader is stimulated by the wise, witty, and sometimes rueful book which Morris Ernst and Alan Schwartz have put together with the patience of a tapestry weaver and the selective eye of the artist.

Because they are lawyers—and justly esteemed lawyers—both these gentlemen may bristle at the comparison of themselves to artisans or artists. But the reader fortunate enough to buy, beg, borrow, or steal this book will soon recognize that the authors are uncommon lawyers, whose ability to carve through the bolus of legal language bears at least a supportable comparison to the ability of a Michelangelo to draw forth a David from a mass of stone.

By their patient scholarship and balanced judgments Messrs. Ernst and Schwartz carve into relief one aspect of legal censorship—that dealing with obscenity. The problem—whether we realize it or not—touches each of us, for we are, as citizens, parents, and civilized human beings, involved in what the courts decide may or may not be made available to the eyes and ears of ourselves and our children, among whom are the artists as well as the art audience of the future.

And at the very heart of the censorship tangle lies the question of freedom—freedom to create in fidelity to the artist's vision, and freedom to share in the vision of the artist if we choose. Almost every great literary artist has been frowned on or frozen out by some official censor at some time or another—precisely because the artist is an eye among the blind, most of whom think darkness light enough. The struggle against censorship recorded in these pages has been a struggle against those forces—often massively official—which would limit the freedom of artist and art audience to the type of work considered unharmful to the judge or police chief's sixteen-year-old daughter.

Reading and viewing are among the principal educational instruments by which we develop that freedom which alone makes maturity possible, and that maturity which alone makes freedom meaningful. It is this realization—as old as recorded Western thought—which shines through the pages of Morris Ernst and Alan Schwartz. They have written a civilized book, in all the connotations of that abused adjective. They have written it from a sense of civic duty, and the reading of it becomes just such a duty for parents and educators as well as for jurists and publishers.

PHILIP SCHARPER

President, The Religious Education
Association of the United States and Canada

Foreword

There can be no peaceful world without some system for the settlement of disputes between man and man, and man and his sovereign —whether city, state, or nation. This arrangement, called Law, is known in our terms to only a small minority of the three billion inhabitants of our world.

Our exercise in law is understandably quite unlike the decision-making decrees under dictatorships, and it has little resemblance to tribal justice. Law among the millions of men and women who as yet have no written language rests on different assumptions than does law in our Republic.

With us the improvement and perfection of the legal process depends to a great extent on an understanding by nonlawyers of the process of arriving at truth through the use of advocates in quiet chambers called courtrooms.

To the extent that law is a mystery, judges and lawyers capitalize on the chasm existing between the public and the officials who operate the legal system. Moreover, we suggest that the public, losing faith in courtrooms, increasingly chooses to "win" on open picket lines or, by secret operations, hopes to gain decisions by emotion and power rather than by rational thought.

In our small towns a constant concern for and familiarity with the law is possible because the knowledge is at firsthand and not exclusively by way of the mass media, which increasingly report with emphasis only the worst of the news, believing that, to invert a legend, Good News Is No News.

In general, our public is kept ignorant of the ordinary difficulties of searching for truth in areas of human conflict. Judges write for lawyers, and lawyers seek to impress their clients. Such are the ways of experts—doctors' prescriptions unreadable by patients, churchmen intoning their dogmas in Latin, and so on.

As lawyers and writers, we are confident that Law can be made intelligible to the laity—can, in fact, be shown to be the fascinating and exciting subject it is. For this reason we agreed to edit the Macmillan "Milestones of Law" Series. The first volume dealt with the Law of Privacy, or the right to be let alone. This new volume treats with the Law of the Obscene—its origins in our culture, the forces that shaped and are still shaping it, and above all, the pivotal opinions —pro and con—rendered by judges high and low.

In writing this book we had to select from hundreds of cases. Other lawyers might well have chosen other skirmishes and battles between the censorious and the unshockable, but we have concentrated on the ones that seemed most significant, most interesting, or both.

David Loth, author of *The Erotic in Literature,* gave us valued editorial aid, and we are also in debt to our wise editor, Al Hart, and to Margaret E. Ernst, author of *In a Word* and *More About Words,* for her gay endpaper etymologies.

MORRIS L. ERNST
ALAN U. SCHWARTZ

Monomoy-Surfside-Nantucket, 1963

part I

Before

Comstock

1
Our
Sexual
Folkway

Lord Byron wrote: "What men call gallantry and the Gods adultery is far more common where the climate's sultry."

The scientific validity of this isotherm theory of sexual behavior is still being debated. And it is only one of the many explanations for man's activities in this field. But it is in these explanations that we must look for an understanding of laws that deal with the sexual. The so-called "obscene" in our society has many changing aspects, but its very vagaries, paradoxes, and anomalies were and are implicit in the conflicting and varied sexual patchwork quilt that covers our couches. We are justly proud of our racial and cultural melting pot, but a brew such as ours has varied genetic spices that are reflected in the laws we create.

First, a brief glance at the laws of two ancient cultures that have greatly influenced the lives of our people—the Judaic and the Grecian. From them we can see in democratic terms how rules of society or laws are created. Perhaps they derive not so much from abstract philosophy as from the condition of the soil, the size of the population, the state of the economy.

Despite the figures in the Book of Numbers, it has been recently estimated that the Jewish population that left Egypt with Moses was about 3,600—very small compared to the productive potential of their acres in the Promised Land, and inadequate in proportion to the enemies at their borders. Hence it became the way of life among the Jews, written into their laws and Bible, to frown upon and forbid all sexual relations and attitudes that would tend to limit the population. What the Jews needed was more people; thus, Solomon with his thousand wives and concubines, a real bit of extreme polygamy, was held up for admiration. On the other hand, the Hebrew ethic and law condemned adultery, onanism, masturbation, homosexuality, and all other practices unlikely to produce offspring and thereby give more fighting strength to the tiny tribes of Israel.

It was not much later that the Greek culture reached its fabulous heights. The Greeks possessed a large population for their relatively small land. We may surmise that they did not want a population explosion. Accordingly, their law condoned sexual relations such as homosexuality and lesbianism, which could not possibly produce offspring. Thus we read of Sappho and the prestige of Lesbia. Male homosexuals held positions of highest esteem. There was no legal prohibition of adultery or fornication because, in some way that we have not yet been able to discern, it was recognized that mistresses were not so likely to become pregnant as were wives.

The Greeks went further—they condoned infanticide. This may seem shocking, but it is a practice not confined to antiquity. According to a recent study, about two decades ago seventeen thousand girl babies were left in the fields to die in one state in India. The motivation in both cultures was similiar. In a society that dooms surplus people to a lifetime of utter misery, it is perhaps kindness rather than cruelty to make the lifetime brief. Girls are selected for infanticide because they cannot produce so much in the fields as boys, because they must be furnished with dowries if they are to marry, and because they would then add still more to the surplus population.

The Greeks and the Jews illustrate one way that laws relating to sex take root. Similar influences may explain our own. In New England, for example, a relatively few colonists seeking to establish prosperous communities on a rocky soil had to put great store by hard work. They professed to live by the proverb "Satan makes mischief for idle hands." At the same time, the great scarcity of women throughout the early migratory colonial period helped to create the rules laid down for the conduct of a man and a maid. Long before

1700, in Connecticut, young men were forbidden to "draw away" the affection of a maid under pretense of marriage without the permission of her parents or the nearest magistrate. Injunctions were issued to restrain such "drawing away of affection," which is not quite a synonym for the modern "alienation of affection" or "seduction." A case is recorded of one Jacob and one Sarah of New Haven who had meetings "not for prayer or fasting," but "his arm was around her and her arm upon his shoulder or about his neck," and "hee kissed her and shee kissed him," maintaining this posture for about half an hour. "Guilty!" the court ruled.

There were many examples of a caste system of romance, but always with a joinder of antisex and propriety. Servant girls mainly were the ones brought into court for folding their hair, "frizzling," and wearing silk scarves. A governor of Massachusetts decreed that the wearing of long hair was contrary, not to taste, if you please, but to God's Word.

Within a dozen years of the first landings of the pilgrims, flirtation became so serious a problem that laws were passed to regulate the menace. In an entrancing volume, *The Not-Quite Puritans,* Henry W. Lawrence refers to no fewer than sixty-six *confessions* to premarital fornication in one small city between 1761 and 1775.

The symbol of the sexual behavior of the churchly Protestant New Englander may well have been "bundling" or "tarrying," a practice imported from Wales. It was quite proper for a courting man and woman to lie together or sleep together in the same bed without undressing, spiritually purified by a dividing piece of wood called a bundling board.

One could list thousands of such instances of compromise or contradiction between prudery and practice. Law was jittery and unsure of itself. The exhortations of the clergy had little effect. As is still the case in small communities, temptations were great but the opportunities for privacy were few. Such a combination spurs man's chicanery and hypocrisy. So the Church preached one code and the lads and lasses, with the light hearts of "cheaters," lived by another.

The excess of these "blue laws" is evidence of the distress of the moral leaders. "No woman shall kiss her child on the Sabbath or Fasting Days" or "make minced Pies" or "play any instrument of music except the drum, the trumpet or the jew's harp." These are sex-directed regulations, although no one has identified the sexual significance of minced pies as against other pies (except perhaps the spices and the brandy!).

There was no limit to the worry and delights of the sexually censorious. Around 1650, in one town a young bachelor was forbidden to keep house, although by 1652 bachelors were granted special permission to keep house together but not to entertain idle persons "to the evil expense of time by day or night."

A century before the Revolution, in one county, penal offenses listed included: fornication, 34; debt, 32; living away from wife, 5; running away from master, 4. The punishments were severe—the lash, the stocks, the jail. These statistics are relatively high; Philadelphia at the time of the Revolution was our largest city, with an estimated 30,000 people. The colonies were run on a caste system—slaves, indentured servants, freemen, landowners, literate aristocrats—and there were clearly defined categories of sexual behavior for the different castes.

Since psychology now recognizes a relation between sadism and sexual pleasure, we can understand the cruel penalties that were inflicted upon those who strayed into forbidden areas—often the public display of the culprit in the marketplace for the satisfaction of the smirking innocent and the uncaught guilty—just as today we play up executions on the front pages of our daily press.

We suggest that the colonists were seeking comfortable sexual mores, in terms of religious precepts and law, for many reasons but above all because there were fewer women than men. History shows that migrations of men without their women produce problems of sexual drive not unrelated to the economics of scarcity. But polyandry could not be the answer in the world of most of our pioneers because religion strongly forbade it. Colonial culture, a truly great force for a higher standard of living, carried alongside its economic ambition stern rules of sexual conduct that, however, could not be attained by "example" or "exhortation." The result was an embarrassing gap between preaching and practice, violations not dissimilar to those during the "Noble Experiment," as Herbert Hoover called the Prohibition Era of this century in the United States. Custom, like law, can help educate a people or bend a folkway, but its scope has limits that, if exceeded, create cynicism and ultimately mass violation.

The stream of religious influence touching on sexual mores has been persistently misconstrued, so that much of it is attributed to the impact of the Roman Catholic Church. If we had traveled by coach as our ancestors did over the rutted roads from Maine southward in our formative years as a nation, we would have found scant Catholic influence. We would have met instead the influence of the New Amsterdamers, the Quakers of William Penn, the literate, aristocratic slaveowning tribe of Freethinkers in Virginia—some censorious, some not. Sexual behavior varied from the harsh Maine coast to the extravagance of the lush soil and sun of the St. James River, but, by and large, Protestants made the rules.

Throughout the colonial era and well into the first century of our national independence, although antisexual mores were emphasized, there was scant feeling in any of these communities for the need of a law to curb the expression of ideas about sex, that is, a law to censor so-called obscenity. This was just as true in Puritan New England and Quaker Pennsylvania (where no one worried about Ben Franklin's several recognized but illegitimate children) as in Virginia. The control of obscenity in print did not get into our law until a generation or more after the Thirteen Colonies became a nation.

We can only wonder at the possible influences that kept censorship of sex ideas from sprouting from the roots of our law in early times. Certainly it was not because indecent writing or indecent pictures were unknown. The most famous American of that day, and one of the most versatile of any day, Franklin, was also American's best-known writer. He had penned ribaldries of high literary merit as far back as the 1740's but, although America's leading printer, he did not publish them. His "Advice to a Young Man on Choosing a Mistress," "Speech of Polly Baker," and "Letter to the Royal Academy at Brussels" were circulated exclusively among friends, (except for "Polly Baker," which two of Franklin's scientific friends in London gave to a British magazine without his knowledge).

This was the situation when delegates from the new states assembled at Philadelphia in 1787 to try to form a single nation. Forty-two of them remained until the last day, September 15th, enduring four months of secret debate presided over by George Washington and the sage Franklin, who was past eighty; invigorated by several under thirty, and architected by James Madison, who kept the most complete notes we have of what was said.

During the great debates not a word was uttered about the basic problems of freedom of the press, of speech, even of religion. No one talked of obscenity. These literate, cultured gentlemen lived in a land of about 4,000,000 population (England had about 8,000,000) where free public education was still unknown and literacy, therefore, a matter of privilege.

The then radicals, such as Sam Adams, Jefferson, Tom Paine, and Patrick Henry, were not among the delegates, but their influence was promptly felt when the draft of the Constitution was submitted for approval to the people in the thirteen states. The draft was accepted by a close vote, although in Philadelphia and elsewhere police were needed to assure a quorum on the adoption vote. Even so, the document would not have been accepted by the quarter of a million who could vote if the radicals had not made what in effect was the first great political trade in our history: The Constitution would be approved if safeguards for certain of their basic ideas were added in the form of amendments. These ten amendments became known as the Bill of Rights, and the matrix of our national experiment is in the First Amendment, which reads:

"Congress shall make no law respecting an establishment of religion, or prohibiting the free exercise thereof; or abridging the freedom of speech or of the press . . ."

Note the joinder of religion and free speech. Note also the first words: "Congress shall make no law . . ." All that the proponents of the Bill of Rights meant was to express their fear of the new Union. They wanted to be very sure that this new United Nation of 1787 would not butt in on the censor business, a business to be reserved to the separate states. The prevalent fear was of national government. The authors of these amendments did not declare, "There shall be no restraint on freedom of the press." In fact, they favored such restraint.

That none of the Founding Fathers mentioned obscenity was not because of ignorance of censorship by law. Many of them were familiar with English law and precedents. Some were aware of censorship in other countries because many colonists had been drawn from the unorthodox of different lands. They knew full well about the censorship powers of the faculties of medieval universities. Even in the sixteenth century this power lay with the universities of Oxford and Cambridge in England, the Sorbonne in Paris, the Berlin Academy of Sciences in Prussia, the University of Padua in the Venetian Republic, the University of Munich in Bavaria. On the Continent, these controls often were entrusted to Colleges of Censors, sometimes attached to "Commissioners on Heresy." American colonists were familiar with the shift of this control in England from the universities to a Stationers' Company founded in 1557. This company had the monopoly of the press to curtail "mischievous printers and authors." Later the licensing of printed matter was taken over by the government itself.

To preserve a proper perspective, we should note that the British system was copied from Venice and the Paris Syndic. Furthermore, in all these countries literacy was very limited, and the controls were designed to prevent unorthodox and unpopular expressions of political or religious opinion. Not until literacy began to spread in England was there any atttempt to apply controls to obscenity.

The first attempt failed. This was in 1708 when an English judge decided, without shocking the public in the least, that a book entitled *The Fyfteen Plagues of a Maidenhead* was not indictable for obscenity at common law. ("Common law" is the body of English law [which we inherited] that is not embodied in statutes but is created by judges to meet various needs. It was called "common" because it was common to all England, not like the local laws or customs that applied only to a particular area.) The judge went so far as to explain that if there was any offense in the book it was only a spiritual one, to be dealt with in the ecclesiastical courts which still had control over moral sins from adultery to swearing. That the common law was not immutable was proved when in 1725 another judge ruled that there was such a crime as publishing obscenity and that Richard Curl had committed it by issuing a volume called *Venus in the Cloister, or the Nun in Her Smock*. Appeals courts upheld the conviction, and by the time of the American War of Independence there had been several other convictions of pornographers under this common-law ruling.

John Wilkes, of political fame, got into trouble in 1768 through "An Essay on Women" and "The Maiden's Prayer," although these writings were prosecuted for impiety, not obscenity. Throughout these earliest English precedents there is a strong link between the prosecution for obscenity and the fear of blasphemy or sedition, mostly blasphemy.

The educated colonists knew about all this. Why, then, we ask again, did we not have statutory censorship laws until the nineteenth century? There is of course no clear answer to this question. As we have seen, the lack of Federal legislation in this field can be traced in part to the First Amendment prohibition on Federal interference with freedom of speech and press. But the First Amendment did not, in those days, apply to the states. What, then, made our colonies, and later the states, legislatively so abstemious in this area? Well, not even our own Supreme Court can agree on the reasons. Some judges think that the colonial lawmakers felt that judge-made law was sufficient in the field of censorship and that statutes would be superfluous. This view is tolerable—but perhaps hard to justify in view of the few instances of such "judge-made law." Other judges say that no statutes were passed in these early times because colonial peoples felt that this was a matter of religion and culture, rather than of law, and that obscene behavior could be adequately dealt with at nonlegal levels. Perhaps; perhaps not—and you can take your choice. The one fact that is clear from all this is that for over a century the governments of our colonies and then our Republic kept their hands off the censorship of obscenity—without visible impairment of national or local morals. The importance of this fact will become evident later in this volume as debates pro and con censorship fill our judicial records.

It was almost a full century after the English example before the courts in our nation were called upon to consider whether or not obscenity was a proper matter for the Law to punish. This was in 1815, just after the close of our second war with the British, when the country was vastly enlarged by the Louisiana Purchase, with six new states added to the original thirteen, when the population had more than doubled to over 8,000,000, and above all when literacy was slowly rising, although a law of compulsory school attendance was still thirty-seven years away.

2

Early Cases

Against this background of illiteracy, it is not surprising that our first obscenity case concerned not a piece of writing but a picture. Was this because the enforcers of law supposed that pictorial obscenity would corrupt the illiterate more easily than the educated? Did they already believe that a picture was more effective than a thousand words?

There was an ideological merger of the law of outrage to religion, or blasphemy, and offenses against sexual decencies. But the law was invoked for the first time partly at least because of an additional motive, the desire to keep the peace or, as it was called, the "dignity" of the community. It is interesting, too, that this first case arose in the country's largest city, Philadelphia, before there was any statute on the books to cover the offense. We insert here, in a form that now seems quaint, a page from the original decision against certain "yeomen" in Philadelphia. The "certiorari" that brought the matter to the Supreme Court of the state is a legal term for an order by which a certified copy of proceedings in a lower court is brought before a higher court for review.

CASES

IN THE

SUPREME COURT

OF

PENNSYLVANIA.

EASTERN DISTRICT, DECEMBER TERM, 1815.

Wednesday,
December 20.

The Commonwealth *against* SHARPLESS and others.

Any offence which in its nature and by its example, tends to the corruption of morals, as the *exhibition of an obscene picture,* is indictable at common law.
In an indictment for exhibiting an obscene picture, it need not be averred, that the exhibition was *public;* if it be stated, that the picture was shewn to sundry persons for money, it is a sufficient averment of its *publication.*
Nor is it necessary that

THE following indictment was found in the Mayor's Court of the city of *Philadelphia,* and removed to this Court by *certiorari.*

" MARCH SESSIONS, 1815.

" City of *Philadelphia,* ss.

" The Grand Inquest of the Commonwealth of *Pennsylva-*
" *nia,* inquiring for the city of *Philadelphia,* upon their oaths
" and affirmations respectively do present, that *Jesse Sharp-*
" *less,* late of the same city yeoman, *John Haines,* late of the
" same city yeoman, *George Haines,* late of the same city yeo-
" man, *John Steel,* late of the same city yeoman, *Ephraim*
" *Martin,* late of the same city yeoman, and —— *Mayo,* also
" late of the same city yeoman, being evil disposed persons,
" and designing, contriving, and intending the morals, as well
" of youth as of divers other citizens of this commonwealth,
" to debauch and corrupt, and to raise and create in their
" minds inordinate and lustful desires, on the first day of
" *March,* in the year one thousand eight hundred and fifteen,

the postures and attitudes of the figures should be minutely described; it is enough if the picture be so described as to enable the jury to apply the evidence, and to judge, whether or not it is an indecent picture.
Nor is it necessary to lay the house, in which the picture is exhibited, to be a *nuisance;* the offence not being a nuisance, but one tending to the corruption of morals.

"at the city aforesaid, and within the jurisdiction of this
" Court, in a *certain house* there situate, unlawfully, wicked-
" ly, and scandalously *did exhibit, and show for money, to*
" *persons, to the inquest aforesaid unknown, a certain lewd,*
" *wicked, scandalous, infamous, and obscene painting, repre-*
" *senting a man in an obscene, impudent, and indecent posture*
" *with a woman,* to the manifest corruption and subversion
" of youth, and other citizens of this commonwealth, to the
" evil example of all others in like case offending, and against
" the peace and dignity of the commonwealth of *Pennsyl-*
" *vania.*"

The law was certainly going through its early birth pangs. The charge was a fumbling one, as you can see. England had struggled with the idea that ecclesiastical courts had ruled on "sin"—not only crime—and here Sharpless was charged with exhibiting for money a picture of a man in an "impudent" posture with a woman. People were worried about the creation of "inordinate" desires. The picture was not preserved in the court record, but, as the judge wrote:

There is no act punishing the offence charged against these offenders, and therefore the case must be decided upon the judge-made principles. That actions against PUBLIC DECENCY were always crimes, as tending to corrupt the public morals, I can have no doubt; because, even in the profligate reign of Charles II SIR CHARLES SEDLEY was punished by imprisonment and a heavy fine, for standing naked in a balcony, in a public part of the city of LONDON. It is true, that, besides this shameful exhibition, it is mentioned in some of the reports of that case, that he threw down bottles, containing offensive liquor, among the people; but we have the highest authority for saying, that the most criminal part of his conduct and that which principally drew upon him the vengeance of the law, was the EXPOSURE OF HIS PERSON.

The courts enjoyed trying to assume the role of guardian of public morals even though Jesse Sharpless and his associates urged they should not be sent to jail except for violation of a law passed by legislators elected by the people. And there had been no enactment of such law. In any event, it was urged without success that the charge was not specific since the picture was not sufficiently described. The judicial answer was:

We do not know, that the picture had any name, and therefore it might be impossible to designate it by name. What then is expected? Must the indictment describe minutely, the attitude and posture of the figures? I am for paying some respect to the chastity of our records. These are circumstances which may be well omitted.

One other aspect of this—one of the few early cases—went to the "private" nature of the exhibition. As the opinion reads:

The question then in this part of the case is narrowed to a single point;—Whether the exhibition of a lewd, wicked, scandalous, infamous and obscene painting, representing, &c. to certain individuals in a private house for money, is punishable by the sound principles of judge-made law? On this question I cannot hesitate. Secret poison cannot be thus disseminated. A slight knowledge of human nature teaches us, that while secrecy is affected in a case like the present, public curiosity is more strongly excited thereby, and that those persons who may ignorantly suppose they have had the good fortune of seeing bawdy pictures, will not content themselves with keeping the secret in their own bosoms.

As to the nature and manner in which the painting is represented to have been made, I hold it to be sufficient to state, that it represented a man in an obscene, impudent, and indecent posture with a woman, either clothed or unclothed, without wounding our eyes or ears, with a particular description of their attitude or posture. Why should it be so described? If the jurors are satisfied on the proof, that the persons represented were painted in an impudent and indecent posture, will not this give the Court all the information they can require?

Would you consider it an essential part of the offense that the picture was exhibited "for money" as both the indictment and the court opinion note? Should the law be concerned if the obscene item is "disgusting," or only if it is "sexually stimulating and arousing"? You may answer either way and find support among later judges, but the one in the *Sharpless* case said:

Some immodest paintings, it is true, may carry grosser features of indecency than others, and in fact, may produce disgust in the minds even of the most debauched; yet if the painting here, tended to the manifest corruption of youth and other citizens, and was of public evil example to others, I think it sufficiently described.

If only we could now look at the picture for which Sharpless took money and was punished! How would it compare with the "girlie" magazines, or with many of the great masterpieces at our most important art museums? Time goes on—attitudes change. Only a few decades ago a woman at a public bathing beach would have been arrested if she were not attired in full-length black stockings and long sleeves to her wrists. Nowadays a woman bathing with stockings and sleeves might well gather a crowd and be arrested for interfering with the dignity and peace of the community.

The First Book

Six years after Jesse Sharpless and his associates were convicted in Philadelphia, the first obscenity case involving a book was heard in Massachusetts. The volume was what is perhaps the best-selling pornographic novel of all time, *Fanny Hill* by John Cleland, appearing in this country in 1821 under its alternative title, *Memoirs of a Woman of Pleasure,* published in America by Peter Holmes. Originally published quite openly in England in the 1740's, it had been outlawed there for many years when our case was brought. It is a detailed account of the life of a prostitute but does not contain a single word that could be considered coarse, let alone "dirty."

Today *Fanny Hill* is once again the center of controversy, and the questions raised by the *Sharpless* case have renewed importance.

Would the reasons given in Philadelphia for convicting those who exhibited a picture hold good for those who sold a book? Was this novel sexually corrupting? Did it disturb the peace and "dignity" of the Commonwealth? Would it have been equally offensive if not illustrated? Would you convict Peter Holmes on a mere description, without having read the text of the book? Chief Judge Parker of the Massachusetts Supreme Court, where Holmes pleaded after his conviction in the lower court, repeated the charges and facts in this way:

Holmes was convicted for publishing a lewd and obscene print, contained in a certain book entitled "Memoirs of a Woman of Pleasure," and also for publishing the same book. It was charged that Holmes, being a scandalous and evil disposed person, and contriving, devising and intending, the morals as well of youth as of other good citizens of said Commonwealth to debauch and corrupt, and to raise and create in their minds inordinate and lustful desires, knowingly, unlawfully, wickedly, maliciously and scandalously, did utter, publish and deliver to A.B. a certain lewd, wicked, scandalous, infamous and obscene printed book, entitled &c. which said printed book is so lewd, wicked and obscene, that the same would be offensive to the court here, and improper to be placed upon the records thereof: wherefore the jurors aforesaid do not set forth the same in this indictment: to the manifest corruption and subversion of the youth and other good citizens of said Commonwealth in their manners and conversation; in contempt of law; to the evil and pernicious example of others in like case offending, and against the peace &c. Holmes was also charged with the publishing and delivering to C.D. the print contained in the same book, describing the print, and averring the same evil intent and tendency.

In other words, they threw the book at him. Holmes, no doubt staggering from the verbal attack, appealed to the higher court, claiming that the jury got only a description of the "print," but never saw the print itself, that what he was charged with was not an offense against the state and that, anyway, all the charges were too vague to be constitutional.

Chief Judge Parker, however, did not agree:

It can never be required that an obscene book and picture should be displayed upon the records of the court: which must be done, if the description in these charges is insufficient. This would be to require that the public itself should give permanency and notoriety to indecency, in order to punish it.

Thus Holmes loses his appeal with a short chop of the judicial ax. The judge's reasoning may seem perhaps a bit circular to some of us moderns. "Holmes was convicted fairly, even though the jury didn't see the obscene material—because the stuff was obviously too obnoxious to show to respectable people"—that's the way the argument runs—and it is still heard in some courts today, but with less success. Holmes obviously, being a pioneer, was born 150 years too soon!

The reader may have noticed that both Holmes and Sharpless were tried under the "common law," a body of prior judge-made decisions that serve as precedents for future cases. As each new case of this kind is decided, it, too, becomes a part of the "common law," to serve, along with its predecessors, as precedents for future cases. At the time of these decisions there were no legislative enactments, called "statutes," to govern obscenity. But as we shall see, even as Judge Parker was deciding the fate of Holmes, the legislatures were joining in the censorship game.

3

Early Statutes–
Here and Abroad

In the years just after these early obscenity decisions under the common law, both the states and Congress began to build statutory bridges of written law between the old colonial blue laws governing blasphemy and the new concept that people could be corrupted sexually by pictures or words. Two factors in the growth of our Republic seem to have been keys to the change. One was the weakening of the clerical domination of community life, even in New England. The other was the growth of literacy among "common" people and the accompanying fear of those who controlled society that somehow these "common" folk were less resistant to the corrupting influence of books than the well-to-do.

So we see some legislatures, notably in New England, attempting to attack what they considered the evil of the obscene by writing new laws against indecent literature. Vermont was the first, passing its statute in 1821, the same year as the case against Peter Holmes was decided in Massachusetts. (Surely it is no coincidence that the first public high school in the United States had opened the year before.) Connecticut followed Vermont's example in 1834 and Massachusetts in 1835, both with laws against indecent literature. By this time the agitation for universal, free, compulsory elementary education was

18

making great strides, and the fear of literacy was obviously linked to the legal moves against obscenity.

The state actions were preludes to the first exercise of Federal power in this field, which took place, on a limited scale, in 1842.

Under the Constitution the states had retained full jurisdiction, generally speaking, over regulations concerning education, the family, and sexual behavior. But no state could enact a law concerned with interstate commerce or foreign imports and exports because the Supreme Court of the United States had early held that such matters were solely the concern of the Federal government.

In its first law on the subject, Congress confined itself to the control of "obscenity" imported from other countries. We include a photostat of several sections of the Customs Law of that year so that the reader can appreciate the conglomeration of provisions into which the ban on foreign indecency was inserted. (See page 20.)

Note that there is no reference in Section 28 to books, pamphlets, or magazines or other printed material. Pictorial art alone, not the printed word, was dangerous in the eyes of our Congress.

This initial Federal approach to the problem of obscenity was a manifestation of the normal human trait of frowning on the folkways of foreigners. For some reason what we do seems always less jarring than the behavior of other people. Furthermore, early in our history Paris had become a symbol of the naughty, the risqué—it still is, although with considerably less justification!

Although we did raise our collective eyebrows at imports from abroad, there was no attempt to exercise the Federal power over the circulation of "obscene" material between states or into the territories over which Congress had sole jurisdiction. These territories were very large in 1842, including, besides the District of Columbia, the whole of eleven present states—Florida, Iowa, Kansas, Minnesota, Montana, Nebraska, North and South Dakota, Oklahoma, Wisconsin and Wyoming.

Perhaps the failure of Congress to interfere with the "obscene" in traffic between states or in the territories in 1842 can be traced to an important debate that had taken place in the Senate seven years earlier. While it was not concerned with indecent literature, it had a bearing on all the arguments for censorship of the mails. In 1835 a proposal had been made to bar from the postbags all material that might incite rebellion among the slaves of the South. The most distinguished senators of both sections, including Clay, Calhoun, and Webster, rose to declare such legislation a violation of the Constitu-

SEC. 25. *And be it further enacted,* That nothing in this act contained shall apply to goods shipped in a vessel bound to any port of the United States, actually having left her last port of lading eastward of the Cape of Good Hope or beyond Cape Horn prior to the first day of September, eighteen hundred and forty-two; and all legal provisions and regulations existing immediately before the thirtieth day of June, eighteen hundred and forty-two, shall be applied to importations which may be made in vessels which have left such last port of lading eastward of the Cape of Good Hope or beyond Cape Horn prior to said first day of September, eighteen hundred and forty-two.

> Act not to apply to vessels having left their last port of lading, beyond the Cape of Good Hope, &c. before 1st Sept. 1842—laws applicable thereto.

SEC. 26. *And be it further enacted,* That the laws existing on the first day of June, eighteen hundred and forty-two, shall extend to and be in force for the collection of the duties imposed by this act on goods, wares, and merchandise, imported into the United States, and for the recovery, collection, distribution and remission of all fines, penalties, and forfeitures, and for the allowance of the drawbacks by this act authorized, as fully and effectually as if every regulation, restriction, penalty, forfeiture, provision, clause, matter, and thing, in the said laws contained, had been inserted in and re-enacted by this act. And that all provisions of any former law inconsistent with this act, shall be, and the same are hereby, repealed.

> Laws existing on 1st June 1842, in force for certain purposes.

> Laws inconsistent herewith repealed.

SEC. 27. *And be it further enacted,* That it shall be the duty of the Secretary of the Treasury, annually, to ascertain whether, for the year ending on the thirtieth of June, next preceding, the duty on any articles has exceeded thirty-five per centum ad valorem on the average wholesale market value of such articles, in the several ports of the United States for the preceding year; and, if so, he shall report a tabular statement of such articles and excess of duty to Congress, at the commencement of the next annual session thereof, with such observations and recommendations as he may deem necessary for the improvement of the revenue.

> Sec. Treas. to ascertain whether the duty on any article has exceeded 35 per cent., and report to Congress.

SEC. 28. *And be it further enacted,* That the importation of all indecent and obscene prints, paintings, lithographs, engravings, and transparencies is hereby prohibited; and no invoice or package whatever, or any part thereof, shall be admitted to entry, in which any such articles are contained; and all invoices and packages whereof any such articles shall compose a part, are hereby declared to be liable to be proceeded against, seized, and forfeited, by due course of law, and the said articles shall be forthwith destroyed.

> Indecent prints and paintings prohibited.

SEC. 29. *And be it further enacted,* That, wherever the word "ton" is used in this act, in reference to weight, it shall be deemed and taken to be twenty hundred weight, each hundred weight being one hundred and twelve pounds avoirdupois.

> Weight of the ton.

tion. They argued that there was a duty to carry all mail. The government monopoly of mail delivery gave neither postman nor Congress the power to censor the contents of the pouches.

President Washington had at one time proposed that all mail be carried without charge because he had feared that someday someone would suggest a Federal power over its content. These senators from

North and South ridiculed (in constitutional terms) the idea of postal censorship even to prevent rebellion, a danger everyone would accept as greater than sexual provocation (or even sexual corruption) by the "obscene," no matter who defines that word.

Would you agree with these senators that use of the mails is a right, or with some later authorities who say it is a privilege? As we shall see, the question even today is far from academic. The same debate rages—both in Congress and in the Supreme Court. During the last hundred years, as obscenity statutes proliferated and convictions mounted, courts and even lawyers seemed to assume as lawful what these senators in 1835 had questioned. As you read on in this volume, watch this assumption fade from view and the old fears of Washington return to prominence. History may not be cyclical—but people, even judges, often behave as if it were.

Thus far the courts have not passed on the scope of the postal censorship power, although they have had many invitations to do so. At the moment, *first-class* mail appears to be sacred and substantially free from examination by postal officials.

The Customs Censorship Law has been doctored from time to time, but it would not be helpful to reprint every amendment. For example, in 1857 the section was reenacted to add the word "articles" to the category of items that could be seized. Two ancient types of reproduction—"images and figures"—were included, and to make sure that nothing slipped through, a ban was put on indecent daguerreographs and photographs. Later, as we shall see, printed matter was added, but not for some time.

We do not know how many tasteless French postcards disturbed or titillated our customs officials, but our courts were not bothered with suits brought against travelers importing obscenity until nearly a century after the original law. How the law operated is indicated in a speech by a member of the British Parliament during a debate in 1857:

> In the United States there was a law which decreed the destruction of any obscene publications which might be imported thither. It happened curiously enough, not long ago, that an American traveler, returning home from Italy, brought with him a copy of that well-known work describing with figures, the principal statues, paintings, etc., of the Royal Museum of Naples. The name of this work is the MUSEO BARBONICA REALE; its value some thirty or forty pounds [then $150 or $200]; and we have it in the Library attached

to this House. Now, this very work was by the Collector of the Customs at New York deemed obscene; and was then and there ruthlessly destroyed.

The speaker had looked over the book again in the Parliamentary library and "would put it to any of the honorable members conversant with its contents whether such a work (published under royal authority) could be called obscene."

The Honourable Member hinted at irony—and it certainly was, and is, ironic that works of art may be considered obscene. But happily, young as we still are, we probably have outgrown the justice of his accusation. As we shall see, our law and our people are now sophisticated enough to welcome a work of art, even if titillating, without declaring it obscene. But more of this later—right now, let us glance across the water to see if our British friend was not indeed committing the cardinal misjudgment of throwing stones from a glass house!

On the other side of the Atlantic, the legal standards of what was called obscene sometimes preceded, sometimes followed, and sometimes were almost simultaneous with ours. But there was a definite similarity, which we might expect because our law had its roots in English law and because of the joint literary heritage of the two countries.

As has been said, England's first obscenity prosecutions were at common law. Earlier than ours, they seem to have been more frequent, too, although averaging only about three a year from 1802 to 1857. England's first special law on the subject was contained in the Vagrancy Act of 1824. This forbade only the exposing of an obscene book or print in any street, road, highway, or place of public resort. (The reader will recall the judicial reference to pubic display in the case of Jesse Sharpless in Philadelphia.)

Eleven years after the United States Customs Law against importation of obscene pictures, England also adopted legislation to ban foreign obscenity, and it too was aimed chiefly at the products of Paris. While booksellers could be prosecuted at common law, their stocks of obscene literature could not be confiscated. Many dealers continued to take chances. One found it profitable to pay nine fines on nine convictions.

Then, in 1857, the same year that our Customs Law was revised, Lord John Campbell, a lover of literature and author of *The Lives of the Lord Chancellors,* introduced a bill in the Parliament to curb obscenity. He was moved to this, he said, because as Lord Chief Justice he had just sentenced a pornographer to jail and felt that the law needed strengthening. The proposed law provided for searches and seizures. Before his bill was passed, some safeguards were incorporated to provide that the offending books had to be "held for sale" and that only a public shop could be raided. Thus private libraries for the well-to-do literates in the population were immune.

While the House of Lords was considering the bill, it made the first attempt in a debate to define the obscene. Lord Campbell declared that his measure was drafted to apply exclusively to words (*a*) written for the single purpose of corrupting the morals of youth and (*b*) of a nature to shock the common feelings of decency in any well regulated mind. Keep this explanation in mind for later use: the motive of the author was an essential element of the crime, and the aim was to protect youth.

During the debate, however, Lord Lyndhurst raised some embarrassing points as to what the effect of Lord Campbell's Act (as the legislation came to be called) would be on literature generally:

"My noble and learned Friend's aim," declared Lord Lyndhurst, "is to put down the sale of obscene books and prints; but what is the interpretation which is to be put upon the word 'obscene'? I can easily conceive that two men will come to entirely different conclusions as to its meaning. I have looked into 'Johnson' to see what definition he gives of the word, and I find that he says it is something 'immodest; not agreeable to chastity of mind; causing lewd ideas.' These are definitions which he gives the word. Suppose now a man following the trade of an informer, or a policeman, sees in a window something which he conceives to be a licentious print. He goes to the magistrate, and describes, according to his ideas, what he saw; the magistrate thereupon issues his warrant for the seizure of the disgusting print. The officer then goes to the shop, and says to the shopkeeper, 'Let me look at that picture of Jupiter and Antiope.' 'Jupiter and what?' says the shopkeeper. 'Jupiter and Antiope,' says the man. 'Oh, Jupiter and Antiope, you mean,' says the shopkeeper; and hands him down the print. He sees the picture of a woman stark naked, lying down, and a satyr standing by her with an expression on his face which shows most distinctly what his feeling are and what is his object.

"The informer tells the man he is going to seize the print, and to take him before a magistrate. 'Under what authority?' he asks;

and he is told—'Under the authority of Lord Campbell's Act.' 'But,' says the man, 'don't you know that it is a copy from a picture of one of the most celebrated masters in Europe?' That does not matter; the informer seizes it as an obscene print. He asks if the shopkeeper has got any more prints like it. 'Oh, yes, I have got several others,' is the reply. Whereupon he searches the shop and in so doing perhaps he stumbles upon a print of the story of Danae. There he sees a naked woman lifting her eyes to heaven, but standing in a very strange attitude, the shower of gold descending upon her, a little Cupid peeping over her shoulder pointing with his dart, and other circumstances which I will not describe.

"Well, is this print also to be brought before the magistrate? These prints come within the description in this Bill as much as any work you can conceive. And yet they are both celebrated pictures; the first is a copy of a famous Correggio which hangs in the large square room of the Louvre, right opposite an ottoman, on which are seated daily ladies of the first rank from all countries of Europe, who resort there for the purpose of studying the works of art in that great gallery. But this is not all. Our informant leaves the print shop and goes into the studio of a sculptor or some statuary and sees there figures of nymphs, fauns and satyrs, all perfectly naked, some of them in attitudes which I do not choose to describe. According to this Bill they may every one be seized.

"Well, I will now go to a third class—the poets—for the informant next proceeds to the circulating libraries. I do not know whether my noble and learned Friend's extensive reading has made him familiar with the poems of Rochester, but I think they would come under the description of this Bill. 'The freedom of ancient satirists,' says Hume, the historian, 'no more resembles the licentiousness of Rochester than the nakedness of an Indian does that of a common prostitute.' Suppose that book is in a certain library lent out for hire; under my noble and learned Friend's bill it may be seized at once—in fact, under the Bill a circulating library may be searched from one end to the other. In the same way the dramatists of the Restoration, Wycherley, Congreve, and the rest of them,—there is not a page in any one of them which might not be seized under this Bill. One of the principal characters in one of Congreve's plays is Lady Wishfor't. Dryden, too, is as bad as any of them. He has translated the worst parts of Ovid—his ART OF LOVE—works for which Ovid was exiled, and died,

I believe, on the shores of the Euxine. There is not a single volume of that great poet which would not come under the definition of my noble and learned Friend's bill."

But Lord Campbell had one book in mind and in his hand. It was none other than *The Lady of the Camellias* by Dumas the Younger, upon which the opera *La Traviata,* then running at Exeter Hall in London, was based. Lord Campbell confessed to the legal dilemma still extant today in England, and even more so in our nation:

"HE DID NOT WISH TO CREATE A CATEGORY OF OFFENSES IN WHICH THIS MIGHT BE INCLUDED ALTHOUGH IT WAS CERTAINLY OF A POLLUTING CHARACTER. IT WAS ONLY FROM THE FORCE OF PUBLIC OPINION AND AN IMPROVED TASTE THAT THE CIRCULATION OF SUCH WORKS COULD BE PUT A STOP TO: but he was glad to inform their Lordships that there was a Society for the Encouragement of Pure Literature of which his noble Friend the Duke of Argyll was President. He was shocked to think that there should be so much circulation for works like the one in his hand—THE LADY OF THE CAMELLIAS. In this work, the Lady described her red camellias and her white camellias; but he would not shock their Lordships by going further."

We do not know how much Lord Campbell's assurance that the law was not meant to apply to works of recognized literary or artistic merit had to do with getting the bill passed. But passed it was, and without anything in it to tell the courts that the exception Lord Campbell supposed to be obvious was there at all. So the law was ready to provide a legal standard of what was then called "obscene libel" that coincided with Victorian literary (and other) prudery. It needed only the right man in the right place to apply the standard, and on both sides of the Atlantic the men were there.

In
Search
of the
Obscene

part II

In
Search
of the
Obscene

4

The Crusader
and the Law

In both legal cultures—England and the United States—the application of standards of obscenity against recognized literature occurred, by coincidence, in the same year, 1868. But the men who had the most to do with imposing the standard were very different. In England it was Lord Campbell's successor, Sir Alexander Cockburn, as Lord Chief Justice. In America it was a twenty-four-year-old grocery clerk, Anthony Comstock. Although history, and hence law, is impelled by social forces, a single human being, often an evangelist, acts as a propeller of the social pressures, and both these men had evangelical qualities.

Tragedy Comes to American Literature

Anthony Comstock was one of ten children, seven living to maturity. When he was eighteen he was clerk in a store and already a crusader in action against what he regarded as a liquor evil. His later diaries, kept during his short enlistment at the time of the Civil War, are precious morsels for any psychiatrist. Obvious it is that he suffered from extreme feelings of guilt because of a habit of masturbation.

29

Our youthful democracy has always invited crusaders of extreme fanaticism. Some of Comstock's contemporaries come readily to mind —Fanny Bloomer, agitating for a more sensible feminine costume; Lucy Stone for the right of a woman to keep her own name; the Claflin girls, Tennessee and her sister, Virginia Woodhull, for women's rights generally; Carrie Nation, for abolition of the liquor traffic. Young Comstock, long before his marriage to a woman ten years his elder, crusaded against sex in all its manifestations. One of his early slogans was "Books Are Feeders for Brothels." To him there was nothing valuable in art unless human figures were clothed. Statues must have fig leaves. He crusaded against Lady Godiva and Peeping Tom. On one occasion he seized 117 masters of classical French art. Looking back on this obvious psychopath, it is plain that suppression gratified his hatred of everything he saw as vice.

Little of value in terms of legal historical background can be found to show why at this moment in time—just after the end of the Civil War—Protestant leaders in New York City became so aroused over obscenity. At this point, the little-understood base of Comstock's support must be declared. Because in the twentieth century Irish Catholics have been the leaders of drives against obscenity, many writers have unjustly blamed nineteenth century censorship laws on Catholic influences. This is totally untrue. It was the top of the non-Catholic social hierarchy in our land that gave Comstock his main, his only support. We find the name of J. P. Morgan at the head of his endorsements.

This group already had prepared the way for the crusader. In 1865, Congress had adopted its first law attempting to bar obscenity from the mails. Ignoring the great debate of 1835 and the principles at stake, Congress declared that mailing obscene publications would be a criminal offense. The Post Office, however, received no power to exclude anything from the mails; to this extent the older principle was upheld. The penalty of fine and jail was to be imposed only after the offending material had gone through the mails. It does not appear that there were very many prosecutions.

The next year, 1866, the Young Men's Christian Association of New York made a survey of conditions in that city affecting young men. It found much to complain about, including "vile newspapers and . . . licentious books." The YMCA thereupon urged the state legislature to outlaw this traffic, and in 1868 a bill for the suppression of what was simply called "obscene literature" was passed.

Comstock, who had moved to New York from Connecticut, was not a member of the YMCA, but he was the man who took most advantage of the new law. Still supporting himself as a clerk, he spent his spare time tracking down dealers of magazines or books that offended him, and getting them arrested.

None of these defendants put up a defense that would have caused a court to interpret the law. But Comstock thought that there was need for a Federal law on the subject so he could get after publishers and not just dealers. So in 1872 he suggested a cooperative drive with the YMCA to get such legislation, and a Committee for the Suppression of Vice was formed, with Comstock as its agent. (Later the "Committee" became the "Society.")

This was the man who went to the halls of our Congress in 1873 and lobbied through both houses, with less than a total of one hour of debate, the law that—with few and relatively trifling changes—still governs "obscenity" in the mails. It was hurried through in the closing hours of a hectic session, the final vote coming about 2:00 A.M. on a Sunday morning, although the clock was stopped to preserve the fiction that it was still Saturday. The law reads:

Tit. 18. CRIMES AND CRIMINAL PROCEDURE
Ch. 71. Obscenity

Section 1461. Mailing obscene or crime-inciting matter.

Every obscene, lewd, lascivious, or filthy book, pamphlet, picture, paper, letter, writing, print, or other publication of an indecent character; and

Every article or thing designed, adapted, or intended for preventing conception or producing abortion, or for any indecent or immoral use; and

Every article, instrument, substance, drug, medicine, or thing which is advertised or described in a manner calculated to lead another to use or apply it for preventing conception or producing abortion, or for any indecent or immoral purpose; and

Every written or printed card, letter, circular, book, pamphlet, advertisement, or notice of any kind giving information, directly or indirectly, where, or how, or from whom, or by what means any of such mentioned matters, articles, or things may be obtained or made, or where or by whom any act or operation of any kind for the procuring or producing of abortion will be done or performed, or how or by what means conception may be prevented or abortion produced, whether sealed or unsealed; and

Every paper, writing, advertisement, or representation that any article, instrument, substance, drug, medicine, or thing may, or can, be used or applied for preventing conception or producing abortion, or for any indecent or immoral purpose; and

Every description calculated to induce or incite a person to so use or apply any such article, instrument, substance, drug, medicine, or thing—

Is declared to be nonmailable matter and shall not be conveyed in the mails or delivered from any post office or by any letter carrier.

Whoever knowingly uses the mail for the mailing, carriage in the mails, or delivery of anything declared by this section to be nonmailable, or knowingly causes to be delivered by mail according to the direction thereon, or at the place at which it is directed to be delivered by the person to whom it is addressed, or knowingly takes any such thing from the mails for the purpose of circulating or disposing thereof, shall be fined not more than $5,000 or imprisoned not more than five years, or both, for the first such offense, and shall be fined not more than $10,000 or imprisoned not more than ten years, or both, for each such offense thereafter.

The term "indecent," as used in this section includes matter of a character tending to incite arson, murder, or assassination.

One of the objects of a law must always be that it can be read and understood. The obscenity law just quoted uses a series of words defining the kind of writing or picture that can land the publisher, author, or seller behind bars. The key words are "lewd," lascivious," "indecent" and "obscene." Do these words describe a single crime or does each describe a separate crime? Are they words everyone uses in the same sense? When in doubt about the meaning of words, we go to the dictionaries, and we find:

Lewd: Characterized by lust or LASCIVIOUSNESS or given to licentiousness; libidinous; unchaste; as lewd actions or lewd persons.

Lascivious: Having or denoting wanton desires; lustful, LEWD; as a lascivious person; lascivious feelings or words. Tending to produce sensual pictures, as lascivious pictures or books.

Indecent: Offensive to common propriety or adjudged to be subversive to morality; offending against modesty or delicacy; unfit
to be seen or heard; immodest; gross; OBSCENE.

Obscene: Offensive to chastity, delicacy, or decency; expressing
or presenting to the mind or view something that decency, delicacy, and purity forbid to be exposed; offensive to morals; INDE-
CENT; impure.

For a more complete etymology see the end papers of this volume.
The legislators were playing with synonyms, no doubt for the joy of
presumed emphasis through repetition. But sometimes when a legis-
lator's mind is only groping for an idea, he is apt to list a variety of
words in shotgun succession, hoping that one word or another will
bring down the legal pigeon. In this case Congress was giving the
courts a wide choice.

With this blessing from the national legislature, state after state
followed with similar laws. These and the Federal statute are still called
the "Comstock Laws." Comstock himself was appointed a special
agent of the Post Office, and on him police power was bestowed. The
Society for the Suppression of Vice, which he headed from 1872 until
he died in 1915, for many years received part of all the fines collected
on successful prosecutions based on the work of the great vice hunter.
Sheriffs had traditionally been allowed to keep a percentage of the fees
they collected, and this financial inducement for Comstock to increase
his raids produced no serious objection from newspaper, magazine, or
book publishers—or anyone.

By 1873, when he lobbied for his bill, Comstock had given up the
grocery business to go into the business of censorship of all the arts.
By January 1, 1874, he bragged that under the new law he had seized
194,000 obscene pictures and photographs, 134,000 pounds of books,
14,200 stereo plates, 60,300 rubber articles (no doubt contraceptives,
mostly condoms—curiously, Comstock himself had only one child by
his marriage), 5,500 sets of playing cards, 31,150 boxes of pills and
powders (mostly "aphrodisiacs").

Very soon nearly all freedom-loving editors had been intimidated
into acquiescence in Comstock's activities. Thus does man lose a bit
of liberty by cowardice. Perhaps it is historically right that law should
push the cowards around.

Parallel in England

Although an English Society for the Suppression of Vice antedated the Comstock organization by no less than seven decades, the law that led to the great Victorian drive against impurity in literature took form in the same year as the New York statute under which Comstock first operated. It was in 1868 that Sir Alexander Cockburn, the Lord Chief Justice, gave expression to a streak of hypersensitiveness to Victorian "sin" that was to have profound effects on the law of obscenity in our country as well as his own.

From the time of Chaucer and before, English writing had been robust, to say the least. On both sides of the ocean, four-letter words were found in translations of Ovid's *Art of Love* and in such novels as Fielding's *Tom Jones* and other books that had enjoyed great prestige among the literate. But in England as in America, the literate were few until the great revolution in reading and writing in the middle of the nineteenth century. For a time, too, the same writings were popular in both countries; in fact, around 1900 some 95 percent of the books circulating in the United States were of British authorship.

The case that introduced Comstockery to England in 1868 began by holding strictly to Lord Campbell's legal theory of what his Act outlawed. An antipapist had published and distributed a pamphlet entitled "The Confessional Unmasked, Showing the Depravity of the Romish Priesthood; the Iniquity of the Confessional, and the Questions Put to Females in Confession." Copies of the pamphlet were seized under Lord Campbell's Act. When an appeal was taken against the warrant, the learned intermediate-appeals judge, Benjamin Hicklin, the Recorder of London (which is a judicial title), held that, while the material was undoubtedly "obscene" in the ordinary meaning of the term, it did not come within the Act because it had been distributed for the honest purpose of exposing the practices of the Catholic confessional. In other words, it had not been published "for the single purpose of corrupting the morals of youth." The reader will remember that this had to be the case before a publication came within the declared intention of Campbell's Act.

This was the last time such a perhaps enlightened doctrine was heard in an Anglo-Saxon court. The prosecution appealed from the Hicklin verdict, and the case came before the Lord Chief Justice,

Cockburn, who overruled Hicklin, and wrote the famous words that have been the bugaboo of our obscenity law ever since:

> I think the test of obscenity is this, whether the tendency of the matter charged as obscenity is to deprave and corrupt those whose minds are open to such immoral influences and into whose hands a publication of this sort may fall.

With this utterance sanity was swept away, and Victorian literary prudery and the law made to coincide. Or rather, law was swept aside to make room for hysteria. Almost any book that might have some evil effect upon any Anglo-Saxon, young or old, moronic or intelligent, male or female, was made criminal. Anon the classics were attacked, and then modern literature. A literary reign of terror had been instituted. No rational being could tell who might be the next victim on either side of the Atlantic.

One must say "either side" because the test that Cockburn devised, and which through the curiosity of legal nomenclature was called the "Hicklin rule" (although exactly opposite to what Hicklin ruled), became the standard in the United States, too. In the first case that went to the Supreme Court of the United States for resolution of basic questions concerning the Comstock Law, the trial judge had charged the jury in these words:

> The test of obscenity is whether the tendency of the matter is to deprave and corrupt the morals of those whose minds are open to such influence and into whose hands a publication of this sort may fall.

The case concerned a New Yorker named Lew Rosen and a publication entitled *Broadway*. The United States Supreme Court decided it in 1896, and we shall meet it later in this volume. The "Hicklin" test for obscenity was so much a recognized part of American jurisprudence by then that the trial judge did not mention that it had come from a famous British case. He used the "rule" as if it were a settled and accepted legal fact, both in England and here.

5

The
Hunt
Begins

The Comstock Laws established the censorship business on a big scale. And the business thrived lustily during the next half-century. Many prosecutors and judges wanted to get into the act. It was a new sport, with virtually no rules or trained referees.

For instance, Walt Whitman's *Leaves of Grass* had been called obscene, impure, and immoral by some ever since it was published in 1855. By others it was called the finest poetry yet written by an American. In 1881 a Boston prosecutor threatened action under the Comstock Laws, and the publisher meekly withdrew a new edition. Mark Twain published *The Adventures of Huckleberry Finn* in 1885 and a half-century later it was removed from some public library shelves after pressure of censorians in our land.

Incidentally, just before he began *Huckleberry Finn,* the genial Twain wrote for a cleric friend one of the outstanding American examples of high literary pornography—*1601*. It was passed around in handwritten copies until, some years later, a cultured Secretary of State, John Hay, had a small edition secretly printed on the presses of the United States Military Academy at West Point.

Meanwhile, dozens of cases were brought in the courts against various kinds of books and papers. Judges had fun but little success in trying to define "obscene," "lewd," "lascivious," "indecent"—a game still seemingly engaged in with pleasure by the courts. Moreover, the indictments seldom contained the objectionable words, paragraphs, or pages.

There is an ancient and valid rule of law that when the State lays a charge against a citizen, the accusation should be set forth with enough precision for the indicted person to be able to make answer. But time and again our jurists explained that in the field of obscenity such precision must be foregone to save the court records from being "defiled" by the obscene. They felt, as did the judge in the *Sharpless* case (1815), that they must "pay some respect to the chastity of the records of the court" (so Sharpless never knew just what part of the picture was objectionable and why!).

The aura of prudery was such that individual defendants were actually embarrassed when arguing to the charges leveled against them, and the law itself was corrupted by failure of the indictments and opinions to refer in specific detail to the material alleged to be "criminally corrupting." Law develops soundly only if based on facts and the comparatives involved in each case. Dozens of times the courts convicted the applicant who cried out: "Please point to the page you deem illegal. Then and only then can I debate the legal significance of 'obscene' and its synonyms."

Even so, judges found themselves faced with the necessity of clarifying certain points on which a man could be jailed or a book legally burned. In both state and Federal courts there was a search for some standard by which the written word could be suppressed or permitted. In the following chapters we shall present some of the landmark cases in this legal quest, samples of the judicial search for the obscene.

6

The Classics

Twenty years after Anthony Comstock became the Post Office's special agent to track down obscenity, he became involved in a test to determine the legal question of whether books were obscene even if they were expensive and also were written by famous dead authors. It happened in New York, and the ruling of Judge Morgan J. O'Brien in the New York Supreme Court settled quite a bit of legal dust.

The facts were simple. The Worthington Book Publishing Company was in financial trouble. The Court appointed a receiver to sell the assets for the benefit of the creditors. Among those assets were books very expensively bound but which included some of the great pornography of the ages. The receiver asked the Court for instructions as to their disposition. No doubt he did not want to be arrested by the Society for the Suppression of Vice even if he was acting as an appointee of the Court. Interestingly enough, Comstock himself, although not an attorney, appeared in the court records as "opposed" to the sale of the volumes. This meant that he wanted an official book burning of all the volumes, thus depriving the creditors of many dollars.

Here, omitting citations and references, is what the Court decided:

O'BRIEN, J. After consultation with some of my brethren, we have concluded that the following views should be expressed con-

38

cerning the merits of this motion: This is an application made by the receiver of the Worthington Company for instructions concerning the final disposition of certain books which were found among the assets of that company, and which are now in his custody, and respecting which it is alleged by certain parties that they are unfit for general circulation, and come under the designation of "immoral literature," and as such should be excluded from sale. That these books constitute valuable assets of this receivership cannot be doubted, and the question before the court for decision on this motion is whether or not they are of such a character as should be condemned and their sale prohibited.

The Classics Under Attack

The books in question consist of Payne's edition of the ARABIAN NIGHTS, Fielding's novel, TOM JONES, the works of Rabelais, Ovid's ART OF LOVE, THE DECAMERON of Boccaccio, THE HEPTAMERON of Queen Margaret of Navarre, THE CONFESSIONS of J. J. Rousseau, and TALES FROM THE ARABIC, AND ALADDIN. Most of the volumes that have been submitted to the inspection of the court are of choice editions, both as to the letter-press and the bindings, and are such, both as to their commercial value and subject-matter, as to prevent their being generally sold or purchased, except by those who would desire them for their literary merit, or for their worth as specimens of fine book-making.

Then Why Not the Bible?

It is very difficult to see upon what theory these world-renowned classics can be regarded as specimens of that pornographic literature which it is the office of the Society for the Suppression of Vice to suppress, or how they can come under any stronger condemnation than that high standard literature which consists of the works of Shakespeare, of Chaucer, of Laurence Sterne, and of other great English writers, without making reference to many parts of the Old Testament Scriptures, which are to be found in almost every household in the land. The very artistic character, the high qualities of style, the absence of those glaring and crude pictures, scenes, and descriptions which affect the common and vulgar mind, make a place for books of the character in question, entirely apart from such gross and obscene writings as it is the duty of the public authorities to suppress.

It would be quite as unjustifiable to condemn the writings of Shakespeare and Chaucer and Laurence Sterne, the early English novelists, the playwrights of the Restoration, and the dramatic literature which has so much enriched the English language, as to place an interdict upon these volumes, which have received the admiration of literary men for so many years. What has become standard literature of the English language—has been wrought into the very structure of our splendid English literature—is not to be pronounced at this late day unfit for publication or circulation, and stamped with judicial disapprobation, as hurtful to the community. The works under consideration are the product of the greatest literary genius. Payne's ARABIAN NIGHTS is a wonderful exhibition of Oriental scholarship, and the other volumes have so long held a supreme rank in literature that it would be absurd to call them now foul and unclean.

Mal y Pense

A seeker after the sensual and degrading parts of a narrative may find in all these works, as in those of other great authors, something to satisfy his pruriency. But to condemn a standard literary work, because of a few of its episodes, would compel the exclusion from circulation of a very large proportion of the works of fiction of the most famous writers of the English language. There is no such evil to be feared from the sale of these rare and costly books as the imagination of many even well-disposed people might apprehend. They rank with the higher literature, and would not be bought nor appreciated by the class of people from whom unclean publications ought to be withheld. They are not corrupting in their influence upon the young, for they are not likely to reach them.

I am satisfied that it would be a wanton destruction of property to prohibit the sale by the receiver of these works—for if their sale ought to be prohibited the books should be burned—but I find no reason in law, morals, or expediency why they should not be sold for the benefit of the creditors of the receivership. The receiver is therefore allowed to sell these volumes.

The opinion gave a green light for the sale. But the reasons why these books were excepted from the legal suppression of obscenity certainly raise some pertinent questions, such as:

a) These were expensive, choice editions. Query: Did the Court mean that the rich, who were the only people who could afford them, were incorruptible or already corrupted? Or that in cheaper editions the same words and pictures would be illegal? If so, how much cheaper?

b) These volumes were the product of "the greatest literary genius." Query: Did the Court mean that if an author wrote without literary genius, the obscenities could not be forgiven? Would mere talent be enough?

c) These were "world-renowned classics," and an author usually must be dead before his work is deemed a classic. Query: How long must he be dead before his "obscenity" is legalized for the wealthy?

These questions are still with us in prosecutions for obscenity. In our nation, the two generally recognized literary masterpieces in the field of pornography are by Benjamin Franklin and Mark Twain. Have these authors been "dead" long enough for their books to be classics? At what price must their works be sold to win immunity? Does the high reputation of the authors entitle them to greater immunity than for similar topics treated by lesser men with lesser skills?

However you answer those questions, you will have a highly reputable, even distinguished, judicial opinion to back you up. The Law is still groping for firm answers.

Of course, in the matter of the Worthington Company the high literary quality was unquestioned. As we shall see next, old-fashioned vulgarity also had its day in court.

7

The Vulgar

Most obscenity statutes use words like "obscene," "lewd," and the rest. Just before the turn of the century, courts were asked to decide for the first time whether these words included writings that were just plain coarse and vulgar.

The first obscenity issues on which the Supreme Court of the United States expressed itself were decided early in the year 1896. It was perhaps a portent of future rulings in this area of the law that the nine learned men did not agree in either of the cases they heard. The one of greater significance and more closely divided opinion involved the question of whether or not the Comstock Law was directed solely against items with sexual connotations. Were there other types of obscenity or indecency or impurity that Congress meant to bar from the mails?

This nice legal point arose because in 1895 Dan K. Swearingen was indicted in Kansas for mailing a copy of *The Burlington Courier,* dated September 21, 1894, "containing a certain article charged to be obscene, lewd, lascivious" and hence nonmailable. The court reprinted the article in a footnote which reads as follows:

About the meanest and most universally hated and detested thing in human shape that ever cursed this community is the red headed mental and physical bastard that flings filth under another man's name down on Neosho Street. He has slandered and maligned every Populist in the State, from the governor down to the humblest voter. This black hearted coward is known to every decent man, woman, and child in the community as a liar, perjurer, and slanderer, who would sell a mother's honor with less hesitancy and for much less silver than Judas betrayed the Saviour, and who would pimp and fatten on a sister's shame with as much unction as a buzzard gluts in carrion.

He is a contemptible scoundrel and political blackleg of the lowest cut. He is pretending to serve Democracy and at the same time in the pay of the Republican party. He has been known as the companion of negro strumpets and has revelled in lowest debauches. He has criminally libelled and slandered such men as ————, ————, ————, ————, ————, ————, ————, ————, ————, and dozens of others whom we might name, who are recognized by all parties as among the oldest and most respected citizens of the county. His soul, if he has a soul, is blacker than the blackest shades of hell. He is the embodiment of treachery, cowardice, and dishonor, and hasn't the physical nor moral courage to deny it. He stands to-day hated, despised, and detested as all that is low, mean, debased, and despicable. We propose to have done with the knave. We have already devoted too much valuable space to him. Time and again has he been proven a wilful, malicious, and cowardly liar, and instead of subsiding he has redoubled his lies. He lies faster than ten men could refute; and for what? A little Republican slush-money! He is lower, meaner, filthier, rottener than the rottenest strumpet that prowls the streets by night. Again we say, we are done with him. The sooner Populists and Populist newspapers snub him, quit him cold, ignore him entirely, the sooner will he cease to be thought of only as a pimp that any man can buy for $1 or less. He is too little and rotten to merit the notice of men. We have been doing wrong in noticing the poltroon at all, and henceforth are done.

Strong words indeed! The lower Court, obviously shocked to its shoe tops, declared it nonmailable. The Supreme Court, or most of it, however, was more concerned with keeping the obscenity statute within more narrow limits. The gist of the High Court decision, delivered on March 9, 1896, by Justice George Shiras, reads:

Assuming that it was within the province of the judge to determine whether the publication in question was obscene, lewd and lascivious, within the meaning of the statute, we do not agree with the court below in thinking that the language and tenor of this newspaper article brought it within such meaning. The offence aimed at, in that portion of the statute we are now considering, was the use of the mails to circulate or deliver matter to corrupt the morals of the people. The words "obscene," "lewd" and "lascivious," as used in the statute, signify that form of immorality which has relation to sexual impurity, and have the same meaning as is given them at common law in prosecutions for obscene libel. As the statute is highly penal, it should not be held to embrace language unless it is fairly within its letter and spirit.

Referring to this newspaper article, as found in the record, it is undeniable that its language is exceedingly coarse and vulgar, and, as applied to an individual person, plainly libelous. But we cannot perceive in it anything of a lewd, lascivious and obscene tendency, calculated to corrupt and debauch the mind and morals of those into whose hands it might fall.

Honorable judges, men of learning and goodwill, could not agree. Five declared the article was not obscene, lewd, and lascivious. Four judges upheld the conviction. Dan Swearingen was saved—by one vote—from his sentence of prison at hard labor for one year, a fine, and the payment of the costs of the prosecution.

This decision was important because it went in the direction of removing the merely tasteless and vulgar from the "obscene." It took many more test cases to limit the obscenity laws to matters touching on sex. Outhouse, toilet, and scatological material, generally speaking, was finally held to be not within the definition of obscenity. One later case went to the single point of whether "Wipe your dirty arse" was to be deemed sexually provocative. The court found no sexual purity or impurity in the phrase. It was outside the Comstock Laws.

By Bread Alone?—The *Rosen* Case, 1896

The fact that the full text of the Swearingen article that the prosecution found offensive was printed in the record was something of an exception in these cases, as has been noted. That the defendant could be kept in ignorance of the salient facts in the charge against him was affirmed by the United States Supreme Court just six weeks before it rendered its decision in the *Swearingen* case. This prior case came to it from New York and was the one in which the trial judge had so clearly accepted the Hicklin rule of what is obscenity, referred to earlier.

The *Rosen* case came to be widely quoted in later legal arguments, but in its own day it was famous chiefly because the application of a bit of bread to a page of the gazette in question would reveal pictures otherwise "invisible," which the defense held were of an innocent hilarity but which the Court called "females in different attitudes of indecency." Lew Rosen had issued his twelve-page paper, *Broadway,* with the figures obscured by lampblack that could be erased with a piece of bread. Mr. Justice John Marshall Harlan, grandfather of the present Justice of the same name, delivered the opinion of the Court:

> Undoubtedly the mere depositing in the mail of a writing paper or other publication of an obscene, lewd or lascivious character is not an offence under the statute if the person making the deposit was, at the time and in good faith, without knowledge, information, or notice of its contents* * * *
>
> However, the indictment on its face implies that the defendant owned or managed the paper "Broadway." He admitted at the trial that he owned and controlled it. He did not pretend that he was ignorant at the time of the contents of the particular number that he caused to be put in the post office at New York. The general charge that he "unlawfully, wilfully, and knowingly deposited and caused to be deposited in the post office . . . a certain obscene, lewd, and lascivious paper"—describing it by its name, volume, number, date of trade-mark, date of issue, and as having on it the name of Lew Rosen, proprietor, the same name borne by the defendant— may, not unreasonably, be construed as meaning that the defendant was, and must have been, aware of the nature of its contents at the time he caused it to be put into the post office for transmission and delivery* * * *

Must the Court Point to the Specific Obscenity?

> Rosen insists that the omission from the indictment of a description of the pictures of female figures found in the paper was in violation of the constitutional guaranty that the defendant in a criminal

case shall be informed of the nature and cause of the accusation against him. Sixth Amendment.

The doctrine to be deduced from the American cases is that the constitutional right of the defendant to be informed of the nature and cause of the accusation against him entitles him to insist, at the outset and after verdict that the indictment shall apprise him of the crime charged with such reasonable certainty that he can make his defence and protect himself after judgment against another prosecution for the same offence; that this right is not infringed by the omission from the indictment of indecent and obscene matter, alleged as not proper to be spread upon the records of the court, provided the crime charged, however general the language used, is yet so described as reasonably to inform the accused of the nature of the charge sought to be established against him; and that, in such case, the accused may apply to the court before the trial is entered upon for a bill of particulars, showing what parts of the paper would be relied on by the prosecution as being obscene, lewd, and lascivious, which motion will be granted or refused, as the court, in the exercise of a sound legal discretion, may find necessary to the ends of justice.

The really important point for the lawyers and judges who were to argue and decide these issues later was less the necessity for quotation in the indictment or charge than the issue of whether or not the defendant knew that what he was mailing or selling was against the law. In the *Rosen* case, there were two dissenters, Justices George Shiras and Edward D. White (who was later to become Chief Justice). They did not raise the issue of whether Rosen knew the material was obscene—although counsel for Rosen had argued the question—and thus this crucial issue had to wait more than sixty years before it was decided, as we shall see later. Instead the Justices confined their dissent to the fact that the indictment did not state exactly what the Grand Jury found indictable. Was it the picture under the lampblack or was it the sly arousing of curiosity by covering up a picture that might have escaped censure if openly displayed? Was it that the alleged obscenity was visible "by bread alone," or did the offense extend to other matters?

Another revealing point about these two early cases before the Supreme Court is that, in spite of them, as will be seen in the stream of later cases, our law is still in doubt as to the difference between sexual purity and what Mr. Justice Shiras called "sexual impurity." For some in our culture even today all public reference to sex is impure—at least for perusal by all members of the public, excepting of course the "censor" himself.

8

Improper,
Intemperate,
Reprehensible—
but Not Indecent

One of the early attempts of the law to come to grips with the meaning of the words used in our obscenity statutes was made by the highest tribunal of New York State in 1907. The seven judges of the Court of Appeals were led to expound some definitions in a case that came to them, not from the big bad city of Gotham but from upstate. Chapter VII of the State Penal Code is headed by this title: "Indecent exposure, obscene exhibitions, books, prints, and bawdy and other disorderly houses." Quite a mishmash of objectionable behavior patterns for a single chapter!

At this time in much of the rural part of New York State, there was an intense anti-Catholicism. The fanatically anti-Romanist American Protective Association was a political power in the region. Fanatics are often notoriously abusive, and an article by one N. L. A. Eastman was in this tradition. The dissenting jurists in his appeal to the highest state court saw fit to incorporate his attack in full so that the writing could speak for itself, and here it is:

THE OPEN DOOR TO HELL

is the confessional box. It is hell's gate. The mainspring to lust. The very embodiment and focus of the virus of hell. It is the very matter and pus that runs from the corpse in hell. It is the pollution and rottenness of the decay of ages. It is the cesspool, the recipient, the reservoirs of lust, of vile thoughts and communication, adultery, the birthplace of sexual criminality, with men's wives and young girls, and the convent is earth's terminus and hell, the lake of fire is the dumping-ground. It is the criminal college. The mother of prostitution. The author of pauperism. From it emanates poison to society, homes, our schools and government. I speak in love. No time to trifle. The Anaconda is drawing itself over many a threshold and stinging thousands to death. Hark! A voice from the tomb, the blood of the innocent crying out, in what sense is the confessional box needed? The Word of God says, in I John, 1, 9, if we confess our sins, He is faithful and just to forgive our sins and to cleanse us from all unrighteousness. You go direct to God Almighty through Jesus Christ to confess your sins. Not in a concealed and secluded place alone. No wife can go with her husband. Here the priest asks the vilest of questions, and of course the husband could not be present. He asks the most delicate and intimate questions. But under what obligation is any one to a priest? What business has he got to go into a box and ask delicate questions that no minister of Jesus Christ or true gentlemen on earth would ask? Right here in the confessional box many have been ruined, and many become mothers as a result; and men, you are paying your money to priests and to a church that is ruining your daughters and stealing the affections of your wife, until he knows more about her than you do. She has many secrets kept from you, husband, but not from that licentious priest. This is all true, dear reader, and can be proven by thousands of witnesses. May it not well be called the open door to hell? Last month a dear brother gave The Gospel Worker to some in the place where he was at work in this city. It was the January number with the article, "Break open the Doors and Look In," and it caused much excitement. Bloody threats and curses were made, and two could not sleep all night, they were so stirred over the truth in it. Was any one ever benefited in any way by going to the confessional box? If it is advice you need why go to that secret place? Dear reader, Jesus Christ never instituted the confessional. Would he call lustful, licentious, drinking men to ask such low, vile questions, which are unbecoming for any one to ask another? I am sure as well confess to a dead dog. The Roman Church teaches you cannot be saved unless you confess to a priest. Read this from their own teaching: "If any one shall say that priests who are in mortal sin have not the power of binding or loosing, or that priests are not the only ministers of absolution, let him be accursed." This does away with Jesus' blood. It makes God second to this fellow in the confessional box. They teach that every sin, the vilest and lowest, the most criminal, by man and woman, must be confessed to the priest. They do not teach it necessary to repent, but to do penance. Notice, this takes the place of repentance. Penance and confession to a wicked priest necessary to salvation? Is there any intelligent person on the earth who believes it? The following is what Margaret L. Shepard, who was for three years an inmate of the Arno's Court Convent, Bristol, England, says: "In a confessional the depth of corruption and womanly degradation is reached. There the seeds of hell are planted in the soul. The thoughts of a young girl are polluted. Her heart is polluted, her mind becomes familiarized with the most revolting sins and impurity. The lessons engraved in the memory, the heart, the thought, the soul, like the sear of a red-hot iron, leaves its scar. In the confessional young unmarried and married women get accustomed to hear and repeat without a scruple things which would cause even a fallen woman to blush." These are the words of one who has been through the above and escaped from their murderous hands. I will close with the above. It is a clincher and positive evidence and witness of all I have said. All unite with me in prayer that the above will open the eyes of many deceived Romanists and come to the blood of Christ.

N. L. A. EASTMAN.

There were two detailed opinions in the court as to the offense Mr. Eastman had committed. One was that his language was highly objectionable but not punishable as obscenity. The other was that the law forbade indecent utterances and was meant to cover just such instances as this. Here are some of the arguments advanced by those who were favorable to Eastman's cause, this opinion being written by Chief Judge Cullen:

That the article is a scurrilous and vile attack on a large and respected body of Christian clergymen is unquestionable. That it is "indecent" from every consideration of propriety is entirely clear, but that is not the indecency condemned by this section of the Code. The preceding section punishes indecent exposure of person, the next section the sale of articles for indecent or immoral use.

Is Truth a Defense?

Since, however, the article is to appear, I may challenge its comparison with many that have been published attacking the Mormon Church. Surely, publication as to that church have gone far beyond the article now before us. It is no answer to say that the Mormons, while they practiced polygamy, were justly subject to such strictures. The truth or falsity of the writing has no bearing on the guilt or innocence of the defendant under this section of the Code. If the charges contained in this article had been made, not against a class but against a single individual, and that individual a layman, not a clergyman, it would, doubtless, if false, have been a gross libel. But it would not be contended that if true it was indecent and should subject the party writing it to the penalties prescribed by the Code.

Does the State Try to Legislate Manners?

It is clear from the manner in which the legislature has used the word "indecent" that it relates to obscene prints or publications; it is not an attempt to regulate manners, but it is a declaration of the penalties to be imposed upon the various phases of the crime of obscenity.

On the other hand, the other opinion had a different interpretation of the legislature's meaning of the word. The three judges who signed this one felt that

the term "indecent" signifies "more than indelicate and less than modest"; that it means "something unfit for the eye or ear."

In reading this statute there may be some danger of falling into the error of construing "indecent" as synonymous with "lewd, lascivious," etc., used in connection with it, but an examination of the language of the section, from its appearance in the original Code of 1881 to the present time, clearly discloses that the word does not necessarily have any reference to morals. The prohibition is against an "obscene OR indecent" publication.

Four judges of the court held to the first point of view and three to the second, so the prevailing sentiment was in favor of Eastman, the majority holding:

> The Court is of opinion that the publication set forth in the indictment is improper, intemperate, unjustifiable and highly reprehensible, nevertheless it is not "indecent" as that word is employed in Section 317 of the Penal Code.

It is worth noting that neither of the opinions discussed the potential harm, if any, at which the law was aiming. Until very recently, seldom if ever did any judge ask in a trial involving obscenity: "What is the antisocial effect of the writing under attack?" "Just who has been damaged or harmed or corrupted and how?"

Much clearer were the lines of battle when Savonarola burned the works of Dante in Florence in 1497 and when Savonarola was tortured on the rack in 1498 until he confessed his error in denouncing papal corruption. Even the Emperor Chi Huang Ti's order in 200 B.C. to burn the Analects and other writings of Confucius rested on diagnosed fears.

These boundaries of the permitted do not seem so simple to us today. Although his judges deplored Mr. Eastman's taste, they did not regard his words as meriting punishment by the law. Like most tools of society, Law has had to learn to grope around in the gray smog produced by an aging and sophisticated civilization. Under our system of law, judges are not allowed to muse in the abstract. Their gropings must be triggered by what lawyers call a "case or controversy"—and it takes two sides to have one. In the context of the persistent success of Comstock and his cohorts in the field of censorship, the subtle distinctions of the courts between "obscenity" and "vulgarity" take on the aspect of a quiet frolic and detour. On the main battlefield the Comstocks kept winning—largely because the other "side" of the controversy usually gave in without a fight. There were exceptions, however, and our next chapter will introduce you to a really good fighter.

9

A Publisher
Fights Back

The law's tendency, in the course of its search for definitions of obscenity, to exempt vulgarity and outhouse humor from punishment did nothing to mitigate the stern prosecutions of literature and art that offended the sexual standards of the Society for the Suppression of Vice, its agents and supporters. The time from the enactment of the Comstock Laws until 1915 was a sad and sorry period for law and all authors in our Republic. During these years the courts had few honorable opportunities to formulate legal concepts of censorship because so many of the leading publishers bowed to Comstock. Manuscripts were submitted to him for his blessing. Even the Peck's Bad Boy of the magazine field, H. L. Mencken, himself traipsed over to the Vice Society office with the manuscript of a book by Theodore Dreiser to beg absolution. The book was *Sister Carrie!*

In 1915, however, a modest publisher with a small list of titles challenged Comstock as none of the great publishing houses had seen fit to do, and his courage turned the tide. He was Mitchell Kennerley, and the book he dared to defend was a novel, *Hagar Revelly,* by Daniel Carson Goodman.

This work shocked the censors for reasons now difficult to imagine. The plot derived from the then prevalent notion that sexual vice had an economic root, that prostitution could be traced to the low wages paid to workingwomen. In this novel there were two shopgirls. Only one went wrong. Comstock presumably read the seduction scenes and skipped the moral lessons.

When Kennerley decided to defend his imprint, a clerk had already been convicted in a New York State court for selling *Hagar Revelly*. Another case was brought in the Federal court, just across City Hall Park from the state court. There, Judge Learned Hand, just recently appointed to the bench, offered the first variation from the test of obscenity pronounced by Lord Chief Justice Cockburn forty-seven years earlier. His opinion must be understood against the background of the Comstock Era. In England even Shakespeare ("homosexual" poems) and Shelley (the incest of *The Cenci*) were under attack, while on our shores Hawthorne (*The Scarlet Letter*) and Mark Twain (*Huckleberry Finn*) brought blushes. The development of legal thinking away from these attitudes had its real start in Judge Hand's opinion in the *Kennerley* case. He wrote:

> I hope it is not improper for me to say that the rule as laid down, however consonant it may be with mid-Victorian morals, does not seem to me to answer to the understanding and morality of the present time, as conveyed by the words, "obscene, lewd or lascivious." I question whether in the end men will regard that as obscene which is honestly relevant to the adequate expression of innocent ideas, and whether they will not believe that truth and beauty are too precious to society at large to be mutilated in the interests of those most likely to pervert them to base uses. Indeed, it seems hardly likely that we are even today so lukewarm in our interest in letters or serious discussion as to be content to reduce our treatment of sex to the standard of a child's library in the supposed interest of a salacious few, or that shame will for long prevent us from adequate portrayal of some of the most serious and beautiful sides of human nature.

Then, in place of the test Cockburn had made the law of both his own country and ours, Judge Hand suggested "the word 'obscene' be allowed to indicate the present critical point in the compromise between candor and shame at which the community may have arrived here and now."

This was the first suggestion in a court of eminence that perhaps the standards of the people have some bearing on what is to be considered corrupting. The decision raised issues that are still troubling our courts. For example:

Times do change. Should definitions of obscenity change with them?

Do "truth and beauty" condone obscenity?

Is the literary diet of adults to be reduced to the mush fit for children or the feebleminded?

In view of Judge Hand's obvious answers to some of these questions, the layman might suppose that he would have dismissed the charge against Kennerley. But the law is not that easily revised. As a lower-court Federal judge, Learned Hand did not feel himself high enough in the judicial hierarchy to upset a test for obscenity that had been accepted without question by high- and low-court judges for nearly half a century. So he said he had no choice, under the precedents established through the years, but to rule against the courageous publisher. However, when a judge makes such a ruling, he is inviting the loser in the case to appeal to a higher court, and the higher court under our system will hear that appeal if only because one of its judicial brethren has doubts about the soundness of the precedents. A Federal Court of Appeals decided that *Hagar Revelly* was not obscene, even under the old test. These judges did not, therefore, expressly approve Judge Hand's proposed definition, but it remained in the record for lawyers to quote with approval from that time forward.

It had been obvious to almost any reader that *Hagar Revelly* was intended to uplift the moral standards of the people. But what if an author's avowed motive was to corrupt the public? This was an issue the courts could not evade, as our next chapter will show.

10

An
Avowed
Corrupter

U sually in obscenity trials defenders of books under attack have
tried to justify the alleged indecencies on the ground that the writer's
motive was pure. But there is one famous case in which the author
frankly stated in his introduction that he wrote the novel to make light
of fornication, adultery, and homosexuality.

The judicial decision, when it came—incidentally more than eighty
years after the book appeared—was an excellent example of the way
our courts, by ruling on relatively narrow points of law, make legal
history over the decades by pecking away at the old standards little by
little, adding a new concept here, weakening an established precedent
there. At the time of this particular case, too, it should be kept in
mind, the country was in the midst of the profound changes in manners and morals accompanying the First World War. Large segments
of the population were ready for greater freedom not only in writing
about sex but also in actual sexual behavior. And other large segments
were deploring this fact.

Legal history in this instance was made by a bookstore clerk, Raymond D. Halsey, although a world-renowned author and a minor
classic of the nineteenth century were also involved. It happened in a
series of simple steps. On November 17, 1917, Halsey sold to an

agent of the Society for the Suppression of Vice, Comstock's successor, John S. Sumner, one copy of *Mademoiselle de Maupin,* by Théophile Gautier. Halsey was arrested for selling an obscene volume. At the trial he was acquitted.

Halsey, an old-fashioned American, did not allow the matter to rest there. He sued for false arrest and malicious prosecution. His case hinged on whether Sumner and the Society had probable cause to believe that the book was sold in violation of the New York State obscenity law. The Court of Appeals, which in New York is the highest tribunal, upheld a lower-court judgment for damages of $2,500 granted to Halsey by a jury. The Court of Appeals had to take a look at the book as well as at the claim for money damages, with the result that it ruled 4 to 2 for Halsey and in effect for the book.

It is significant that the Court took into consideration these points: (*a*) the reputation of the author; (*b*) the regard in which the novel had been held by eminent critics since its first publication in 1835; (*c*) a reading of the book in its entirety and not just selected passages; (*d*) the fact that even the language complained of was not "of the street"; (*e*) the effect of the translation from the French. When reading the relevant portions of the opinion, be ready for the dissenting view of Judge Crane, who was later to be Chief Judge of this court. And note that by neither the majority nor minority was any attention paid to the motive that Gautier had so frankly avowed!

RAYMOND D. HALSEY V. THE NEW YORK SOCIETY FOR THE SUP-PRESSION OF VICE. (New York 1922.)

ANDREWS, J. On November 17, 1917, in the City of New York, Halsey sold to Sumner an English translation of "Mademoiselle de Maupin." Mr. Sumner submitted the book to City Magistrate House who, however, took no action. He then on November 22d presented a marked copy to Magistrate Simms with a letter calling attention to certain pages which he thought deserved examination. On the 28th he also charged that the book was obscene and indecent, referring not only to the marked pages but to the entire work. Thereupon an order was issued stating that it appeared "from the within depositions and statements that the crime therein mentioned has been committed" and holding Halsey to answer. Halsey was arrested at the direction of Sumner and arraigned. He waived examination, was held for the action of the Court of Special Sessions, tried and acquitted. The record of that trial is not before us, but it was conceded that the copy of "Mademoiselle de Maupin" had been sold by Halsey and the acquittal was for the reason, apparently, that the book was not obscene or indecent. This action to recover damages for malicious prosecution was then begun. At the close of the evidence the case was submitted to the jury which found in favor of Halsey.

The entire book was offered in evidence. We are asked to say from its bare perusal that probable cause existed for the belief on the part of Sumner that Halsey was guilty by its sale of a violation of the Penal Law.

The question of "probable cause" is important here because a prosecution cannot, under the law, be "malicious" if the prosecuting person had good reason to believe that a law had been violated. Thus, if Sumner had "probable cause" to believe that Halsey had indeed violated the law (or, to put it another way, that a reasonable man would think the book to be obscene), Halsey would lose his case.

Although Judge Andrews was a man of the judicial cloth, he was also, as he shows us, a man of literature:

The Distinguished Author

Théophile Gautier is conceded to be among the greatest French writers of the nineteenth century. When some of his earlier works were submitted to Sainte-Beuve, that distinguished critic was astonished by the variety and richness of his expression. Henry James refers to him as a man of genius (North American Review, April, 1873). Arthur Symons (Studies in Prose and Verse), George Saintsbury (A Short History of French Literature), James Breck Perkins (Atlantic Monthly, March, 1887) all speak of him with admiration. They tell of his command of style, his poetical imagery, his artistic conceptions, his indescribable charm, his high and probably permanent place in French literature. They say that in many respects he resembles Thackeray.

The Book Has a Place in the Literature of France

This was the man who in 1836 published "Mademoiselle de Maupin." It is a book of over four hundred pages. The moment it was issued it excited the criticism of many, but not all of the great Frenchmen of the day. It has since become a part of French literature. No review of French writers of the last one hundred years fails to comment upon it. With the author's felicitous style, it contains passages of purity and beauty. It seems to be largely a protest against what the author, we believe mistakenly, regards as the prudery of newspaper criticism. It contains many paragraphs, however, which taken by themselves are undoubtedly vulgar and indecent.

The Book Must Be Judged in Its Entirety

No work may be judged from a selection of such paragraphs alone. Printed by themselves they might, as a matter of law, come within the prohibition of the statute. So might a similar selection from Aristophanes or Chaucer or Boccaccio or even from the Bible. The book, however, must be considered broadly as a whole. So considered, critical opinion is divided. Some critics, while admitting that the novel has been much admired, call it both "pornographic and dull." (The Nation, Nov. 2, 1893.) Mr. Perkins writes that "there is much in Mademoiselle de Maupin that is unpleasant, and is saved only by beauty of expression from being vulgar. Though Gautier's style reached in this novel its full perfection, it is far from his best work and it is unfortunate that it is probably the one best known." An article in the June, 1868, issue of the Atlantic Monthly says that this is Gautier's representative romance. James calls it his one disagreeable performance but "in certain lights the book is almost ludicrously innocent, and we are at a loss what to think of those critics who either hailed or denounced it as a serious profession of faith." Finally in "A Century of French Fiction," Benjamin W. Wells, professor of modern languages in the University of the South, says: "Mademoiselle de Maupin is an exquisite work of art, but it spurns the conventions of received morality with a contempt that was to close the Academy to Gautier forever. With a springboard of fact in the seventeenth century to start from, he conceives a wealthy and energetic girl of twenty, freed from domestic restraints and resolved to acquire, by mingling as man among men, more knowledge of the other sex than the conventions of social intercourse would admit. He transfers the adventures from the real world to a sort of forest of Arden, where the Rosalind of Shakespeare might meet a Watteau shepherdess and a melancholy Jacques. Thus he helps us over the instinctive repulsion that we feel for the situation, and gives a purely artistic interest to the self-revelation that comes to his heroine and to Albert from their prolonged association. Various forms of love reaching out for an attainable ideal occupy the body of the book, and when once the actors learn to know themselves and each other Gautier parts them forever. In its ethics the book is opposed to the professed morality of nearly all, and doubtless to the real morality of most, but as Sainte-Beuve said of it: 'Every physician of the soul, every moralist, should have it on some back shelf of his library,' and those who, like Mithridates, no longer react to such poisons will find in Mlle. de Maupin much food for the purest literary enjoyment."

After this virtuoso performance, Judge Andrews turns his aesthetic profile toward his judicial brethren. Who are they—he asks—to cast the first stone? The question is still pertinent. Should a judge or a jury decide whether something is worth reading? Or should a literary critic decide what is or is not obscene? As you now read further in our book you will see this judicial-literary tennis match proliferate into many matches, with judge, jury, author, critic, sociologist, and more, in the game. And all too often the audience gets little more than a stiff neck. But now—"Service, Judge Andrews!"

Endurance for a Century Is Meaningful in Law

We have quoted estimates of the book as showing the manner in which it affects different minds. The conflict among the members of this court itself points a finger at the dangers of a censorship entrusted to men of one profession, of like education and similar surroundings. Far better than we, is a jury drawn from those of varied experiences, engaged in various occupations, in close touch with the currents of public feeling, fitted to say whether the defendant had reasonable ground to believe that a book such as this was obscene or indecent. Here is the work of a great author, written in admirable style, which has become a part of classical literature. We may take judicial notice that it has been widely sold, separately and as a part of every collection of the works of Gautier. It has excited admiration as well as opposition. We know that a book merely obscene soon dies. Many a Roman poet wrote a Metamorphoses. Ovid survives. So this book also has lived for a hundred years.

On the other hand, it does contain indecent paragraphs. We are dealing too with a translation where the charm of style may be attenuated. It is possible that the morality of New York City today may be on a higher plane than that of Paris in 1836—that there is less vice, less crime. We hope so. We admit freely that a book may be thoroughly indecent, no matter how great the author or how fascinating the style. It is also true that well-known writers have committed crimes, yet it is difficult to trace the connection between this fact and the question we are called upon to decide. Doctor Dodd was hanged for forgery, yet his sermons were not indecent. Oscar Wilde was convicted of personal wrongdoing and confined in Reading Gaol. It does not follow that all his plays are obscene. It is also true that the work before us bears the name of no publisher. That the house which issued it was ashamed of its act is an inference not perhaps justified by any evidence before us.

Regarding all these circumstances, so far as they are at all material, we believe it is for the jury, and not for us, to draw the conclusion that must be drawn. Was the book as a whole of a character to justify the reasonable belief that its sale was a violation of the Penal Law? The jury has said that it was not. We cannot say as a matter of law that they might not reach this decision. We hold that the question of probable cause was properly submitted to them.

The judgment must, therefore, be affirmed.

To us, at least, Judge Andrews is quite convincing—as well as erudite. But Judge Crane, writing for the dissenting minority, is perhaps only a shade less erudite—and certainly as qualified to speak:

CRANE, J. (dissenting). Would reasonable, careful, prudent men acting with caution, and environed with the conditions of life as they exist to-day, and not in some past age, be justified in believing "Mademoiselle de Maupin" a filthy and indecent book and published for no useful purpose, but simply from a desire to cater to the lowest and most sensual part of human nature?

Publisher—Anonymous!

In order to justify my conclusion that Sumner had probable cause to believe this book such an one, it is not necessary to spread upon our pages all the indecent and lascivious part of this work. Some facts, however, may be mentioned to give point and direction to this inquiry. In the first place the Society for the Suppression of Vice was confronted with the fact that the publisher, whoever he was, does not put his name to the book.

Counseling Vice Is Obscene

The book consists of certain letters purported to be written by a young man of twenty-two as a sort of a satire on virtue and in praise of the sensual passions, adultery and fornication. It counsels vice. He tells his friend of his love for certain women, describes them, and relates the scenes leading up to immoral practices and to intercourse. To have a mistress in the eyes of this young man is the first qualification of a gentleman, and adultery to him appears to be the most innocent thing in the world. He writes: "I deem it quite a simple matter that a young girl should prostitute herself."

No doubt many books of fine literature known as standard works have passages in them which may shock the moral sensibilities of some people of this day, but they appear as expressions of the times and not to my knowledge as in praise of vice and derision of virtue. Most works, wherever prostitution appears, condemn or confess it as a vice or admit its evil effects and influences. The purport of this book seems to be to impress upon the readers that vice and voluptuousness are natural to society, are not wrongs but proper practices to be indulged in by the young.

Condemned by the People of His Time and Culture

Théophile Gautier published Mlle. de Maupin in 1835. The people of his time condemned it, and by reason of its lasciviousness and bad taste he was forever barred from the French Academy. He acquired a reputation as a writer, but it was not because of this book. The New International Encyclopedia has this to say about Gautier and his Mlle. de Maupin: "Théophile Gautier 1811–1872. Gautier's next book, Mlle. de Maupin (1835), a curious attempt at self-analysis, was a frank expression of Hedonism. Its art is fascinating, but it treats the fundamental postulates of morality with a contempt that closed the Academy to him for life."

Literary Reputation Is the Defense

In the Encyclopaedia Britannica we read the following: 'His first novel of any size, and in many respects his most remarkable work, was Mlle. de Maupin. Unfortunately this book while it establishes his literary reputation on an imperishable basis, was *unfitted* by its subject, and in parts by its treatment, *for general perusal,* and created even in France, a prejudice against its author which he was very far from really deserving." (Article by George Saintsbury.) [Italics mine.]

In the Encyclopedia Americana may be read: "Gautier's whole philosophy is a philosophy of paradox, his ideal of life hardly more than a picturesque viciousness. His besetting sin was a desire to say something clever and wicked to shock the Philistines (see Mlle. de Maupin). The academy was forever closed to him."

When the people of France and Gautier's time condemned his book as being vicious and unfit for general perusal, are we going to say that Sumner did not have probable cause to believe the same thing, when the translation was published in America by a publisher who was ashamed to put his name to it?

Many things have moved in the past century, and with the teachings of church, synagogue and college, we, at least, have the right to expect that the general tone of morality in America in 1922 is equal to that of France in 1835.

It may be true that Gautier's style is fascinating and his imagination rich, but neither style, imagination or learning can create a privileged class, or permit obscenity because it is dressed up in a fashion difficult to imitate or acquire.

Our Literature Has Been Clean!

American literature has been fairly clean. That the policy of this state is to keep it so is indicated by Section 1141 of the Penal Law. The legislature has declared in this section that no obscene, lewd, lascivious or disgusting book shall be sold. Language could not be plainer.

If the things said by Gautier in this book of Mlle. de Maupin were stated openly and frankly in the language of the street, there would be no doubt in the minds of anybody, I take it, that the work would be lewd, vicious and indecent. The fact that the disgusting details are served up in a polished style with exquisite settings and perfumed words makes it all the more dangerous and insidious and none the less obscene and lascivious.

Gautier may have a reputation as a writer, but his reputation does not create a license for the American market.

Oscar Wilde had a great reputation for style, but went to jail just the same. Literary ability is no excuse for degeneracy.

Sufficient to say that a reading of this book convinces me that as a matter of law the Society for the Suppression of Vice had probable cause to believe Halsey guilty of violating the Penal Law in selling this book.

HISCOCK, ch. J., POUND and MCLAUGHLIN, JJ., concur with ANDREWS, J.; CRANE, J., reads dissenting opinion in which HOGAN, J., concurs.

This case had great importance. Since these judges relied on literary authorities—either dead authors such as Henry James or the anonymous contributors to a famous encyclopedia—it was soon to be urged in many cases that living critics should be permitted to offer testimony for or against any book. The example in the *Halsey* case, therefore, was of great influence, although the majority had said that a jury, because of its variety of experience, was better fitted to decide the issues than a group of judges. Experts were used in later cases in various ways. In some instances this "opinion testimony" was presented to the judge in a separate printed brief on the ground that if the Court of Appeals was aided by the views of the dead, lower tribunals might be assisted by expressions of then living experts such as Sinclair Lewis, Carl Van Doren, or Heywood Broun. At times supplemental opinions came from book reviewers, English professors in colleges, and even religious leaders.

Whenever a Court is trying to appraise vague words of peculiarly subjective meaning, such as "obscenity," the door opens with special grace to the opinions of community leaders. These can make a contribution in aid of the jury, although it still is argued that a jury, as a cross section of our public, is competent to order the burning of any book and needs no advice except as to the law itself from a judge. The

Halsey decision was the gatekeeper that opened the door to opinions of representative people in the community to assist both judge and jury. But the meaning of "obscenity" remained uncertain, thoroughly subjective, even when the judge who sought to define it was absolutely sure of his own definition. Read on—and see what we mean!

11

The Word Obscenity

"Defies Misunderstanding"

In 1924, an honorable judge, later to be an important senator from New York, Robert F. Wagner, wrote an opinion with a startlingly fresh approach to the New York statute on obscenity. The book involved in the opinion of Judge Wagner was *Casanova's Homecoming,* by Arthur Schnitzler. It circulates freely in our city, state, and nation. By now it is a minor but recognized classic. The case was *People* v. *Seltzer*—and here is the judge:

> The Obscenity Law does not attempt to define the meaning of the words "obscene" or "indecent" or the others set forth therein, it seems to me that such definitions would be entirely unnecessary, for these words are in common use and their meaning is readily comprehended by men of ordinary intelligence. The difficulty that has arisen with respect to this section lies not in the particular test to be applied thereto in determining the question as to whether a particular book comes within the provisions or not, but in the misconception that there can be any judge-made or constant test at all established by way of formularization.

This makes law look like a living, growing art; but then, from the same pen:

The lack of symmetry of prior interpretation and misapprehension of a decision by our highest court, due in a large measure to the human difficulty of dealing with the abstract as well as the breadth of the law's scope, have left the subject in what I consider a confused state, justifying, perhaps, a brief RÉSUMÉ of the principles and considerations useful to its interpretation.

The inexactness of the law as a science is never more pointedly instanced than as here, when it is sought to chisel from abstractions of legal survey precise and mathematical-like rules for the analysis and admeasurement of the concrete. The important but not sole test, as taken from the case of REGINA v. HICKLIN, is one that I think should in part guide the law-enforcing authority and a court and jury in determining whether a book offends the law against obscene publications, namely: "Is the tendency of the matter charged as obscene to deprave or corrupt those whose minds are open to such immoral influences and who might come in contact with it?" keeping in full view the consideration that the law looks to the protection not of the mature and intelligent, with minds strengthened to withstand the influences of the prohibited data, but of the young and immature, the ignorant and sensually inclined.

At first reading it is hard to quarrel with the judge. But be careful; there is an imposing assumption to be recognized. By stating that the purpose of the Obscenity Law is to protect the young and innocent rather than the mature adult, is not Judge Wagner limiting the literary diet of the average adult to those works that children might safely read? The question of what community standards are to be applied in obscenity cases is still with us—although, as we shall see later in the volume, the tide has gone against Judge Wagner in recent years.

But the judge is just picking up steam. He goes on to hold that literary criticism is irrelevant; acceptance in other places or countries has no persuasive force; expert opinion is inadmissible. He then states positions which it has taken authors and publishers decades to expunge from legal theory:

Charm of language, subtlety of thought, faultless style, even distinction of authorship, may all have their lure for the literary critic, yet these qualities may all be present and the book be unfit for dissemination to the reading public. Frequently these attractive literary qualities are the very vehicles by which the destination of illegality is reached. Neither literary artistry nor charm and grace of exquisite composition may cloak protectively these obnoxious impulses that subtly creep unaware to a point of approval, which on patent appearance would be abhorred.

> "So may the outward shows be least themselves;
> The world is still deceiv'd with ornaments.
> In law, what plea so tainted and corrupt
> But, being seasoned with a gracious voice,
> Obscures the show of evil? * * *
> There is no vice so simple but assumes
> Some mark of virtue on its outward parts."

We, therefore, cannot accept a book's adoption by another land or the approval of critics as conclusive of non-obscenity under the statute, for we may assert with pride—though not boastfully—that we are essentially an idealistic and spiritual nation and exact a higher standard than some others. Aside from the purely spiritual and idealistic viewpoint, the enforcement of this section is of great materialistic concern to our government. The future of a nation depends upon its youth. Our more enlightened conception of the need of protective measures to preserve our youth is reflected in the great progress that has taken place in recent years in the enactment of laws for the protection of the health of our women and children to save them from exploitation by the unscrupulous employer, and even sometimes, though rarely, the unscrupulous parent, in order that the child may become a healthy and useful citizen and the woman preserved for motherhood. We have the compulsory education laws; we have the laws prohibiting child labor, and when children are permitted by law to work we limit their hours of employment; we have the laws limiting the hours women may toil, and others prohibiting them from working in factories during the night time; we have laws insuring proper sanitary conditions under which they may be employed, the Widows' Pension Law and many others, here unnecessary to enumerate, of the same purport.

And while their enactment was actuated largely by our enlightened conceptions of social justice and motives altruistic, yet these laws also exist because the fostering of the health of women and children is one of grave governmental concern. Just as it is of national concern and interest to protect their health, it is equally important to protect our youth against the corruption of their morals, so that we may do everything within governmental power to afford them physical, mental and moral virility and not have their development arrested in these respects during the formative period. It is a national duty to prevent the moral or physical weakening of the family— "The Nursery of Mankind." History warns us that in the wake of a moral deterioration comes physical deterioration and national destruction. Hence our interest in the strict enforcement of all laws to prevent the publication and distribution of corrupt literature. As it is the duty of our law-enforcing branches of government to enforce with vigor these laws, so it is the co-relative function of the courts not to narrow the law's application by accepting tests restrictive of the commonly accepted meaning of the words.

This honest though bewildered judge says what few men on the bench have ever dared say. It's not easy for a judge to declare that law must be a "feeling" and not a result of rational, logical, sober thought.

Feeling Versus Rational Thought

The meaning of the section to the ordinary mind defies misunderstanding. It deals with subjects which are felt, understood and appreciated by the layman. Instantaneous is the reaction, instinctive the revolt to better feelings when disregard occurs. It addresses itself largely to the good judgment, common sense, knowledge of human nature and its weaknesses. For this reason there can be established no absolute test to guide those responsible for its enforcement. No sentence, paragraph or opinion can set forth adequately and completely all the elements to be considered and the prevailing considerations to be applied. Moral standards of thought are not of static or plastic nature. Thought once accepted of course, may to-day be repelled. It follows that the current opinion as to whether or not a publication falls within the prohibitions of the section may better be ascertained by a jury of varied occupations and of different experiences, yet all in touch with the currents of views and opinions. As was said in PEOPLE V. MULLER, the question whether a writing "is obscene is one of the plainest that can be presented to a jury, and under the guidance of a discreet judge there is little danger of their reaching a wrong conclusion."

To this judge it was all so, so simple.

History has proved Judge Wagner to have been a pretty poor prophet in this case. But the Law of Obscenity had to go through many different phases before it could reach the degree of sophistication and eclecticism it has today. Courageous defendants and their lawyers had to chip away at the great stone monument to Comstockery piece by piece. Each judicial theory had to be isolated and challenged before the law could be liberalized.

12

On Banning a Theme

The censorious seldom, if ever, had placed a taboo upon an entire subject matter or theme, a whole area of thought. Usually, the attack had been against a specific technique used in presenting the theme, such as four-letter words of Anglo-Saxon origin or specific sexual descriptions. Until after the middle of the 1920's, no court opinion had been addressed directly to the question of banning the literary expression of an entire area of human knowledge or human behavior.

Then, in both drama and the novel, the question was raised: Should the public be denied the right to read a book or see a play on the subject of female homosexuality?

Curiously enough, the test of the subject arose first on the stage. In our culture the theater has been substantially unmolested by the censors except in just the period we are now discussing, the 1920's and 1930's. Social scientists may tell us the basis of this immunity. Perhaps it is the high price of tickets, conveying an exemption that in literature is traditionally assured to expensive editions, at least since the *Worthington* case. The fact that children were less likely to be exposed may have distracted the leers of the "Comstocks" to more fertile fields of attack. In this connection a quote from Father Murray, a great Catholic writer on taste, morals, and the law, seems appropriate, although he was not talking specifically about the theater:

"Society has an interest in the artist's expression which is not necessarily shared by the family. If adult standards of literature could be dangerous for children, a child's standard is rather appalling for an adult."

Even at the peak of Comstock's power, he had not been able to force upon theatrical producers the yoke in which he held book publishers. In 1905 he had made the attempt. His target was George Bernard Shaw's new play, *Mrs. Warren's Profession,* which scandalized many people because it dealt with prostitution. It had already been banned from the British stage where the Master of the Revels (the Lord Chamberlain) had (and still has) precensorship powers over all plays publicly produced. Comstock announced that if anyone staged the play by "the Irish smut-dealer," he would prosecute. He did, too, but a three-man court ruled by a vote of 2 to 1 that *Mrs. Warren's Profession* did not fall within the scope of the New York State Obscenity Law.

However, female homosexuality was another matter. Lesbian-oriented plays such as Edouard Bourdet's *The Captive* in 1927 were closed down, and the resulting furor led the New York Legislature—since New York City is the center of the thespian arts—to pass a law against the performance of any drama that dealt with sexual perversion.

The law, interestingly, was directed not only against the offending play but also against the theater in which it was performed. The theater owner could lose his license and the theater be closed.

Two years later, in 1929, the courts were called upon to consider whether the same objections applied to a novel, specifically, *The Well of Loneliness,* by Radclyffe Hall. This was a work of "restraint and literary merit," to use the words of the most horrified of the judges who presided over its fate. The prosecutor objected not to any identified episode of lesbian lovemaking but to its mere idea. In that era all discussions of sexual relations other than those between male and female were illegal in the eyes of the State. There had been a few novels touching on the love of man and man, or woman and woman. But no law had been made as to the lines of permissibility or impermissibility. Nevertheless, in *The Well of Loneliness* case the cultural taboo frightened many editors of our mass media. One of our most distinguished publishers had actually set up *The Well of Loneliness* in type. He was then advised by an able attorney to desist from publication because the book was, or at least might be held to be, obscene and illegal.

Donald Friede, of Covici, Friede, a couragous publisher, took over the publishing rights and dared the legal conventions. When brought into the Magistrate's Court in New York City, he not only defended his imprimatur but defended it stoutly and, what is still more important, without the least trace of apology. Unlike many other publishers before and after him, he acted as if he really believed what the Constitution guaranteed—freedom of the printed word. The case came to court without any dispute as to facts such as "Was the book published?" "Was it sold?" "Who sold it?" and all the other details that are really irrelevant in most battles over freedom for the mind of man.

The judge who first heard the case addressed himself to it in terms of that familiar text of Lord Chief Justice Cockburn in 1868: Would the book corrupt those into whose hands it was likely to fall?

Psychiatrists of esteem differed widely as to its possible influence or effect. Leaders of that profession were afraid to testify, some going so far as to indicate that the book might conceivably corrupt our culture, some suggesting that it might turn our nation into an "Isle of Lesbos." Others with great sobriety of thought replied with questions: Do we favor forcing this problem or issue or situation into dirty, secret underground avenues for future discussion? If there be a problem, since sexual relations between men and women are deemed to be preferable, do we still believe that man has his best chance of finding a wise solution by open debate in the marketplace of thought, or by suppression of all writings on the subject? Do we sweep the entire problem under the bed?

When the case came before Judge Hyman Bushel sitting without a jury in the Magistrate's Court of New York City, he wrote a lengthy opinion. For those who have not read the book itself and who may be interested in techniques of testing for the obscene, Judge Bushel's view is set forth at length to show what he read *in* and *out* of the volume. He does point out that there are no unclean words, that the book is well written and carefully constructed as a piece of fiction. He decides, however, that the book should be banned because the "depraved" relationships are idealized and extolled and, what bothers him most, because lesbian love and lesbian lovers are not held up to shame. We assume that the good judge might have concluded that the book was legal if Radclyffe Hall, the author, had had the characters apologetic for what they did to life and what life did to them.

This opinion should be read with care. The judge was offended, shocked, and discouraged. He will not object if we add that he was not a man who had lived in an ivory tower. He was married and he had grown up in the hurly-burly of a big city. But we must be gentle with him, for in 1929 few women in our land had ever heard the word "lesbian." If the mass media of that era referred at all to such a way of life, it was only by indirection or with euphemisms. It was understandable that Judge Bushel might conclude that the volume was offensive, according to his own likes.

PEOPLE V. FRIEDE

City Magistrate's Court of New York City (1929)

BUSHEL, City Magistrate. Friede and another person are charged with having violated the New York Penal Law by their possession and sale of a book entitled "The Well of Loneliness." Evidence proving possession and sale of the book by Friede had been introduced and is not controverted by him.

This court in a prosecution of this character is not the trier of the fact. Its judicial province is limited to a determination of the question as to whether as matter of law it can be said that the book which forms the basis of the charge in question is not violative of the statute. The evidence before me, however, is the same as that which would be presented to the tribunal vested with the power of deciding the facts as well as the law.

An "Unnatural" Crew

The book here involved is a novel dealing with the childhood and early womanhood of a female invert. In broad outline the story shows how these unnatural tendencies manifested themselves from early childhood; the queer attraction of the child to the maid in the household, her affairs with one Angela Crossby, a normally sexed, but unhappily married, woman, causing further dissension between the latter and her husband, her jealousy of another man who later debauched this married woman, and her despair, in being supplanted by him in Angela's affections, are vividly portrayed. The book culminates with an extended elaboration upon her intimate relations with a normal young girl, who becomes a helpless subject of her perverted influence and passion, and pictures the struggle for this girl's affections between this invert and a man from whose normal advances she herself had previously recoiled, because of her own perverted nature. Her sex experiences are set forth in some detail and also her visits to various resorts frequented by male and female inverts.

Literary Merit—Yes

The author has treated these incidents not without some restraint; nor is it disputed that the book has literary merit. To quote the people's brief: "It is a well-written, carefully constructed piece of fiction, and contains no unclean words." Yet the narrative does not veer from its central theme, and the emotional and literary setting in which they are found give the incidents described therein great force and poignancy. The unnatural and depraved relationships portrayed are sought to be idealized and extolled. The characters in the book who indulge in these vices are described in attractive terms, and it is maintained throughout that they be accepted on the same plane as persons normally constituted, and that their perverse and inverted love is as worthy as the affection between normal beings and should be considered just as sacred by society.

Moral Value—No

The book can have no moral value, since it seeks to justify the right of a pervert to prey upon normal members of a community, and to uphold such relationship as noble and lofty. Although it pleads for tolerance on the part of society of those possessed of and inflicted with perverted traits and tendencies, it does not argue for repression or moderation of insidious impulses. An idea of the moral tone which the book assumes may be gained from the attitude taken by its principal character towards her mother, pictured as a hard, cruel, and pitiless woman, because of the abhorrence she displays to unnatural lust, and to whom, because of that reaction, the former says: "But what I will never forgive is your daring to try and make me ashamed of my love. I'm not ashamed of it; there's no shame in me."

The theme of the novel is not only antisocial and offensive to public morals and decency, but the method in which it is developed, in its highly emotional way attracting and focusing attention upon perverted ideas and unnatural vices, and seeking to justify and idealize them, is strongly calculated to corrupt and debase those members of the community who would be susceptible to its immoral influence.

Justice Cockburn Rides Again

Although the book in evidence is prefaced by a laudatory commentary by Havelock Ellis, yet it is he who, in his scientific treatise on the subject, states: "We are bound to protect the helpless members of society against the invert." The court is charged with that precise duty here. The test of an obscene book laid down in *Regina* v. *Hicklin,* is "whether the tendency of the matter charged as obscenity is to deprave or corrupt those whose minds are open to such immoral influences, and who might come into contact with it." Although not sole and exclusive, this test is one which has been frequently applied. It may be accepted as a basis for judicial decision here.

Its application and soundness are assailed by learned counsel for Friede, who argue that it seeks to gauge the mental and moral capacity of the community by that of its dullest-witted and most fallible members. This contention overlooks the fact that those who are subject to perverted influences, and in whom that abnormality may be called into activity, and who might be aroused to lustful and lecherous practices are not limited to the young and immature, the moron, the mentally weak, or the intellectually impoverished, but may be found among those of mature age and of high intellectual development and professional attainment.

Men may differ in their conceptions as to the propriety of placing any restrictions upon a literary work or absolute freedom of expression and interchange of ideas. This conflict between liberty and restraint is not new to the law. However, the Legislature has spoken on that subject in the enactment of the law in question. Even if the courts were not (as a matter of fact they are) in accord with the public policy it declares, they would not be free to disregard it, because it may be founded upon conceptions of morality with which they disagree. Moreover, the Legislature has not sought to set up a literary censorship, or attempted to confine thought and discussion in a strait jacket of inflexible legal definition, but has imposed upon the courts the duty of protecting the weaker members of society from corrupt, depraving, and lecherous influences, although exerted through the guise and medium of literature, drama or art. The public policy so declared was reaffirmed by the Legislature by its recent amendment to the Penal Law, making it a misdemeanor to prepare, advertise, or present any drama, play, etc., dealing with the subject of sex degeneracy or sex perversion.

Defendants' counsel urge that the book is to be judged by the mores of the day. The community, through this recent legislation, has evinced a public policy even more hostile to the presentation and circulation of matter treating of sexual depravity. The argument, therefore, that the mores have so changed as to fully justify the distribution of a book exalting sex perversion is without force. The amendment to the Penal Law just referred to followed closely upon the decision of the Appellate Division of this department in a case which involved a dramatization of the same theme as this novel. In the language there employed by McAvoy, J., "It cannot be said dogmatically that the morals of youth, or even of adults would not be affected by presenting a theme of the character here exhibited," and that it might not "give to some minds a lecherous swing causing a corruption of the moral tone of the susceptible members" of the community.

The defendants' brief refers the court to eminent men of letters, critics, artists, and publishers who have praised "The Well of Loneliness." Were the issue before the court the book's value from a literary standpoint, the opinions of those mentioned might, of course, carry great weight. However, the book's literary merits are not challenged, and the court may not conjecture as to the loss that its condemnation may entail to our general literature, when it is plainly subversive of public morals and public decency, which the statute is designed to safeguard. Moreover, it has been held that the opinions of experts are inadmissible.

I am convinced that "The Well of Loneliness" tends to debauch public morals, that its subject-matter is offensive to public decency, and that it is calculated to deprave and corrupt minds open to its immoral influences and who might come in contact with it, and applying the rules and recognized standards of interpretation as laid down by our courts, I refuse to hold as matter of law that the book in question is not violative of the statute. Accordingly, and under the stipulation entered into in this case, that the testimony taken upon the summons shall be the testimony taken upon the complaint, if one is ordered, I hereby order a complaint against these defendants.

Friede carried on the fight. On April 19, 1929, a three-man appellate court, after reading the opinion of the lower court and after reading the book, unanimously came to a contrary opinion and held that the book was not obscene in a very brief decision. The difference of opinions of the lower and appellate jurists in this case shows how subjective the legal test for obscenity was at that time—and still is. The judicial mind reviewing this particular book came out 3 to 1 in its final verdict, with no facts in dispute—the same book, the same words, the same basic theme.

There have been obscenity cases where nearly twoscore of jurisprudential minds have been applied to interpreting the law. Twelve jurors and a judge, three judges on appeal, five judges on further appeal, seven judges on further appeal, and finally nine judges on final appeal. To be sure, in all fields of law some human beings must make the decisions, since if men were angels there would be no need of law. Nor are we disturbed by divided votes in the United States Supreme Court or any other appellate tribunal. We prefer a forthright avowed split vote and division of opinion to the practice that was in existence some decades ago when a Chief Justice of the United States felt apologetic at every division in the Court and tried to press the Court into acting like a committee to find the lowest common denominator of compromises so as to come out and affirm the values of unanimity.

But court splits in this field, however honest, are disquieting because they show that we really don't have any objective standards for testing the obscene. In the final analysis the managers of our National Censorship Index are the nine members of our Supreme Court in Washington, nine men who sit increasingly (and reluctantly) as a Board of Censorship Review, reading this magazine or that book, seeing a motion picture once in a while—but always reflecting their own very personal backgrounds in their view of the law.

We may be willing to rely on the "taste" of the Supreme Court. But we must take the whole package, not just the fancy ribbon. We must also, like it or not, rely on the "taste" of local- and lower-court judges at each level of an obscenity proceeding. And not all those accused and convicted can afford an appeal to the "taste" of the Supreme Court of the United States. The secret of progressive growth in other fields of law has been the lagging but unerring adjustment to changing community tastes and morality made by the great majority of our judges. This element is, of course, present in the field of obscenity; but, as we shall continue to note, the road to progress here has been diverted by the strangely personal relationship between these cases and the men who decide them. Taste is, of course, an essentially subjective method of appraisal—all too often dependent upon the particular sensibilities, or lack of them, of each person. Taste and law are really two different elements—so let us pity the poor judges who had to—and still have to—mash them together and keep a wise face!

The reversal of Donald Friede's conviction in *The Well of Loneliness* case was the victory of three judges over their lower brother—a timely imposition of perhaps more sophisticated taste and jurisprudence in order to free an important book.

The great significance of *The Well of Loneliness* case is that since the book was allowed open circulation no theme, as a theme, has been banned by our courts. The censors have had to find other reasons for suppressing the written word—and of course they have not run out of pretexts.

13

Is

Sex

Education

Obscene?

While *The Well of Loneliness* case upset the desire of prosecutors to ban an entire theme from print, the law enforcement of obscenity statutes came perilously close to preventing the publication of books dealing with the theme of education. Action against Radclyffe Hall's novel had been taken because, as one judicial opinion held, the matter was basically "unhealthy." But what would you say about simple heterosexual sex education? How far can one go in explicit descriptions before the censor steps in? Who is to decide whether in a given case the text has been prepared with taste and accuracy?

To understand the background of the pivotal case over sex education, one must go back a few years before the actual legal test, to the year 1919. Most children in our culture received their information about sex in the gutters from their companions. Parents then, as now, usually took up the subject too late, and were less than frank. Church and school were as ineffective.

Mary Ware Dennett, a distinguished woman, therefore wrote a pamphlet for the instruction of her two growing sons. In it she abandoned the American folkway of analogizing human behavior to birds and bees. The pamphlet took the position:

1. That the main evil of masturbation is an excess of the habit

and the feelings of guilt about it. This at a time when masturbation was generally deemed to be an almost exclusively male practice, before scientific studies showed its high prevalence among women.

2. That venereal disease is curable. Many spiritual leaders still believed fear of syphilis was the best tactic to preserve virginity among boys. Not until a decade later did General Hugh Johnson, of Blue Eagle fame, gain the honor of being the first person to mention that disease on the radio.

3. That the sex act is the "nicest" thing in the world when used with taste, since sex relations belong to love, and love is never a business.

The pamphlet, containing much more than these three points, was so well liked by worthy religious and educational institutions that it was printed for their distribution, and for some time was unmolested. In 1926 a copy was received from the author by a Mrs. Carl A. Miles, a married woman from Virginia. Mrs. Miles was an entrapper for the Post Office Department, which proceeded with a Federal prosecution in Brooklyn. A Grand Jury was persuaded to charge Mrs. Dennett with violation of the old Comstock mail law. Tried before a judge and jury, Mrs. Dennett was convicted and sentenced to a $300 fine. To her credit, she stood at the bar and told the judge that if in fact she had corrupted youth, $300 would be too light a penalty, and that she would go to jail if the conviction were sustained on appeal.

On March 5, 1930, the Federal Circuit Court of Appeals reversed the conviction. The reasons are important. To appreciate them, it must be kept in mind that there are always two facets to a lawsuit. One is the determination of the facts. The other is the application of the rules of law to those established facts. In Mrs. Dennett's case, the appeal court did not find that the jury was mistaken on the facts. Rather, and more significantly, it found unanimously that the case never should have been presented to the jury at all, for as a matter of law the pamphlet was not obscene and therefore could not be in violation of the Postal Obscenity Law.

The reporting of the opinion appears in two sections. First are the background factual material and quotations from the pamphlet, the names of endorsers, and so on. This is followed by the clear, gracious opinion of Judge Augustus N. Hand, a cousin of Learned Hand of *Hagar Revelly* fame. In reading it, look for the following points:

Is the motive of the writer a factor? Is it relevant that the writer was not selling it for profit? Should the jury be allowed to listen to authorities pro and con? Should the aggregate standards of a com-

munity, as determined by a jury, control? Such queries still are relevant because, despite this and other judicial rulings, they have not
yet been finally and irrevocably settled in our law.

UNITED STATES V. DENNETT

CIRCUIT COURT OF APPEALS, SECOND CIRCUIT

March 3, 1930

Mary W. Dennett was convicted of mailing obscene matter in
contravention of the United States Criminal Code, and she appeals.

The Court Sets Forth the Facts:
Mrs. Dennett and the Publication

Mrs. Dennett is the mother of two boys. When they had reached
the respective ages of eleven and fourteen, she concluded that she
ought to teach them about the sex side of life. After examining
about sixty publications on the subject and forming the opinion that
they were inadequate and unsatisfactory, she wrote the pamphlet
entitled "Sex Side of Life," for the mailing of which she was afterwards indicted.

The defendant allowed some of her friends, both parents and
young people, to read the manuscript which she had written for
her own children, and it finally came to the notice of the owner
of the Medical Review of Reviews, who asked if he might read it
and afterwards published it. About a year afterwards she published
the article herself at twenty-five cents a copy when sold singly,
and at lower prices when ordered in quantities. Twenty-five
thousand of the pamphlets seem to have been distributed in this
way.

At the trial, Mrs. Dennett sought to prove the cost of publication
in order to show that there could have been no motive of gain
on her part. She also offered to prove that she had received orders
from the Union Theological Seminary, Young Men's Christian
Association, the Young Women's Christian Association, the Public
Health Departments of the various states and from no less than
four hundred welfare and religious organizations, as well as from
clergymen, college professors, and doctors, and that the pamphlet
was in use in the public schools at Bronxville, N.Y. The foregoing
offers were rejected on the ground that the defendant's motive in

distributing the pamphlet was irrelevant, and that the only issues were whether she caused the pamphlet to be mailed and whether it was obscene.

The Content of the Pamphlet

The pamphlet begins with a so-called "Introduction for Elders" which sets forth the general views of the writer and is as follows:

"In reading several dozen books on sex matters for the young with a view to selecting the best for my own children, I found none that I was willing to put into their hands, without first guarding them against what I considered very misleading and harmful impressions, which they would otherwise be sure to acquire in reading them. That is the excuse for this article.

"It is far more specific than most sex information written for young people. I believe we owe it to children to be specific if we talk about the subject at all.

"From a careful observation of youthful curiosity and a very vivid recollection of my own childhood, I have tried to explain frankly the points about which there is the greatest inquiry. These points are not frankly or clearly explained in most sex literature. They are avoided, partly from embarrassment, but more, apparently, because those who have undertaken to instruct the children are not really clear in their own minds as to the proper status of the sex relation.

"I found that from the physiological point of view, the question was handled with limitations and reservations. From the point of natural science it was often handled with sentimentality, the child being led from a semi-esthetic study of the reproduction of flowers and animals to the acceptance of a similar idea for human beings. From the moral point of view it was handled least satisfactorily of all, the child being given a jumble of conflicting ideas, with no means of correlating them—fear of venereal disease, one's duty to suppress 'animal passion,' the sacredness of marriage, and so forth. And from the emotional point of view, the subject was not handled at all.

"This one omission seems to me to be the key to the whole situation, and it is the basis of the radical departure I have made from the precedents in most sex literature for children.

"Concerning all four points of view just mentioned, there are certain departures from the traditional method that have seemed to me worth making.

The Human Body

"On the physiological side I have given as far as possible, the proper terminology for the sex organs and functions. Children have had to read the expurgated literature which has been specially prepared for them in poetic or colloquial terms, and then are needlessly mystified when they hear things called by their real names.

"On the side of natural science, I have emphasized our unlikeness to the plants and animals rather than our likeness, for while the points we have in common with the lower orders make an interesting section in our general education, it is knowing about the vital points in which we differ that helps us to solve the sexual problems of maturity; and the child needs that knowledge precisely as he needs knowledge of everything which will fortify him for wise decisions when he is grown.

Disease and Morality

"On the moral side, I have tried to avoid confusion and dogmatism in the following ways: by eliminating fear of venereal disease as an appeal for strictly limited sex relations, stating candidly that venereal disease is becoming curable; by barring out all mention of 'brute' or 'animal' passion, terms frequently used in pleas for chastity and self-control, as such talk is an aspersion on the brute and has done children much harm in giving them the impression that there is an essential baseness in the sex relation; by inviting the inference that marriage is 'sacred' by virtue of its being a reflection of human ideality rather than because it is a legalized institution.

"Unquestionably the stress which most have laid upon the beauty of nature's plans for perpetuating the plant and animal species, and the effort to have the child carry over into human life some sense of that beauty has come from a most commendable instinct to protect the child from the natural shock of the revelation of so much that is unesthetic and revolting in human sex life. The nearness of the sex organs to the excretory organs, the pain and messiness of childbirth are elements which certainly need some compensating antidote to prevent their making too disagreeable and disproportionate an impress on the child's mind.

"The results are doubtless good as far as they go, but they do not go nearly far enough. What else is there to call upon to help out? Why, the one thing which has been persistently neglected by practically all the sex writers,—the emotional side of sex experience. Parents and teachers have been afraid of it and distrustful of it. In not a single one of all the books for young people that I have thus far read has there been the frank, unashamed declaration that the climax of sex emotion is an unsurpassed joy, something which rightly belongs to every normal human being, a joy to be proudly and serenely experienced. Instead there has been all too evident an inference that sex emotion is a thing to be ashamed of, that yielding to it is indulgence which must be curbed as much as possible, that all thought and understanding of it must be rigorously postponed, at any rate till after marriage.

"We give to young folks, in their general education, as much as they can grasp of science and ethics and art, and yet in their sex education, which rightly has to do with all of these, we have said, 'Give them only the bare physiological facts, lest they be prematurely stimulated.' Others of us, realizing that the bare physiological facts are shocking to many a sensitive child, and must somehow be softened with something pleasant, have said, 'Give them the facts, yes, but see to it that they are so related to the wonders of evolution and the beauties of the natural world that the shock is minimized.' But none of us has yet dared to say, 'Yes, give them the facts, give them the nature study, too, but also give them some conception of sex life as a vivifying joy, as a vital art, as a thing to be studied and developed with reverence for its big meaning, with understanding of its far-reaching reactions, psychologically and spiritually, with temperant restraint, good taste and the highest idealism.' We have contented ourselves by assuming that marriage makes sex relations respectable. We have not yet said that it is only beautiful 'sex' relations that can make marriage lovely.

Guidance

"Young people are just as capable of being guided and inspired in their thought about sex emotion as in their taste and ideals in literature and ethics, and just as they imperatively need to have their general taste and ideals cultivated as a preparation for mature life, so do they need to have some understanding of the marvelous place which sex emotion has in life.

"Only such an understanding can be counted on to give them the self-control that is born of knowledge, not fear, the reverence that will prevent premature or trivial connections, the good taste and finesse that will make their sex life when they reach maturity a vitalizing success."

After the foregoing introduction comes the part devoted to sex instruction entitled, "An Explanation for Young People." It proceeds to explain sex life in detail both physiologically and emotionally. It describes the sex organs and their operation and the way children are begotten and born. It negatives the idea that the sex impulse is in itself a base passion, and treats it as normal and its satisfaction as a great and justifiable joy when accompanied by love between two human beings. It warns against perversion, venereal disease, and prostitution, and argues for continence and healthy mindedness and against promiscuous sex relations.

A Man and a Woman

The pamphlet in discussing the emotional side of the human sex relation, says:

"It means that a man and a woman feel that they belong to no one else; it makes them wonderfully happy to be together; they find they want to live together, work together, play together, and to have children together, that is, to marry each other; and their dream is to be happy together all their lives. * * * The idea of sex relations between people who do not love each other, who do not feel any sense of belonging to each other, will always be revolting to highly developed sensitive people.

"People's lives grow finer and their characters better, if they have sex relations only with those they love. And those who make the wretched mistake of yielding to the sex impulse alone when there is no love to go with it, usually live to despise themselves for their weakness and their bad taste. They are always ashamed of doing it, and they try to keep it secret from their families and those they respect. You can be sure that whatever people are ashamed to do is something that can never bring them real happiness. It is true that one's sex relations are the most personal and private matters in the world, and they belong just to us and to no one else, but while we may be shy and reserved about them, *we are not ashamed.*

"When two people really love each other, they don't care who knows it. They are proud of their happiness. But no man is ever proud of his connection with a prostitute and no prostitute is ever proud of her business.

"Sex relations belong to love, and love is never a *business*. Love is the nicest thing in the world, but it can't be bought. And the sex side of it is the biggest and most important side of it, so it is the one side of us that we must be absolutely sure to keep in good order and perfect health, if we are going to be happy ourselves or make any one else happy."

The government proved that the pamphlet was mailed to Mrs. C. A. Miles, Grottoes, Va.

In the Trial Court

Upon the foregoing record, of which we have given a summary, the trial judge charged the jury that the motive of Mrs. Dennett in mailing the pamphlet was immaterial, that it was for them to determine whether it was obscene, lewd, or lascivious within the meaning of the statute, and that the test was "whether its language has a tendency to deprave and corrupt the morals of those whose minds are open to such things and into whose hands it may fall; arousing and implanting in such minds lewd and obscene thought or desires."

The court also charged that, "even if the matter sought to be shown in the pamphlet complained of were true, that fact would be immaterial, if the statements of such facts were calculated to deprave the morals of the readers by inciting sexual desires and libidinous thoughts."

The jury returned a verdict of guilty upon which Mrs. Dennett was sentenced to pay a fine of $300, and from the judgment of conviction she has taken this appeal.

THE OPINION OF THE COURT
Before SWAN, AUGUSTUS N. HAND, and CHASE,
AUGUSTUS N. HAND, Circuit Judge (after stating
the facts as above):

The Author's Motive Doesn't Matter

It is doubtless true that the personal motive of Mrs. Dennett in distributing her pamphlet could have no bearing on the question whether she violated the law. Her own belief that a really obscene pamphlet would pay the price for its obscenity by means of intrinsic merits would leave her as much as ever under the ban of the statute. * * *

Accidents of Distribution Don't Matter

It was perhaps proper to exclude the evidence offered by her as to the persons to whom the pamphlet was sold, for the reason that such evidence, if relevant at all, was part of the government's proof. In other words, a publication might be distributed among doctors or nurses or adults in cases where the distribution among small children could not be justified. The fact that the latter might obtain it accidentally or surreptitiously, as they might see some medical books which would not be desirable for them to read, would hardly be sufficient to bar a publication otherwise proper. Here the pamphlet appears to have been mailed to a married woman. The tract may fairly be said to be calculated to aid parents in the instruction of their children in sex matters. As the record stands, it is a reasonable inference that the pamphlet was to be given to children at the discretion of adults and to be distributed through agencies that had the real welfare of the adolescent in view. There is no reason to suppose that it was to be broadcast among children who would have no capacity to understand its general significance. Even the court in the HICKLIN case, which laid down a more strict rule than the New York Court of Appeals was inclined to adopt in the EASTMAN case, said that "the circumstances of the publication" may determine whether the statute has been violated.

What Does Matter

But the important consideration in this case is the meaning and scope of those words of the statute which prohibit the mailing of an "obscene, lewd or lascivious * * * pamphlet." It was for the trial court to determine whether the pamphlet could reasonably be thought to be of such a character before submitting any question of the violation of the statute to the jury. * * *

Arousal of Lust

It may be assumed that any article dealing with the sex side of life and explaining the functions of the sex organs is capable in some circumstances of arousing lust. The sex impulses are present in everyone, and without doubt cause much of the weal and woe of human kind. But it can hardly be said that, because of the risk of arousing sex impulses, there should be no instruction of the young in sex matters, and that the risk of imparting instruction outweighs the disadvantages of leaving them to grope about in mystery and morbid curiosity and of requiring them to secure such information, as they may be able to obtain, from ill-informed and often foul-minded companions, rather than from intelligent and high-minded sources. It may be argued that suggestion plays a large part in such matters, and that on the whole the less sex questions are dwelt upon the better. But it by no means follows that such a desideratum is attained by leaving adolescents in a state of inevitable curiosity, satisfied only by the casual gossip of ignorant playmates.

Changing Mores

The old theory that information about sex matters should be left to chance has greatly changed, and, while there is still a difference of opinion as to just the kind of instruction which ought to be given, it is commonly thought in these days that much was lacking in the old mystery and reticence. This is evident from the current literature on the subject, particularly such pamphlets as "Sex Education," issued by the Treasury Department United States Public Health Service in 1927.

The statute we have to construe was never thought to bar from the mails everything which *might* stimulate sex impulses. If so, much chaste poetry and fiction, as well as many useful medical works would be under the ban. Like everything else, this law must be construed reasonably with a view to the general objects aimed at. While there can be no doubt about its constitutionality, it must not be assumed to have been designed to interfere with serious instruction regarding sex matters unless the terms in which the information is conveyed are clearly indecent.

Truth a Test

We have been referred to no decision where a truthful exposition of the sex side of life, evidently calculated for instruction and for the explanation of relevant facts has been held to be obscene. In DYSART V. UNITED STATES * * * it was decided that the advertisement of a lying-in retreat to enable unmarried women to conceal their missteps, even though written in a coarse and vulgar style, did not fall within prohibition of the statute, and was not "obscene" within the meaning of the law.

Sincerity a Test

Mrs. Dennett's discussion of the phenomena of sex is written with sincerity of feeling and with an idealization of the marriage relation and sex emotions. We think it tends to rationalize and dignify such emotions rather than to arouse lust. While it may be thought by some that portions of the tract go into unnecessary details that would better have been omitted, it may be fairly answered that the curiosity of many adolescents would not be satisfied without full explanation, and that no more than that is really given. It also may reasonably be thought that accurate information, rather than mystery and curiosity, is better in the long run and is less likely to occasion lascivious thoughts than ignorance and anxiety. Perhaps instruction other than that which Mrs. Dennett suggests would be better. That is a matter as to which there is bound to be a wide difference of opinion, but, irrespective of this, we hold that an accurate exposition of the relevant facts of the sex side of life in decent language and in manifestly serious and disinterested spirit cannot ordinarily be regarded as obscene. Any incidental tendency to arouse sex impulses which such a pamphlet may perhaps have is apart from and subordinate to its main effect. The tendency can only exist in so far as it is inherent in any sex instruction, and it would seem to be outweighed by the elimination of ignorance, curiosity, and morbid fear. The direct aim and the net result is to promote understanding and self-control.

Mrs. Dennett is acquitted.

Looking back, it is difficult to think of anyone prosecuting Mrs. Dennett for her tasteful and valuable pamphlet. Though 1930 doesn't seem very far away, if we measured time by standards of prudery it is an age away, and then some. All the more reason to relish the grace and good sense of Judge Augustus N. Hand. It is important to note that early in his opinion the judge decides that it is for the trial judge to determine in the first instance whether a work can reasonably be thought to be obscene before submitting any question of actual violation to the jury. In other words, the question of what constitutes obscenity is one of "law" rather than of "fact"—and it is for the judge and not the jury to determine.

The significance of this view cannot be overestimated. It is now generally held to be the law in most jurisdictions. And it is just because the definition of obscenity is considered a "matter of law" rather than of "fact" that it is reviewable by higher courts, since appellate courts characteristically may not themselves alter a jury's conclusion as to the facts of a case.

Whether a particular book is obscene, therefore, depends on (1) what the judge says "obscenity" means and (2) whether the jury decides that the book fits the definition. And appellate courts, by subsuming the second determination into the first, have the power to redecide the whole case.

It is also interesting to note Judge Hand's assumption that the postal obscenity law was constitutional. As we shall see later in this volume, the question was not decided by the United States Supreme Court until 1957, some twenty-seven years after the *Dennett* case— and the life of that later decision is threatened almost every day by new attacks on the constitutionality of Post Office censorship.

The *Dennett* case was a pivotal decision for other and more practical reasons. From this time on, honorable education of children had a chance. Parents could be informed; teachers were released from ancient legal fears (although not necessarily social fears) that sex was dirty and unmentionable.

Law is only one of the techniques for control of a folkway. Not every youth after March 4, 1930, received all the sexual knowledge made lawful by Mrs. Dennett's fight in the courts. At best, law can do little in an affirmative sense. But in the area discussed in this volume, obscenity laws have had a mighty negative effect upon social development. In the days of Bruno, Galileo, and Copernicus, man was afraid of a round and moving globe. Centuries later, man shifted to fear of an honest search for a way for adults to explain the mysteries and beauties of sex and birth. It is the achievement of Mrs. Dennett and also of Judge Hand that in this one decision they did help to eliminate that fear insofar as it was produced by law.

14

Four-Letter Words
and the Unconscious

Law has its own unique small secrets. One of the most imponderable and attractive is the mystery of how—as often happens—a case that seems unimportant at the time is appraised at a later date as having vast significance. Such a case was the legal battle against suppression in this country of James Joyce's novel *Ulysses*.

From the date of its original publication in Paris in 1922, the book had been in endless legal troubles, but we shall consider here only those it encountered in the United States. Here it was a prime target of the censorious. But the more our postal and customs officials burned copies, the greater the inducement for smuggling and bootlegging. It became a vogue to own one of those blue-paper-jacketed copies of *Ulysses* from Paris—a vogue that soon led to prices in the hundreds of dollars for one such copy. Men went to jail for publishing or vending the book in the United States of America.

Even then some eminent critics thought the book was an important literary experiment. Nevertheless when, after twelve years of suppression, *Ulysses* faced once more the test of the obscenity law, as Random House prepared to challenge the official ruling that it was not importable, the entire court proceeding was viewed more as a stunt than as an opportunity to lay down new rules of law. Within a few years the opinion of Judge John M. Woolsey was hailed as a landmark in the battle of freedom for books. And yet, after more than a quarter of a century, it is difficult even today to find any new principle laid down by the Court on the *Ulysses* case. As we have indicated, general rules come hard in this field of law, mainly because the standards remain essentially subjective. If anything, the *Ulysses* case set a precedent not so much because of any rule it enunciated as because it represented a psychological breakthrough in the censorship field. After the *Ulysses* case the general community notion of what was "dirty" became just a little more sophisticated—a process that, despite recidivism here and there, has thankfully continued.

The case opened in the Federal Court in New York City under the Tariff Law of 1930 that allowed the authorities to proceed against a book itself instead of against the person who published, bought, or sold it. It was tried before Judge John M. Woolsey. A copy of *Ulysses* had been ordered for import. In fact, it slipped through Customs by oversight and had to be returned to them in order to have the case tested in court.

There were two grounds for opposition to the importation of *Ulysses.* First, the use of four-letter Anglo-Saxon words. This is not the first or the last case to involve the use of "suspect" words. A few years before *Ulysses,* a book entitled *What Happens* was convicted because, as the jurors later said, the word used was "masturbation" instead of a term acceptable to them—such as "self-abuse." The counsel for *Ulysses* took the offensive on this score, explaining in court the sad hypocrisy and lack of reality displayed by people in our culture, and indeed in all cultures, where certain functional and historical words are concerned.

Counsel for the book gave an exposition on the words used by Joyce. Each four-letter word was explained in historic terms. It has been said by some that the turning point in the battle came when shame was removed from the mind of the judge in respect to these words in the book. This was accented in a dialogue between Judge Woolsey and Joyce's lawyer, which went something like this:

COUNSEL: Judge, as to the word "fuck," one etymological dictionary gives its derivation as from *facere*—to make—the farmer fucked the seed into the soil. This, your honor, has more integrity than a euphemism used every day in every modern novel to describe precisely the same event.

JUDGE WOOLSEY: For example . . .

COUNSEL: Oh—"They slept together." It means the same thing.
JUDGE WOOLSEY (smiling): But, Counselor, that isn't even usually the truth!

Some believe the case was determined at that precise moment. Who knows?

In this connection, the fate of *Strange Fruit* (a novel by Lillian Smith) in Massachusetts provides a relevant sidelight. The book, a highly praised best seller, was denied circulation in Massachusetts in 1945 by the highest court of that Commonwealth. The story is told that one of the judges of that great bench felt he had to vote for suppression because the defense attorney said he could not mention in court or print in his brief an Anglo-Saxon word used in the novel several times by one of the characters. The jurist explained:

"He wanted us to legalize for general circulation the word 'fucking,' a word he was ashamed to print in a brief for our eyes alone."

Although this is less than sound law, we understand the judge to mean that freedom is for the brave; those who run deserve to be chased. The lawyer's prudish shame had contributed to the ban on his client's book.

The other ground of opposition to *Ulysses* concerned the frankness of the unconscious stream of thought depicted by Joyce in the dreams of important characters in the volume such as Mollie Bloom. Here again there was a colloquy between lawyer and judge that may have had significance in the case:

JUDGE WOOLSEY: Did you really read this entire book? It's tough going, isn't it?
COUNSEL [fearing the judge might suppress on the theory that nothing much will be lost if an unreadable volume is prevented entrance to our shores]: I tried to read it in 1923 when it had just come out but could not get far into it. Last summer, however, I had to read it—in preparation for this trial. And while lecturing in the Unitarian Church in Nantucket on the bank holiday . . .
JUDGE WOOLSEY: What has that to do with my question—have you read it?
COUNSEL: Will your honor let me explain how I was able to plough through it? While talking in that Church I recalled after my lecture was finished that while I was thinking only about the banks and the banking laws I was in fact, at that same time, musing about the clock at the back of the Church, the old woman in the front row, the tall

shutters at the sides. Just as now, Judge, I have thought I was involved only in the defense of the book, this one cause—I must admit at the same time I was thinking of the gold ring around your tie, the picture of George Washington behind your bench and the fact that your black judicial robe is slipping off your shoulder. This double stream of the mind is the contribution of *Ulysses*.

JUDGE WOOLSEY [rapping on the bench]: Now for the first time I appreciate the significance of this book. I have listened to you as intently as I know how. I am disturbed by the dream scenes at the end of the book, and still I must confess, that while listening to you I have been thinking at the same time about the Hepplewhite furniture behind you.

The judge, it appeared, was a collector of antique furniture and for quite a while the audience in the court was entertained by a discourse on furniture manufacture in colonial times.

Seldom is a case capable of being acted out in this fashion. But the double stream of consciousness was acted in the courtroom on that occasion.

These two episodes may have helped make the law in the case. But surely the opinion of Judge Woolsey made history in the sense that it was read by a multitude of people, as incorporated as a Foreword in *Ulysses* editions that have sold close to a half-million copies. Perhaps the clarity of the judicial pen made *Ulysses* a pivotal case. We should like to think that gracious writing made the contribution:

UNITED STATES V. ONE BOOK CALLED "ULYSSES"

District Court, New York
1933

WOOLSEY, District Judge.

I have read "Ulysses" once in its entirety and I have read those passages of which the Government particularly complains several times. In fact, for many weeks, my spare time has been devoted to the consideration of the decision which my duty would require me to make in this matter.

"Ulysses" is not an easy book to read or to understand. But there has been much written about it, and in order properly to approach the consideration of it, it is advisable to read a number of other books which have now become its satellites. The study of "Ulysses" is, therefore, a heavy task.

The reputation of "Ulysses" in the literary world, however, warranted my taking such time as was necessary to enable me to satisfy myself as to the intent with which the book was written, for, of course, in any case where a book is claimed to be obscene it must first be determined whether the intent with which it was written was what is called, according to the usual phrase, pornographic,—that is, written for the purpose of exploiting obscenity.

If the conclusion is that the book is pornographic that is the end of the inquiry and forfeiture must follow.

But in "Ulysses," in spite of its unusual frankness, I do not detect anywhere the leer of the sensualist. I hold, therefore, that it is not pornographic.

In writing "Ulysses," Joyce sought to make a serious experiment in a new, if not wholly novel, literary genre. He takes persons of the lower middle class living in Dublin in 1904 and seeks, not only to describe what they did on a certain day early in June of that year as they went about the City bent on their usual occupations, but also to tell what many of them thought about the while.

Joyce has attempted—it seems to me, with astonishing success —to show how the stream of consciousness with its ever-shifting kaleidoscopic impressions carries, as it were on a plastic palimpsest, not only what is in the focus of each man's observation of the actual things about him, but also in a penumbral zone residue of past impressions, some recent and some drawn up by association from the domain of the subconscious. He shows how each of these impressions affects the life and behavior of the character which he is describing.

What he seeks to get is not unlike the result of a double or, if that is possible, a multiple exposure on a cinema film which would give a clear foreground with a background visible but somewhat blurred and out of focus in varying degrees.

To convey by words an effect which obviously lends itself more appropriately to a graphic technique, accounts, it seems to me, for much of the obscurity which meets a reader of "Ulysses." And it also explains another aspect of the book, which I have further to consider, namely, Joyce's sincerity and his honest effort to show exactly how the minds of his characters operate.

If Joyce did not attempt to be honest in developing the technique which he has adopted in "Ulysses," the result would be psychologically misleading and thus unfaithful to his chosen technique. Such an attitude would be artistically inexcusable.

It is because Joyce has been loyal to his technique and has not funked its necessary implications, but has honestly attempted to tell fully what his characters think about, that he has been the subject of so many attacks and that his purpose has been so often misunderstood and misrepresented. For his attempt sincerely and honestly to realize his objective has required him incidentally to use certain words which are generally considered dirty words and has led at times to what many think is a too poignant preoccupation with sex in the thoughts of his characters.

The words which are criticized as dirty are old Saxon words known to almost all men, and, I venture, to many women, and are such words as would be naturally and habitually used, I believe, by the types of folk whose life, physical and mental, Joyce is seeking to describe. In respect of the recurrent emergence of the theme of sex in the minds of his characters, it must always be remembered that his locale was Celtic and his season Spring.

Whether or not one enjoys such a technique as Joyce uses is a matter of taste on which disagreement is futile, but to subject that technique to the standards of some other technique seems to me to be little short of absurd.

Accordingly, I hold that "Ulysses" is a sincere and honest book and I think that the criticisms of it are entirely disposed by its rationale.

Furthermore, "Ulysses" is an amazing *tour de force* when one considers the success which has been in the main achieved with such a difficult objective as Joyce set for himself. As I have stated, "Ulysses" is not an easy book to read. It is brilliant and dull, intelligible and obscure by turns. In many places it seems to be disgusting, but although it contains, as I have mentioned above, many words usually considered dirty, I have not found anything that I consider to be dirt for dirt's sake. Each word of the book contributes like a bit of mosaic to the detail of the picture which Joyce is seeking to construct for his readers.

If one does not wish to associate with such folk as Joyce describes, that is one's own choice. In order to avoid indirect contact with them one may not wish to read "Ulysses"; that is quite understandable. But when such a great artist in words, as Joyce undoubtedly is, seeks to draw a true picture of the lower middle class in a

European city, ought it to be impossible for the American public legally to see that picture?

To answer this question it is not sufficient merely to find, as I have found above, that Joyce did not write "Ulysses" with what is commonly called pornographic intent, I must endeavor to apply a more objective standard to his book in order to determine its effect in the result, irrespective of the intent with which it was written.

The statute under which the book is attacked only denounces, in so far as we are here concerned, the importation into the United States from any foreign country of "any obscene book." It does not marshal against books the spectrum of condemnatory adjectives found, commonly, in laws dealing with matters of this kind. I am, therefore, only required to determine whether "Ulysses" is obscene within the legal definition of that word.

The meaning of the word "obscene" as legally defined by the courts is: tending to stir the sex impulses or to lead to sexually impure and lustful thoughts.

Whether a particular book would tend to excite such impulses and thoughts must be tested by the Court's opinion as to its effect on a person with average sex instincts—what the French would call *l'homme moyen sensuel*—who plays, in this branch of legal inquiry, the same role of hypothetical reagent as does the "reasonable man" in the law of torts and "the man learned in the art" on questions of invention in patent law.

The risk involved in the use of such a reagent arises from the inherent tendency of the trier of the facts, however fair he may intend to be, to make his reagent too much subservient to his own idiosyncrasies. Here, I have attempted to avoid this, if possible, and to make my reagent herein more objective than he might otherwise be, by adopting the following course:

After I had made my decision in regard to the aspect of "Ulysses," now under consideration, I checked my impressions with two friends of mine who in my opinion answered to the above-stated requirement for my reagent.

These literary assessors—as I might properly describe them—were called on separately, and neither knew that I was consulting the other. They are men whose opinion on literature and on life I value most highly. They had both read "Ulysses," and, of course, were wholly unconnected with this cause.

Without letting either of my assessors know what my decision was, I gave to each of them the legal definition of obscene and asked each whether in his opinion "Ulysses" was obscene within that definition.

I was interested to find that they both agreed with my opinion: that reading "Ulysses" in its entirety, as a book must be read on such a test as this, did not tend to excite sexual impulses or lustful thoughts but that its net effect on them was only that of a somewhat tragic and very powerful commentary on the inner lives of men and women.

It is only with the normal person that the law is concerned. Such a test as I have described, therefore, is the only proper test of obscenity in the case of a book like "Ulysses" which is a sincere and serious attempt to devise a new literary method for the observation and description of mankind.

I am quite aware that owing to some of its scenes "Ulysses" is a rather strong draught to ask some sensitive, though normal, persons to take. But my considered opinion, after long reflection, is that whilst in many places the effect of "Ulysses" on the reader undoubtedly is somewhat emetic, nowhere does it tend to be an aphrodisiac.

"Ulysses" may, therefore, be admitted into the United States.

Judge Woolsey's erudite and beautifully written opinion has been often read and well remembered—and with reason. If judges are, in the nature of the judicial process, to be the final censors, we are relieved when we find one who attempts, and with success, to understand what the artist is doing and saying. Because Woolsey knew how to read he realized, as he says, that for Joyce to abandon his "stream of consciousness" technique from time to time in order to satisfy the more Victorian among us would be dishonest and "artistically inexcusable."

In addition to his firm understanding of the book, Woolsey quietly takes a large step in the direction of freedom to read. He states clearly and unequivocally that a book must be judged not by its effect on the abnormal or the young but rather on the average man, his *"l'homme moyen sensuel."* This view is a far cry from that of Judge Wagner in the *Seltzer* case. Rather it stands with Judge Hand's opinion in the *Dennett* case as the "modern view" of obscenity law.

The government appealed Judge Woolsey's decision in the *Ulysses* case to the next highest court, the Circuit Court of Appeals, only to come face to face with Judge Augustus Hand! We print here excerpts from Hand's opinion as well as others from the dissenting opinion of Judge Manton. Incidentally, you will note that there were two "Hands" ruling for the book, Augustus and Learned. They were cousins—and two of the most brilliant jurists and lucid writers ever to sit in judgment in the United States. Here now are parts of the appellate decisions:

| L. HAND, and AUGUSTUS N. HAND, Circuit Judges:

The Author and the Book

James Joyce, the author of Ulysses, may be regarded as a pioneer among those writers who have adopted the "stream of consciousness" method of presenting fiction, which has attracted considerable attention in academic circles. In this field Ulysses is rated as a book of considerable power by persons whose opinions are entitled to weight. Indeed it has become a sort of contemporary classic, dealing with a new subject-matter. It attempts to depict the thoughts and lay bare the souls of a number of people, some of them intellectuals and some social outcasts and nothing more, with a literalism that leaves nothing unsaid. Certain of its passages are of beauty and undoubted distinction, while others are of a vulgarity that is extreme and the book as a whole has a realism characteristic of the present age. It is supposed to portray the thoughts of the principal characters during a period of about eighteen hours.

We may discount the laudation of Ulysses by some of its admirers and reject the view that it will permanently stand among the great works of literature, but it is fair to say that it is a sincere portrayal with skillful artistry of the "stream of consciousness" of its character. Though the depiction happily is not of the "stream of consciousness" of all men and perhaps of only those of a morbid type, it seems to be sincere, truthful, relevant to the subject, and executed with real art. Joyce, in the words of Paradise Lost, has dealt with "things unattempted yet in prose or rime"—with things that very likely might better have remained "unattempted"—but his book shows originality and is a work of symmetry and excellent craftsmanship of a sort. The question before us is whether such a book of artistic merit and scientific insight should be regarded as "obscene."

That numerous long passages in Ulysses contain matter that is obscene under any fair definition of the word cannot be gainsaid; yet they are relevant to the purpose of depicting the thoughts of the characters and are introduced to give meaning to the whole, rather than to promote lust or portray filth for its own sake. The net effect even of portions most open to attack, such as the closing monologue of the wife of Leopold Bloom, is pitiful and tragic, rather than lustful. The book depicts the souls of men and women that are by turns bewildered and keenly apprehensive, sordid and aspiring, ugly and beautiful, hateful and loving. In the end one feels, more than anything else, pity and sorrow for the confusion, misery, and degradation of humanity. Page after page of the book is, or seems to be, incomprehensible. But many passages show the trained hand of an artist, who can at one moment adapt to perfection the style of an ancient chronicler, and at another become a veritable personification of Thomas Carlyle. In numerous places there are found originality, beauty, and distinction. The book as a whole is not pornographic, and, while in not a few spots it is coarse, blasphemous, and obscene, it does not, in our opinion, tend to promote lust. The erotic passages are submerged in the book as a whole and have little resultant effect. If these are to make the book subject to confiscation, by the same test Venus and Adonis, Hamlet, Romeo and Juliet, and the story told in the Eighth Book of the Odyssey by the bard Demodoeus of how Ares and Aphrodite were entrapped in a net spread by the outraged Hephaestus amid the laughter of the immortal gods, as well as many other classics, would have to be suppressed. Indeed, it may be questioned whether the obscene passages in Romeo and Juliet were as necessary to the development of the play as those in the monologue of Mrs. Bloom are to the depiction of the latter's tortured soul.

Read a Book as a Whole

It is unnecessary to add illustrations to show that, in the administration of statutes aimed at the suppression of immoral books, standard works of literature have not been barred merely because they contain SOME obscene passages, and that confiscation for such a reason would destroy much that is precious in order to benefit a few.

It is settled, at least so far as this court is concerned, that works of physiology, science, and sex instruction are not within the statute, though to some extent and among some persons they may tend to promote lustful thoughts. We think the same immunity should apply to literature as to science, where the presentation, when viewed objectively, is sincere, and the erotic matter is not introduced to promote lust and does not furnish the dominant note of the publication. The question in each case is whether a publication taken as a whole has a libidinous effect. The book before us has such portentous length, is written with such evident truthfulness in its depiction of certain types of humanity, and is so little erotic in its result, that it does not fall within the forbidden class.

We do not think that Ulysses, taken as a whole, tends to promote lust and its criticized passages do this no more than scores of standard books that are constantly bought and sold. Indeed a book of physiology in the hands of adolescents may be more objectionable on this ground than almost anything else.

Dominant Effect

We believe that the proper test of whether a given book is obscene is its dominant effect. In applying this test, relevancy of the objectionable parts to the theme, the established reputation of the work in the estimation of approved critics, if the book is modern, and the verdict of the past, if it is ancient, are persuasive pieces of evidence; for works of art are not likely to sustain a high position with no better warrant for their existence than their obscene content.

Offensive to Many but Not Obscene

It may be that Ulysses will not last as a substantial contribution to literature, and it is certainly easy to believe that, in spite of the opinion of Joyce's laudators, the immortals will still reign, but the same thing may be said of current works of art and music and of many other efforts of the mind. Art certainly cannot advance under compulsion to traditional forms, and nothing in such a field is more stifling to progress than limitation of the right to experiment with a new technique. The foolish judgments of Lord Eldon about one hundred years ago, proscribing the works of Byron and Southey, and the finding by the jury under a charge by Lord Denman that the publication of Shelley's "Queen Mab" was an indictable offense are a warning to all who have to determine the limits of the field within which authors may exercise themselves. We think that Ulysses is a book of originality and sincerity of treatment, and that it has not the effect of promoting lust. Accordingly it does not fall within the statute, even though it justly may offend many.

Decree affirmed.

MANTON, Circuit Judge, dissents.

I dissent.

Who can doubt the obscenity of this book after a reading of the pages referred to, which are too indecent to add as a footnote to this opinion? Its characterization as obscene should be quite unanimous by all who read it.

In the year 1868 Regina v. Hicklin stated that "the test of obscenity is this, whether the tendency of the matter charged as obscenity is to deprave and corrupt those whose minds are open to such immoral influences, and into whose hands a publication of this sort may fall."

Judge Manton goes on to cite a number of Supreme Court cases, dating from 1879, which, to his mind at least, show that the Supreme Court had consistently followed the Hicklin rule. Since most judicial opinions are a mixture of the *decision* in the case (that is, "Mr. X is right and the case should be affirmed") and a variety of comment on the decisions (that is, "Mr. X wins because of *a, b* and *c* . . . and also, it is worth noting that . . .") not all of which are necessary to reach the *decision,* it is not always easy to agree on what a Court is saying in a particular case. Whether the cases and theory used by Judge Manton actually support the rule he says they do is open to question. But his interpretation is certainly not an unsupportable one. Nor, in this field of relativity, would a contrary interpretation be wholly right or wholly wrong.

Manton now turns his guns on *Ulysses,* and opens fire:

Thus the court sustained a charge having a test as to whether or no the publications depraved the morals of the ordinary reader or tended to lower the standards of civilization. The tendency of the matter to deprave and corrupt the morals of those whose minds are open to such influence and into whose hands the publication of this sort may fall, has become the test thoroughly entrenched in the federal courts.

Ulysses is a work of fiction. It may not be compared with books involving medical subjects or description of certain physical or biological facts. It is written for alleged amusement of the reader only. The characters described in the thoughts of the author may in some instances be true, but, be it truthful or otherwise, a book that is obscene is not rendered less so by the statement of truthful fact. It cannot be said that the test above has been rejected by United States v. Dennett, nor can that case be taken to mean that the book is to be judged as a whole. If anything, the case clearly recognizes that the book may be obscene because portions thereof are so, for pains are taken to justify and show not to be obscene portions to which objection is made. The gist of the holding is that a book is not to be declared obscene if it is an "accurate exposition of the relevant facts of the sex side of life in decent language and in manifestly serious and disinterested spirit." A work of obvious benefit to the community was never intended to be within the purview of the statute. No matter what may be said on the side of letters, the effect on the community can and must be the sole determining factor. "Laws of this character are made for society in the aggregate, and not in particular. So, while there may be individuals and societies of men and women of peculiar notions or idiosyncrasies, whose moral sense would neither be depraved nor offended, * * * yet the exceptional sensibility, or want of sensibility, of such cannot be allowed as a standard." United States v. Harman, supra.

And are we to refuse to enforce the statute Congress has enacted because of the argument that "obscenity is only the superstition of the day—the modern counterpart of ancient witchcraft?" Are we to be persuaded by the statement, set forth in the brief, made by the judge below in an interview with the press, "Education, not Law, must solve problems of taste and choice (of books)," when the statute is clear and our duty plain?

The prevailing opinion states that classics would be excluded if the application of the statute here argued for prevailed. But the statute, Tariff Act 1930, Section 305, provides as to classics that they may be introduced into the commerce of the United States provided "that the Secretary of the Treasury * * * in his discretion, admit the so-called classics or books of recognized and established literary or scientific merit, but may, in his discretion, admit such classics or books only when imported for non-commercial purposes." The right to admission under this proviso was not sought nor is it justified by reason thereof in the prevailing opinion.

Congress passed this statute against obscenity for the protection of the great mass of our people; the unusual literator can, or thinks he can, protect himself. The people do not exist for the sake of literature, to give the author fame, the publisher wealth, and the book a market. On the contrary, literature exists for the sake of the people, to refresh the weary, to console the sad, to hearten the dull and downcast, to increase man's interest in the world, his joy of living, and his sympathy in all sorts and conditions of men. Art for art's sake is heartless and soon grows artless; art for the public market is not art at all, but commerce; art for the people's service is a noble, vital, and permanent element of human life.

The public is content with the standard of salability; the prigs with the standard of preciosity. The people need and deserve a moral standard; it should be a point of honor with men of letters to maintain it. Masterpieces have never been produced by men given to obscenity or lustful thoughts—men who have no Master. Reverence for good work is the foundation of literary character. A refusal to imitate obscenity or to load a book with it is an author's professional chastity.

Good work in literature has its permanent mark; it is like all good work, noble and lasting. It requires a human aim—to cheer, console, purify, or ennoble the life of people. With this aim, literature has never sent an arrow close to the mark. It is by good work only that men of letters can justify their right to a place in the world.

Under the authoritative decisions and considering the substance involved in this appeal, it is my opinion that the decree should be reversed.

The excerpts we have run from the Circuit Court of Appeals decision are significant in comparison to the dissent of Judge Manton, who ends his opinion by reverting to the "noble and lasting." His plea for professional chastity did little to lead the law to a more precise standard for burning books or sending authors or purchasers to jail.

And still, after all, the historic impress of the *Ulysses* case may be only: (*a*) If literary persons of repute value a writing it shall be allowed to circulate. This rule of law is not far from the anti-law concept of counting noses or bowing to pressure of a picket line or being swayed by people in a sit-in or sit-down—scarcely the reaching for truth by reason or logic; and (*b*) ideas may be expressed in combination of letters—that is, words—which at any one moment of history are not considered agreeable for parlor use. Scarcely an adult legal test for more than "taste." Certainly the "less coarse" or the "more polite" may have a more potent influence on the mind and glands of a man or woman in the direction of romance and lovemaking, or—if you please—"sleeping together."

You will note that Judge Woolsey was sustained on appeal by a vote of 2 to 1—and the Government of the United States did not choose to appeal to the Supreme Court of the United States to see if that final censor power would pass on the obscenity of *Ulysses* by James Joyce.

Judge Hand may confuse you—he weighs, as you have noted, Pity as an antidote to Obscenity and Portentous Length as an antidote to the Libidinous, and asks: Is a book in effect only a little erotic—as if man, or at least this great judge had, as we suspect every human has, his own private erotica meter. Fortunately, this same court had held, as you have read in the *Dennett* case, that works under attack must be read as a whole.

Perhaps it would be unfair for us to chuckle at the majority's statement, "It may be that Ulysses will not last as a substantial contribution to literature." Hindsight is a terribly unfair weapon. Nevertheless, the obvious incorrectness of that statement does point up that even the best of judges do not necessarily make good literary critics—and if we put criticism in their hands, or in the hands of a jury, we are risking unjust results.

15

A
Passable
Compromise

One of the doubts left by the *Ulysses* decision—and one not yet finally settled—concerns the book with a frankly sexual content that is not so well written that it can win much critical acclaim. The law also takes into account matters other than artistic merit. After all, the courts can hardly abdicate their judicial function in favor of literary experts any more than they can base their decisions on numbers or pickets or other pressures. But should there be one rule of law for the "obscenities" of great or highly acclaimed authors and another for the mediocre writer? Did the philosophy of the *Ulysses* decision apply to publication in general?

The same three judges who had heard the government's appeal on the Joyce novel approached these questions, and a few more, in 1936 when one Esar Levine sought reversal of his conviction for sending obscene advertisements through the mail. On his trial, one of his defenses had been to attempt to offer in evidence a list of those to whom the advertisement—circulars describing books he had for sale —was mailed. This was the usual list of army officers, professional people, judges, and others at the top of our social ladder. No one would contend, claimed Levine's lawyer, that this sophisticated audience was likely to be corrupted either by the advertisements or by the material advertised. Consequently, even assuming the material might be legally "obscene" if sent to children, for example, it couldn't possibly be "obscene" in the hands of those on Levine's "blue-ribbon" mailing list.

The trial judge did not allow the list to be presented in evidence. He held that the standard of obscenity was, in effect, absolute, and didn't depend upon the particular potential audience in a given case. Levine's other defenses got similar treatment, and he was convicted. Then he, like many before and many still to come, turned to the Federal Second Circuit Court of Appeals.

By now, the reader might think that the Second Circuit Court of Appeals was a special "obscenity" court. Not true! Aside from certain specialized courts, like our Court of Claims, family courts, and others, most of our Federal and state courts have jurisdiction over a fairly wide and varied field of cases. Of no court is this truer than of the Second Circuit Court of Appeals. Being a Federal "Circuit Court," it covers more than one state—New York, Connecticut, and Vermont —and since New York is the commercial center of the country the court is quite a busy one. In addition, since New York is the center of most publishing in this country, it is not surprising that the "Second Circuit," as lawyers call it, gets the lion's share of "obscenity" cases. Fortunately for most of us, the judges on the court have been, on the whole, of exceptionally high ability and graceful expression.

For that we, and you, thank them. And now, with credentials presented, we turn with relish to the graceful prose of Judge Learned Hand speaking for a majority of the court in the case of *U.S.* v. *Levine.*

The Books in Question

The circular was alleged to have advertised five books, of which only three are before us: they are entitled, "Secret Museum of Anthropology," "Crossways of Sex" and "Black Lust." The first is a reproduction of a collection of photographs, for the most part of nude female savages of different parts of the world; the legitimacy of its pretensions as serious anthropology is, to say the most, extremely tenuous, and, while in the hands of adults it could not be considered obscene, it might be undesirable in those of children or youths. The second book professes to be a scientific treatise on sexual pathology; again its good-faith is more than questionable; for example, the author, a supposititious scientist, remains anonymous. It could have no value to psychiatrists or others genuinely interested in the subject, and in the hands of children it might be injurious. The third is a work of fiction of considerable merit, but patently erotic, describing the adventures of an English girl captured by the Dervishes at the fall of Khartoum and kept in a harem until the Battle of Omdurman, when she is killed. It purports to be a study in sadism and masochism, and would arouse libidinous feelings in almost any reader. It did appear that the addressees were minors, but the judge declared that the buyer's age was immaterial.

"Ulysses" v. *The Hicklin Rule*

The trial judge first said that the statute was directed against stimulating sensuality, and that this was not to be measured by its effect, either upon "the highly educated" or upon the "highly prudish," but "on the usual, average human mind." This was well enough, so far as it went, but later he in substance took it back. There was a class, he said, "found in every community, the young and immature, the ignorant and those who are sensually inclined"; the statute was meant to protect these and the jury should regard the effect of the books on their minds, rather than on those of "people of a high order of intelligence and those who have reached mature years." If the books contained a "single passage" such as would "excite lustful or sensual desires" in the minds of those "into whose hands they might come," the statute condemned them. The standard so put before the jury was indeed within the doctrine laid down in *Regina* v. *Hicklin* in England.

This earlier doctrine necessarily presupposed that the devil against which the statute is directed so much outweighs all interests of art, letters or science, that they must yield to the mere possibility that some prurient person may get a sensual gratification from reading or seeing what to most people is innocent and may be delightful or enlightening. No civilized community not fanatically puritanical would tolerate such an imposition, and we do not believe that the courts that have declared it, would ever have applied it consistently. As so often happens, the problem is to find a passable compromise between opposing interests, whose relative importance, like that of all social or personal values, is incommensurable. We impose such a duty upon a jury because the standard they fix is likely to be an acceptable mesne, and because in such matters a mesne most nearly satisfies the moral demands of the community. There can never be constitutive principles for such judgments, or indeed more than cautions to avoid the personal aberrations of the jurors. We mentioned some of these in *United States* v. *Ulysses,* the book must be taken as a whole, its merits weighed against its defects; if it is old, its accepted place in the arts must be regarded; if new, the opinions of competent critics in published reviews or the like may be considered; what counts is its effect, not upon any particular class, but upon all those whom it is likely to reach. Thus "obscenity" is a function of many variables, and the verdict of the jury is not the conclusion of a syllogism to which they are to find only the minor premise but really a small bit of legislation *ad hoc.*

There Is No Absolute Standard

The case was not tried on this theory; on the contrary the judge supposed that a book or picture was obscene or innocent by an absolute standard independent of its readers; moreover he thought that a single passage might condemn it, regardless of its merits as a whole. He was in error as to both points, and the only question is whether the mistakes were serious enough to upset the conviction. Judge Manton and I think that they were; Judge Augustus N. Hand believes that "Crossways of Sex" was so plainly obscene that the errors may be disregarded. Our reversal does not mean that on another trial the proper standard can under no circumstances refer to adolescents. It may appear that the prospective buyer was a youth and that the accused had reason to suppose that he was. The evil against which the statute is directed, would then be the possible injury to such a youthful reader. It is when the crime consists of importing the work, or offering it for general sale, that the test cannot be found in the interests of those to whom it is sent, though abnormally susceptible, lest in their protection the interests may be sacrificed of others who might profit from the work; and that some compromise must be made. But even when the crime consists of a single sale, and so may be judged by possible injury to the buyer, the book must be taken as a whole. In this case the jury may find "Crossways of Sex" and "Black Lust" obscene when sent to any reader; "Secret Museum of Anthropology" can be so regarded only if sent to youths. The standard must be the likelihood that the work will so much arouse the salacity of the reader to whom it is sent as to outweigh any literary, scientific or other merits it may have in that reader's hands; of this the jury is the arbiter.

Respectable People Have Their Salacious Moments

The judge refused to allow in evidence a list of purchasers of the books, among whom were a number of well-known persons. He was right. Such a list taken alone told nothing of the standing of the works in the minds of the community; even respectable persons may have a *taste for salacity.* Obviously it would be impossible without hopelessly confusing the issues to undertake any analysis of such a list by finding out why each buyer bought. On the other hand it is reasonable to allow in evidence published reviews of qualified critics—quite another thing incidentally from expert witnesses at the trial—for such evidence does not lead far afield and is rationally helpful, though in the end it is the jury who must declare what the standard shall be. So far as that may be a menace to the free development of the arts, it is a risk which Congress has seen fit to impose, and which we cannot gainsay, even if we could.

Judgment reversed; new trial ordered.

MANTON concurs in the result and AUGUSTUS HAND disagrees.

This is a classic opinion—because it lets us see how a particular set of facts (a "case") serves as a meeting ground for opposing forces in a court of law.

There is, in any attempt at *social* justice as opposed to *absolute* justice, an element of compromise, for without that element society would break (and indeed has been broken) apart from the collision of irreconcilable "absolutes." Learned Hand, more than most, was keenly aware that a courtroom is a meeting ground for conflicting pressures and that, in some way, a Court must resolve each conflict by striking a balance between the pressures.

Thus, in the *Kennerley* case, he talked about a compromise between "candor and shame," and here, in the *Levine* case, he refers to "a passable compromise between opposing interests." And because Hand has shown us this process so clearly we understand him when he refers to a jury verdict as "really a small bit of legislation *ad hoc*"— all social decisions are.

As for Learned Hand's colleague, Judge Manton, he later left the bench under charges of corruption—which shows that not all judges, not even on the Second Circuit, are good men. As for Augustus Hand, he dissented because he believed one of the books was "plainly obscene," which shows that the sensitivity of judges, even if they are cousins, can differ.

So much for Levine. But questions raised by Judge Hand's opinion linger on. If we are to judge a work by the *standards* of the community, which vary with the place and the times, shall the law also change with the times, and, if so, who is to be the keeper (and expositor) of society's moral-temperature chart?

In 1938 *Life* magazine had to face these issues—and bet the freedom of its publisher on the decision.

16

Changing
Community
Standards

Early in 1938, *Life* magazine was being harried in several states
and many cities because of an article, profusely illustrated with photographs, dealing with and entitled "The Birth of a Baby." This was an
article, accompanied by stills from a motion picture of the same name,
and two sets of anatomical diagrams, aimed at educating the public to
the avoidable dangers of childbirth. It was dignified and scientific in
writing and illustration. The attacks, charging obscenity, had been
generated in the main by an important Catholic lay organization. In
New York State, for example, dozens of newsstand dealers had been
arrested. Pennsylvania State Police also had rounded up vendors.

During the 1920's publishers of books and magazines had come
forward and had defended their imprints with pride, following the
example set by Mitchell Kennerley in 1915. But in the late thirties
they began to be more timid, preferring to stay in the background.
Although they paid the booksellers' defense costs, they were seemingly reluctant, as they are today, to be associated with the book as
publishers. Such timidity naturally encourages the censorious. More
important, it helps produce unconsidered law on censorship. A street-
corner newsstand owner does not make enough profit on the sale of
any magazine to warrant the expense of a court defense. It is cheaper

114

to plead guilty. Moreover, a retailer seldom if ever has an opportunity to read and inspect a book or magazine before he displays it, and so cannot appraise the desirability of a defense. No wonder vice hunters and police usually level their guns, not at the wealthier publisher who selects the manuscript (and who is really responsible for its publication), but at relatively impecunious retailers who order a few copies, often as samples, and usually on consignment.

In historic terms, perhaps these publishers do not deserve the richness of our freedom of the press. Perhaps freedom of speech and press should belong only to those who dig their heels into the ground and say: "This is my own imprint. I and I alone shall defend it. I do not choose to hide behind the bookseller or the newsstand dealer."

Roy Larsen, who was the publisher of *Life,* was one publisher who earned this freedom. He could have tested the issue by proffering free legal counsel to any one of the dozens of retailers who had been arrested. To his credit, he stood on the First Amendment, as was his right and duty. In effect he told the Court: "Forget about the newsstand; if anyone is guilty, I am the one, for I am responsible for the article, and I am proud to have published it." Although Law is supposed to be impersonal, we prefer to believe that this frank offer of full and total responsibility influenced the Court in Larsen's favor. Perhaps, if there is real meaning to the word "obscene," an essential ingredient of such meaning consists of a sense of shame and secrecy on the part of those responsible for the publication.

This particular case was brought by the chief prosecutor of Bronx County, New York City, before the lower Criminal Court in New York City. Three judges sat on the case. Their opinion was brief, and except for references to prior cases in other courts, we print it in full.

PEOPLE V. LARSEN
April 26, 1938

Argued before KOZICKE, MCDONALD and PERLMAN, JJ.

NATHAN D. PERLMAN, Justice.

Roy Larsen is a publisher of a weekly newspicture magazine of general circulation. He is charged with having violated the Penal Law, which reads in part as follows: "A person who sells * * * any obscene, lewd, lascivious, filthy, indecent or disgusting * * * magazine * * * is guilty of a misdemeanor." The charge is predicated upon a picture story consisting of stills, taken from a moving picture film entitled "The Birth of a Baby." In addition to the stills, there are two sets of anatomical diagrams.

Section 1141, which purports to define the material condemned by the law, exhausts practically all of the synonyms for the word obscene. An analysis of the meaning of the adjectives appearing in this section will serve no useful purpose and there is an inherent impossibility of verbal precision in matters of this kind.

Conceptions of what is decent or indecent are not constant. The early attitude of the Courts upon this subject is not reflected in the recent cases. The trends to be observed in the cases have mirrored changing popular attitudes. Recent cases illustrate the caution with which Courts have proceeded in this branch of the law to avoid interference with a justifiable freedom of expression. * * *

The gravamen of obscenity is the tendency of the matter to corrupt morals or to lower the standards of right or wrong concerning sexual behavior. * * * The normal person must serve as a criterion, not the abnormal. * * *

Upon the trial of this action, Larsen produced as witnesses responsible public health authorities, welfare workers and educators who testified to the sincerity, honest and educational value of the picture story complained of. The prosecution objected to the admission of this testimony. * * * Strictly speaking, the contention of the People is correct. In a case such as this the jury or the triers of the facts must declare what the standard shall be. Such evidence is, however, rationally helpful and in recent years Courts have considered the opinions of qualified persons.

The Court is aware of the fact that the prosecution might well have produced honest and responsible individuals who may differ widely as to the expediency of presenting this type of picture story. This honest difference of opinion, however, demonstrates the necessity of avoiding arbitrary censorship by a Court.

My own conclusion is that the picture story, because of the manner in which it was presented, does not fall within the forbidden class. The picture story was directly based on a film produced under the auspices of a responsible medical group. There is no nudity or unnecessary disclosure. The subject has been treated with delicacy.

I vote to acquit Larsen.

All concur.

This case, although not the decision of a high court, did more to educate the bench and bar to the practice of offering testimony of informed witnesses. Such authorities are called, not to testify as to the Law of Obscenity, but to give their opinions as to the educational, literary, scientific, or other value (or lack of value) of the words or pictures under attack. This is now quite a common procedure whether the trial is held before a judge sitting alone or a judge and jury, or whether witnesses appear in court or proffer statements included in a brief of counsel on either side.

Expert witnesses have their recognized place in both civil and criminal trials. The experts are not there as judges of the facts, which is what the jury is for, but to help the jury reach an understanding of what the facts are and what they mean. Thus medical men will be called to explain an injury or an ailment; engineers to describe the strength of a beam or the power of an engine, and so on. Then they also may give their opinions, as experts, as to whether a certain wound or disease would have been fatal or a certain bridge would have supported a certain load. Judges in many situations have the power to decide whether or not expert testimony is relevant and how far experts may go in expressing opinions. In the Law of Obscenity, there is less settled precedent than in other areas of litigation, and so practice varies widely. In some courts, the judge holds that the jury needs no help in deciding whether or not a given book or picture is obscene. In others, wide latitude is allowed. England is experimenting with an obscenity law, passed in 1959, which specifically induces expert testimony. In the most celebrated case to be tried under the new law, *Lady Chatterley's Lover,* the defense summoned seventy religious, literary, educational, and artistic experts and put thirty-five of them on the stand.

The *Life*-magazine ruling, although it referred to the standards of the "normal" reader, did not decide who is to say what these standards are. What if a prosecutor is a decade behind his time? That, too, has happened, as our next chapter will show.

17

An
Attorney General
Out of Step

Between October, 1944, and January, 1947, 1,300,000 copies of a book were sold in the United States. A British edition had run over 100,000 copies. Our armed services published a special edition of 140,000. Translations had appeared in thirteen foreign languages. Condensed versions were printed in many magazines, and fourteen radio stations had reviewed it. The volume itself ran to 652 double-column pages.

Then, in 1948, a state of historic cultural roots tried to suppress the book. The state was the Commonwealth of Massachusetts, and the book was *Forever Amber*. The case went to the highest court of the state as a civil rather than a criminal action under a new law. This law provided that "whenever there is a reasonable cause to believe" that a book is "obscene, indecent or impure," the attorney general or any district attorney could ask a justice of the Superior Court to rule on the book. The judge, if he agreed that some people might reasonably believe the book to be obscene, could order anyone who wished to defend the book (and had an interest in it) to appear within thirty days to show why "said book should not be judicially determined to be obscene, indecent or impure."

The law outlined decent procedures for a fair trial and partly resolved one procedural controversy by providing that the Court might, in its discretion, hear expert evidence on the merits of the book. It was presumed that with this legislative "encouragement," judges would permit this expert testimony, and so it was with *Forever Amber.* In a unanimous opinion, the highest Court of the state wrote:

> At the hearing the Attorney General introduced in evidence the novel, which has its setting in England during the Restoration. The publisher, Macmillan, introduced evidence as to its publication and advertising, and called as witnesses two experts in psychiatry. The association of Boston book merchants and Johnson's Book-store, Inc., called as a witness an expert on the literature of the period. A third expert in psychiatry testified on behalf of the Attorney General.

The use of such witnesses is an advance of a subtle nature in the law, but there were other considerations. This was the same Court that had ruled against *Strange Fruit,* as mentioned in a previous chapter. At that time, the Court said:

> But sincerity and literary art alone do not bring it beyond reach of the statute. The question will commonly be one of fact in each case, and if, looking at the book as a whole, the bad is found to persist in substantial degree alongside the good, as the law now stands, the book will fall within the statute.

In its *Forever Amber* opinion, the Court affirmed this concept. At the same time, however, the judges showed due regard for the opinions of the experts, saying:

> The expert on literature testified that as a historical romance of the period, and "in giving the small group of persons with whom it deals," *Forever Amber* is at least as correct as the romances of Cooper or Scott; that it is evident from the book that the author has stated with great care the manner of the period in these respects; that the dialogue more or less faithfully reflects what we have recorded of the language and conversation of the period; that these matters indicate a certain amount of study and research; that it is a work of secondary order but with considerable narrative drive; that it is somewhat similar to *Roxana* and *Moll Flanders* by Daniel Defoe; that these and other works of Restoration literature,

commonly found in college libraries, "essentially hold a thorough understanding of the age," which was extremely cynical; that *Forever Amber* is sufficiently accurate for the purpose of representing a portrait of the period and its customs and morals; that it does not exaggerate or falsify any traits of the Restoration, if by that is meant the conduct and language of the small group around Charles II, which is the subject of the book; and that it would not be possible to write a historically accurate novel about the Restoration with reference to the court, ignoring the sexual theme. *We find the foregoing to be the facts.* [Italics ours.]

Perhaps those "facts" helped the judges to rule that in *Forever Amber* the "bad" did not persist alongside the "good." Here is the part of the opinion in which the Court explained why it felt that way:

The book in this case, when read in its long entirety, in the opinion of a majority of the court, does not offend against the law. It undoubtedly has historical purpose, and in this is adequately accurate in achievement. The career of the heroine, an illegitimate child of noble blood, is traced from an upbringing in a rustic environment through the vicissitudes of her life in or near London until she becomes a duchess and the mistress of Charles II. She has numerous lovers and bears three children by men whom she does not marry. She enters into four marriages, of which only the first appears to have been lawful. She fails in her main objective of marriage to the one man she genuinely loves. There are detailed descriptions of Newgate Prison, the Great Plague, and the Great Fire. A real attempt is made to portray life at the Court of Charles II, the stage, and the costumes of the period. Some descriptions the Attorney General in his brief concedes to be excellent. Many notable figures prominent in the Restoration appear from time to time, and their imaginary conversations are recorded. Unfortunate it is that sexual episodes abound to the point of tedium. For the most part, however, such episodes are lacking in realistic detail, although some are coarse and in a taste foreshadowed by the advertising. We are not required to decide whether standing by themselves any are obscene, indecent, or impure. Once the full task of reading the total six hundred and fifty-two double-column pages has been completed, the paramount impression is of an unfortunate country and its people as yet unfreed of the grasp of the Stuarts, whom Charles Dickens appraised as "a public nuisance altogether," and of its great city ravaged by disaster and by disease. As to the individual characters, the reader is left with an estimate of an unattractive, hedonistic group, whose course of conduct is abhorrent and whose mode of living *can* be neither emulated nor envied.

Law is here trying to approach nonsubjective tests. Here are a few of the "objective" tests to which the Court referred in this passage. But in considering them, how would you react about a book which had a batting average of only .500 on these ten? Or more than .500? Or less? The ten are:

1. Its overall purpose
2. Its historical purpose
3. Its historical accuracy
4. Its excellent descriptions of the court under Charles II
5. The tedium of its sexual episodes
6. Comparative absence of realistic detail
7. Its description of unfortunate people unfreed from the Stuarts
8. Its unattractive hedonist characters
9. Its abhorrence of coarse conduct
10. Its description of a mode of living which can neither be emulated nor envied.

The vast popularity and worldwide acceptance of *Forever Amber* had not prevented the highest law officer of a state proud of its culture from putting the publisher to the expense and hazard of a defense. A less wealthy or courageous defendant than The Macmillan Company, the publisher, might have crumbled before such an attack. As we have said, not all publishers have been devoted to the defense of their imprint in these cases. Fear of an indictment or charge of obscenity, even if it does not hold up in court, is an increasing danger to the freedom of the printed word. If the attorney general of Massachusetts could be so utterly misguided as to the Law of Obscenity, policemen and prosecutors in villages and counties with less tradition of culture can hardly be expected to do better. Their targets, the local newsdealer or bookstore keeper, are even less likely to have the money or incentive to put up a strong legal defense.

Forever Amber, of course, was a book with a wide appeal to a very large audience. However one may deplore censorship, the concern of the censorious with the effect of particular works on a "mass" audience cannot be said to be entirely frivolous. But what of works directed solely to scholars engaged in serious study of special fields of inquiry that require the use of so-called "pornographic" or "obscene" material? Should sociologists, anthropologists, psychologists, and others like them be prevented from obtaining information because of the indiscriminate application of censorship laws? Clearly the answer should be in the negative—for any restriction upon the source of scientific information is antithetical to the scientific method. And yet, in the field of obscenity it was not until 1957, 115 years after our first customs ban on obscenity, and centuries after the Renaissance, that science won its right to knowledge.

18

The Scientist's
Right to Read

Over the years, the squeamish follies of the Customs officials in denying entrance to material on the grounds of obscenity became so ludicrous that shortly after 1933 a special "assessor" was employed by the Treasury Department. This cultured man, Huntington Cairns, soon prevented repetition of bannings of the classics. But while the excesses of zeal were curbed, the question of importing frankly obscene matter under any definition for scientific use was still open.

Alfred Kinsey, who contributed much to the new science that may enable us to correlate the causal relation—if any—between obscene expression and human behavior, was the man who forced an answer. He had purchased for the library of his great project on the study of human sexual behavior, under the auspices of the University of Indiana, pictures and books from many lands depicting sexual attitudes and practices. Some of them were obscene by any standard we have discussed. But they were of value in the Kinsey studies. They were denied admission to the United States for the good professor and his staff. In 1957 Dr. Kinsey took his case to court.

It was heard by Judge Edmund L. Palmieri in the Federal Court at New York. Shortly before this the United States Supreme Court, in its search for the obscene, had evolved a new definition, as will be explained in more detail in a later part of this book. Something is obscene, this definition ran, if "to the average person, applying contemporary community standards, the dominant theme of the material taken as a whole appeals to prurient interest." So the Courts had a new word to play with, "prurient." According to a dictionary, "prurient" means "impure in thought and desire; having lustful cravings and desires."

Judge Palmieri felt bound to apply this new definition to the *Kinsey* case; and, undeniably, the material under consideration fell squarely within the definition. But the case could not end there, because a limited and specialized audience was involved. Says the judge:

> Material is obscene if it makes a certain appeal to the viewer. It is not sufficient that the material be "merely coarse, vulgar, or indecent in the popular sense of those terms." Its appeal must be to "prurient interest." "Obscene material is material which deals with sex in a manner appealing to prurient interest."
>
> But the search for a definition does not end there. To whose prurient interest must the work appeal? While the rule is often stated in terms of the appeal of the material to the "average person," it must be borne in mind that the cases applying the standard in this manner do so in regard to material which is to be distributed to the public at large. I believe, however, that the more inclusive statement of the definition is that which judges the material by its appeal to "all those whom it is likely to reach." Viewed in this light, the "average man" test is but a particular application of the rule, often found in the cases only because the cases often deal with material which is distributed to the public at large.

Once more a judge was called on to guess as to the effect on an audience. But what audience was intended?

> Of course, this rule cuts both ways. Material distributed to the public at large may not be judged by its appeal to the most sophisticated, nor by its appeal to the most susceptible. And I believe that the cases established that material whose use will be restricted to those in whose hands it will not have a prurient appeal is not to be judged by its appeal to the populace at large.

Then the opinion states:

> Another court has held that the human body might be exhibited be-
> for a medical class for the purposes of instruction, "but that if the
> same human body were exposed in front of one of our medical col-
> leges to the public indiscriminately, even for the purpose of opera-
> tion, such an exhibition would be held to be indecent and obscene."

After deciding that science may not be denied, the Court had to
be concerned with the souls of the men of science in Indiana, the
postal clerks who would ship the material, and the poor Customs
officials no doubt condemned long ago to the corruption of prurience.

Thus did the judge cope with this inevitable quandary—enduring
until the *effect,* if any, of the books and pictures be examined by the
Law:

> The Government also raises a CONCURSUS HORRIBILIUM [hue
> and cry], maintaining that there are no workable criteria by which
> the section may be administered if it is interpreted as I do today. It
> is probably sufficient unto this case to point out that there is no
> dispute in this proceeding as to the fact that there is no reasonable
> likelihood that the material will appeal to the prurient interest of
> those who will see it. But I will add that I fail to see why it should
> be more difficult to determine the appeal of matter to a known
> group of persons than it is to determine its appeal to hypothetical
> average man. The question is not whether the materials are neces-
> sary, or merely desirable for a particular research project. The
> question is not whether the fruits of the research will be valuable
> to society. The Tariff Act of 1930 provides no warrant for either
> customs officials or this court to sit in review of the decisions of
> scholars as to the bypaths of learning upon which they shall tread.
> The question is solely whether, as to those persons who will see
> the material, there is a reasonable probability that it will appeal to
> their prurient interest.

The Treasury lost, and Kinsey got his research material. The government did not appeal. Thus did laymen—that is, nonscientists; that
is, judges—decide that science must be served even though there is
no study so far as we can find to prove that scientists do not enjoy the
prurient. Or are we to assume that the nonprurient go into science as

a profession, or that the medicos do not enjoy off-color sexual stories, or that lawyers are impervious to those law cases involving the "salacity" of rape and seduction—reported fully in their buckram-bound libraries? Or is the theory rather that we must take a chance—sacrifice the souls of some scientists, lawyers, scholars, or even clerics in confessionals, as a small price to pay in our desire to expand all knowledge to all professional men dealing in knowledge—prurient or not?

Such questions show how far we are from ending what, at the beginning of this part of the book, we called the judicial search for the obscene, a search for definitions and standards which still is going on and may never end. Since community, or even personal, standards and definitions of the "obscene" change constantly, if imperceptibly, it is impossible to state with certainty what is "legally obscene" at any given time. However, in order to get some idea of where the judicial search for the obscene has taken us to date we present in our next chapter another scene in this episode—entitled: "The Lady, The Gamekeeper, and the Erudite Judge."

19

The Lady,
The Gamekeeper,
and the Erudite Judge

Over one hundred years of obscenity prosecutions had produced, in 1959, a potpourri of judicial definitions and standards, some showing a clear progression from narrowness to liberality, while others were revolving irrationally in a vortex of irreconcilability.

The case of *Lady Chatterley's Lover,* known in the law books as *"Grove Press* v. *Christenberry* (Grove being the publisher and Christenberry the then Postmaster General), although it introduced no new theories or standards of the Law of Obscenity, did serve as a platform upon which Judge Frederick van Pelt Bryan could present an admirably clear and graciously written opinion of the state of Federal obscenity law circa 1959.

In that year, after thirty years of being acclaimed as a masterpiece while banned as an obscenity, D. H. Lawrence's *Lady Chatterley's Lover* was published in full in the United States by the Grove Press. Although various expurgated versions had previously been available, none of them contained the complete catalogue of four-letter words and rugged love scenes used by Lawrence to portray the violent, strangely beautiful relationship between Lady Chatterley and her gamekeeper lover, Mellors.

Because of its frankness, and despite Lawrence's high literary reputation, the Post Office Department banned *Lady Chatterley's Lover* from the mails. The publisher challenged the ban, and Judge Bryan agreed with the publisher and lifted the ban. In his opinion, Judge Bryan carefully outlined the tests he applied in reaching his decision. They were:

1. That the work had to be read as a whole.
2. That literary merit could be considered for the purpose of discovering if it outweighed alleged pornographic features.
3. That honesty and seriousness of the author be taken into account as possibly justifying obscenity that would offend many readers.
4. That the theme is not "morbid" interest in sex (odd word, "morbid," since it really means diseased).
5. That the effect on immature readers is not controlling. (What if a few such are harmed?)
6. That four-letter words and sex as a major theme are not controlling either.
7. That a book may be noncensorable even if it is in bad taste and shocks many readers.
8. That surely a free society must limit severely the restrictions it places on ideas expressed through artistic media.

Judge Bryan was writing, it should be noted, after the Supreme Court of the United States had decided in the *Roth* case (to be discussed later) that whether a writing was obscene or not depended on its effect on the average man according to contemporary community standards. Since Judge Bryan's court was only a Federal "District Court," the lowest court in the Federal judicial hierarchy, he had, of course, to pay obeisance to *his* appellate judges. In the course of his opinion Judge Bryan evidences satisfaction with the application of the "contemporary community standards" rule of obscenity cases, and yet, at the same time, he is quick to realize how subjective a rule it must necessarily be. He says, in part:

> However, the Postmaster General's finding that the book is non-mailable because it offends contemporary community standards bears some discussion.
> I am unable to ascertain upon what the Postmaster General based this conclusion. The record before him indicates general acceptance of the book throughout the country and nothing was

shown to the contrary. The critics were unanimous. Editorial comment by leading journals of opinion welcomed the publication and decried any attempts to ban it.

It is true that the editorial comment was excluded by the Judicial Officer at the hearing. But it seems to me that this was error. These expressions were relevant and material on the question of whether the book exceeded the limits of freedom of expression in matters involving sex relations tolerated by the community at large in these times.

The contemporary standards of the community and the limits of its tolerance cannot be measured or ascertained accurately. There is no poll available to determine such questions. Surely expressions by leading newspapers, with circulations of millions, are some evidence at least as to what the limits of tolerance by present-day community standards are, if we must embark upon a journey of exploration into such uncharted territory.

Quite apart from this, the broadening of freedom of expression and of the frankness with which sex and sex relations are dealt with at the present time require no discussion. In one best selling novel after another frank descriptions of the sex act and "four-letter" words appear with frequency. These trends appear in all media of public expression, in the kind of language used and the subjects discussed in polite society, in pictures, advertisements and dress, and in other ways familiar to all. Much of what is now accepted would have shocked the community to the core a generation ago. Today such things are generally tolerated whether we approve or not.

I hold that, at this stage in the development of our society, this major English novel does not exceed the outer limits of the tolerance which the community as a whole gives to writing about sex and sex relations.

Judge Bryan's opinion is reminiscent both in tone and in emphasis of the *Ulysses* decision. And it is in this spirit of aesthetics mixed with freedom that the judge concludes:

One final word about the constitutional problem implicit here.

It is essential to the maintenance of a free society that the severest restrictions be placed upon restraints which may tend to prevent the dissemination of ideas. It matters not whether such ideas be expressed in political pamphlets or works of political, economic or social theory or criticism, or through artistic media. All such expressions must be freely available.

A work of literature published and distributed through normal channels by a reputable publisher stands on quite a different footing from hard core pornography furtively sold for the purpose of profiting by the titillation of the dirty minded. The courts have been deeply and properly concerned about the use of obscenity statutes to suppress great works of art or literature.

The Circuit Court of Appeals agreed with Judge Bryan, and found that the Postmaster General was not a wise interpreter of "present community standards" when he barred *Lady Chatterley's Lover* from the mails. However, one of the three judges who decided the appeal, Judge Leonard Moore, while agreeing with the result, raised some disturbing questions about "community standards," "literary merit," "definitions of obscenity," and Lawrence's "intentions." Speaking of one "principal message," apparent in *Lady Chatterley's Lover,* Moore noted:

> The third message of "repression of the natural man," said to be inveighed against by the author, is the "inhibited sex relations between man and woman." Whether "natural man" should be somewhat inhibited in this activity presents a sociological and moral problem thus far not solved by society. If the author wishes to plead "for greater freedom and naturalness" for man and woman in their sexual diversions uninhibited by law or convention, it is for the lawmakers and not the courts to rule how far this objective should properly be pursued.

And then as to changing mores and the theory of climate of opinion, he writes:

> The fallacy of "the changing climate of opinion" argument is that it rotates in a circle. During recent years authors of the so-called school of "realism" vied with each other to depict with accuracy all that could be observed by peeking through hypothetical keyholes and by hiding under beds.

He then "reluctantly" concurs, but only after writing these cautionary words:

The Supreme Court (not the Postmaster General) chose the test of "contemporary community standards" and appealing to prurient interest. But what is "community" and what is "prurient interest"? And is a single judge or a group of judges in any one restricted geographic district all-knowing as to community standards? At least the Postmaster General by virtue of his office and his staff of inspectors in every State of the Union is mindful of the type of questionable material found in the mails and the reaction thereto of each community. Parenthetically a conjecture that juries in a substantial number of communities throughout the country would support the Postmaster General's conclusion in this case would not be too erroneous. As to "prurient interest" one can scarcely be so naïve as to believe that the avalanche of sales came about as a result of a sudden desire on the part of the American public to become acquainted with the problems of a professional gamekeeper in the management of an English estate.

Discussing the value of contemporary opinion of experts, Judge Moore said:

Can it be doubted that there is a great difference in what is to be deemed obscene in 1959 compared with what was deemed obscene in 1859?

Unless we disbelieve that the literary, psychological or moral standards of a community can be made fruitful and illuminating subjects of inquiry by those who give their life to such inquiries, it was violative to exclude the constitutionally relevant evidence proffered in this case. The importance of this type of evidence in prosecutions for obscenity has been impressively attested by the recent debates in England in the House of Commons dealing with the insertion of such a provision in the enactment of the English Obscene Publication Act of 1959.

Closing with a bitter legal question still undecided, Moore asks:

But should the literary merit of the product of an author's pen give him carte blanche in case he chooses to venture into forbidden fields?

Unless those who really represent all communities and are best able to speak for their standards, namely, the legislative bodies, take some more definite action, the courts will have to continue to struggle with the problem of some vague and ever-retreating boundary line. Certain it is that if the trend continues unabated, by the time some author writes of "Lady Chatterley's Granddaughter," Lady Chatterley herself will seem like a prim and puritanical housewife.

However, this case must be decided in accordance with contemporary judicial standards and therefore I reluctantly concur.

So Judge Moore, whose wry sense of humor is well known to friends and associates, went down, not without a struggle, and bowed, finally, to what he perhaps all too aptly calls "contemporary judicial standards"—but he emphasizes once again the seemingly unavoidable subjectivity of reflections on sex and promiscuity.

No appeal was taken by the prosecutor to the Supreme Court, and the book was freed. It is interesting to note also that a French motion picture based on the book had been through the courts and had also been cleared. The lady and the gamekeeper thus seem destined forever to play out their scene for all to read and see.

Lady Chatterley's Lover caused a debate, a great to-do, and several paperback cheap editions; but, since the love episodes were between a lady and her gamekeeper, the last word came during a House of Lords debate on a trial in England which cleared the same novel. Viscount Gage quoted a fellow peer "who, on being asked whether he did not object to his daughter reading the book, replied that he had no such objection, but that he had the strongest objection to the book being read by his gamekeeper."

part III

The Law
in Search
of Remedies

20

An
Overflowing
Medicine Box

Aside from the definition of the area known as The Obscene, our society has been concerned in a kind of bewildered way with the problem of the proper punishment to fit the crime, or method to prevent it—what lawyers call Process and Sanction.

For example, in simple terms, the sovereign, whether city, state, or nation, in all matters of a presumed antisocial nature has an eye on retribution or vengeance against the wrongdoer, reformation through incarceration of a violator, or a sanction—by fine or jail sentence—which it is hoped will act as a deterrent to others inclined to similar misbehavior.

In the field of obscenity the problem is complicated even if there were a tidy and clear definition of the illegality. In the first place, our Federal system of government calls for fifty separate state controls, each with its own variety of Process and Sanction. Then again, if the dissemination of the "obscene" material is accomplished by use of the mails, or by importation, our Constitution provides that only the Federal government, and not the states, has the power to regulate and punish. But whether state or Federal action, a choice of remedies is possible under our legal process. For example, we can stop material at the Customs and either prosecute the person who ordered the import, and, if he is found guilty, impose a fine or jail sentence, or we might proceed only against the book itself, with the ultimate sanction being impersonal and resulting only in an order to destroy the book if it is illegally obscene.

The search for remedies and preventives for obscenity—led by legislators and judges—has been as imaginative as it has been varied. Law here too has proven itself viable and ripe for experimentation—if somewhat confused and sometimes downright dangerous. In the pages that follow we shall encounter some of these experiments—old standbys like motion-picture precensorship, and postal stop orders, as well as more modern sophistications.

Recently the difficulty of successfully prosecuting a publisher or bookseller criminally has led states to experiment with the injunctive process. Forget fines or imprisonment, they say; simplify the censorship business by a proceeding to hold up the dissemination of books and magazines. This is in effect precensorship or distribution—a modification of the precensorship of motion pictures that we shall encounter shortly.

All kinds of remedies and processes have been explored: attempts to proceed against the publisher or the buyer of an offending book, attempts to proceed against the newsdealer or bookstore that sells the book whether they have read it or not, and attempts to proceed by public pressure or even police intimidation.

It is important to note that most of these remedies avoid criminal sanctions. Do not be too hasty to applaud them for this—such avoidance presents a concomitant danger. Under our system of law a person accused of a crime has certain inalienable protections to ensure a fair trial, such as the right to counsel and often the right to have a jury, in serious cases. But his most important protection is that the burden of proof of his crime is with the prosecution, which must prove it *beyond a reasonable doubt.* By avoiding criminal sanctions in the field of obscenity through the use of so-called civil processes, some state and local governments often also avoid the necessity of proving their case beyond a reasonable doubt or otherwise affording the accused, whether man or book, the protection to which he or it would otherwise have been entitled.

Much of this portion of our volume may seem technical, but there is, we assure you, strictly speaking, no technicality in the law. What seems to be a technicality is only that part of the law which lawyers and judges have failed to explain to the layman because, as doctors write prescriptions so that no patient knows what medicine he is taking, so most lawyers seemingly enjoy and profit from their needless gobbledygook.

Because of the interrelation between the definition of obscenity and its proposed remedies, it is not completely possible to separate cases into one or the other category. The cases we have just read, although concerned primarily with a definition of the obscene, nevertheless also had to involve a choice of remedies. And the cases that follow, although set down here primarily to give the reader some idea of what remedies the law has pursued in this field, also necessarily touch upon questions of what is obscene.

Most of the remedies that have been tried in the field of obscenity have been attempts by governments at legal shortcuts to the slower and more formal process of a criminal trial. Before we watch their passing parade, we thought it might be refreshing to take a look at an individual, and a famous one, trying his own brand of legal shortcut. You will find him, standing firm as always, in the next chapter.

21

Looking for
a Legal Shortcut

The first attempted new remedy we shall consider was set against the background of the Comstock Era. The principal works condemned by the courts during the half-century 1880–1930 were accepted later, often with great acclaim and without judicial reconsideration. The rejection or later nullification of court rulings in this field led to disrespect and increasing cynicism toward the law in the field of obscenity.

However, as we have said, during the peak of the power of the Society for the Suppression of Vice, distinguished editors and publishers timidly presented to the society manuscripts on which they asked a reading opinion, or they bowed to the society's edicts and withdrew books that already had been printed. They did not care to gamble on winning an expensive contest in the criminal courts, not even after Mitchell Kennerley's successful defiance of the society in the *Hagar Revelly* case in 1915.

The year after this decision there was a historic attempt to introduce a legal shortcut to bypass the control of the marketplace of ideas exercised by the society. The medium used was *The Genius* by Theodore Dreiser. Dreiser was already a very highly acclaimed writer for his novels *Sister Carrie* and *Jennie Gerhardt,* although not yet of the stature he would attain with *An American Tragedy*. *The Genius* had elements of autobiography, and also was concerned with the sex life of the principal characters. The facts in the case are simple, set forth in the unanimous decision of an appellate court in New York State:

Dreiser Against His Publisher, John Lane Co.

Dreiser is the author of a book entitled "The Genius." The publisher John Lane Co. is a domestic corporation engaged in the business of selling, advertising, and publishing books and periodicals. On the 30th day of July, 1914, Dreiser and Lane entered into a contract for the sale, advertisement and publication of the book, under which Dreiser guaranteed Lane that it contained nothing of a scandalous, immoral, or libelous nature. Lane agreed to publish and sell the book, and pay Dreiser 20 per cent of the retail price on all copies sold in the United States and England. Lane commenced the sale, advertisement, and publication, and up to July 28, 1916, sold approximately 8,000 copies thereof. On or about that date the New York Society for the Suppression of Vice notified Lane that it claimed that the sale, advertisement, and publication of "The Genius" violated the laws of the state against obscene literature, and threatened to prosecute criminally if further sale thereof were not discontinued. Thereupon the publisher Lane withdrew the book from the market and discontinued its publication, and refused to sell, advertise, or publish it unless and until it be judicially determined that it is not a violation of the law to do so.

The then much discussed author, Dreiser, sued his publisher. To simplify the work of the court they both agreed on the basic facts, and instead of putting witnesses on the stand to testify, drew up a statement that was jointly submitted to the court.

The Court's opinion refers to this submission as follows:

The author claims that the book is not scandalous, immoral, libelous, or obscene, and does not tend to corrupt the morals, and that its sale, advertisement, and publication are not a violation of the law; and the author claims that the publisher's refusal to go ahead with sales is in breach of the contract. The publisher conceded that its action is in violation of its contract with Dreiser if the sale, advertisement, or publication of the book does not violate the law.

> The parties agree that this court shall render such judgment as
> shall be proper on the foregoing facts, and the parties stipulate that,
> if it shall be determined that the sale, advertisement, or publication
> of the book is a violation of law, in that event the publisher's action
> is justified under the contract, and the author shall lose his case;
> that if the sale, advertisement, or publication of the said book is
> not a violation of the law, in that event the publisher's action is
> not justified, but is a breach of contract, and that a decree may
> be entered preventing the publisher from further violation of the
> contract, and granting the author such other and further relief as
> may be justified.

The Court then states the real purpose of the suit.

> It is apparent that what the author and the publisher of the book
> in question desire is an expression by this court of its opinion as to
> whether the book violated the criminal law against obscene litera-
> ture.

Surely this sounds like a gentlemanly attempt to resolve a murky
problem. But the Court refused to pass on the question of obscenity,
and Lane was not required to publish the book. The opinion said that
obscenity is a crime and that the existence of a crime must be determined in a *criminal* proceeding where one party must be the state, as
accuser, against some author or publisher or vendor as the accused.

The reasonable procedure attempted by Dreiser and Lane to have
a Court determine in a noncriminal way whether the book was obscene was held to be not within the intention of the legislature, which
hoped to simplify the testimony in civil but not criminal lawsuits. The
Court said that Author Dreiser and his publisher Lane were asking
the Court to render an advisory judgment on a *criminal* affair, a
technique employed in some states but not available in New York.

Underlying this rejection of the Lane-Dreiser submission there
rests a profound rule of law. In a litigation between two citizens in
a dispute of a noncriminal nature, the judge or jury is called upon
to hold the scales of justice and see which scale tips down and which
tips up. The difference in the levels may be, and often is, only of the
slightest degree. There is no such concept as a judge announcing a
tie. And if the jury disagrees, the one who sues—the claimant—loses
his case. His argument must prevail or he is out of court. To be sure,
some states do not ask for unanimous votes of jurors—but whatever

minimum number of jurors is fixed by law, that number must decide on the evidence, even if only by a legal wisp of a hair. But justly and wisely the rule of weighing testimony is far different in a criminal case where liberty is at stake—that is, where the state—the government—has a direct concern and proceeds against a person. In a criminal prosecution the title of the case would have been *People of the State of New York* v. *Lane and Dreiser.* Just because the power of the state is always a peril to free men, the Court's decision in a criminal case—whether by judge or jury—cannot be by the tip of a scale, but must be, as lawyers call it, "beyond a reasonable doubt." Not just against the weight of the evidence, but beyond a reasonable doubt, or "the doubt of reasonable men."

So this sound rule to protect freedom evoked by the Court in the *Dreiser* case was not "technical" at all. A Court asked to pass on obscenity in a civil case would not render a judgment "beyond a reasonable doubt." Moreover, in this kind of verdict, involving a crime, a defendant—the person accused—is ordinarily entitled to a jury. Thus, the proposed shortcut of Dreiser and Lane failed, and a relatively painless remedy was, wisely, not allowed. *The Genius,* however, was reissued in 1923 by another, less timid, publisher, and has now passed pretty much into literary (and legal) history—never challenged and remembered mostly by scholars of Dreiser.

The Genius, as we have seen, was only a short dead end in the history of legal remedies for "obscenity." We now, having backed onto the Main Path, turn to the world of entertainment where, curiously enough, raged (and still rages) a great debate concerning judicial and legislative remedies for that ever present (some say purely psychosomatic) alleged societal illness called "obscenity."

22

In the World
of Entertainment

Censorship of the theater is truly an anomaly. The traveling minstrels were the first to arouse fears of sovereign or churches, and so became targets for suppression. Until the days of mass literacy, the theater was the main vehicle for the spread of ideas, and we have seen that only those who are secure enough to relish conflict of thought tolerate the expression of unorthodox ideas.

In England as early as 1605 the courts at Westminster could try actors, playwrights, directors, and producers for profanities on the stage. In 1702 actors were indicted for appearing in Jonson's *Volpone,* Crowne's *Sir Courtly Nice,* Congreve's *Love for Love,* and so on.

In 1843 England passed the Theaters Act, which is essentially the law governing plays in England today. Under this law a theater may be closed if a justice of the peace feels it has abused its license. Further, every new play must be submitted to the Lord Chamberlain in advance of its proposed public performance. This gentleman can prohibit the performance if he is of the opinion that such prohibition is "fitting for the preservation of good manners, decorum, or public peace." It is not surprising that the lists of the last hundred years are full of important plays that have been seen by a relative few within the protection of "private clubs" not subject to the Lord Chamber-

142

lain's power. These plays have included, in recent years, works by our leading playwrights, such as Tennessee Williams's *The Rose Tattoo* and Arthur Miller's *View from the Bridge*.

Needless to say, England is only one of a number of countries that provide for governmental precensorship of the theater. But in our country, the stage has been relatively unmolested by censors. It is true that there were occasional "drives" for "cleanliness." Burlesque was closed in New York by a liberal but publicly prudish mayor, Fiorello La Guardia, who also arrested women for playing pinochle in a city park. There is some evidence that coincidental with the closing of burlesque there was an increase in Peeping Toms and molestation of underage girls.

In the main, our censors concentrated upon newer forms of entertainment. Each new medium frightens man. Just imagine the panic created in Germany in the fifteenth century by Mr. Gutenberg and his novelty of movable type. In this country, in this century, several changing forms of communication were introduced that the law had to digest in a few years: in 1905 the first newsreel, a fight between Young Griffo and Battling Barnett; 1920, the first commercial radio, in Detroit; 1938, the first television theater (in Boston, for twenty-five cents); 1938, the first radio facsimile newspaper issued in St. Paul. But the medium that bore the brunt of attacks on grounds of obscenity or indecency or immorality was the new entertainment, movies, appearing at the same time as the first newsreel. Even with our then high literacy, the impact of visual material frightened many people more than did the printed word. By 1905 movies were seen in dark rooms. It was thought that this visual effect would have greater influence on public morals than the reading of any book could have.

Perhaps the censors, despite their history of continuous attack upon the printed word, really didn't put much faith in the effects of reading on the public. Perhaps they were farsighted enough to realize the great attraction movies were to become. Perhaps they just felt that there was bound to be something sinister about William S. Hart, Pearl White, and their kind. At any rate, whatever the reason, they applied to movies perhaps the most severe method of intellectual suppression known in modern times—prior restraint. This form of censorship is in reality a precensorship that occurs before a particular film is shown to the public. Without allowing the theater owner or producer the meager luxury of showing his film and taking his chances on going to jail if it is later declared to be "obscene," precensorship makes him submit his film to a governmental board in advance of public display. If the board feels the film is not proper for display, the public never gets to see it.

The astounding endurance of precensorship of films as a supposed guarantor of cleanliness to the mind and eye of man, in the light of its decided illegality when applied to other forms of expression, such as newspapers and books, is due to two reasons: first, the appalling timidity of the so-called Hollywood tycoons, and, second, the reluctance of our Supreme Court to overrule state legislatures and state court decisions.

Not only did the old-time Hollywood moguls raise no substantial outcry when hit with precensorship; they actually joined in it. Thus was established a unified Industry Board of Censors—a curious instrument of communal masochism established by an obviously guilt-ridden motion-picture industry that still today presumes to set down rules of so-called morality that motion pictures should follow.

In the early days of motion pictures, in 1915, the Supreme Court decided that the free-speech and free-press guarantees of our Constitution did not apply to movies. Apparently, as the Court had it, since the Founding Fathers of our Constitution had not dreamed of movies, they obviously did not intend them to be protected by the Bill of Rights. And there were other reasons too, as stated in a case that arose in Ohio:

> It cannot be put out of view that the exhibition of moving pictures is a business pure and simple, originated and conducted for profit, like other spectacles, not to be regarded, nor intended to be regarded by the Ohio Constitution, we think as part of the press of the country or as organs of public opinion. They are mere representations of events, of ideas and sentiments published and known, vivid, useful and entertaining no doubt, but, as we have said, capable of evil, having power for it, the greater because of their attractiveness and manner of exhibition. It was this capability and power, and it may be in experience of them, that induced the State of Ohio, in addition to prescribing penalties for immoral exhibitions, as it does in its Criminal Code, to require censorship before exhibition, as it does by the act under review. We cannot regard this as beyond the power of government.
>
> It does not militate against the strength of these considerations that motion pictures may be used to amuse and instruct in other places than theatres—churches, for instance, and in Sunday schools and public schools. Nor are we called upon to say on this record

whether such exceptions would be within the provisions of the statute nor to anticipate that it will be so declared by the state courts or so enforced by the state officers.

So movies were spectacles, and no more. To this day our lawyers and judges are struggling over words such as "educational" or "entertainment," as if education could not be entertaining, and entertainment could not be intellectually educational! It was to take quite a few decades before the Supreme Court came to the conclusion that the silver screen was protected by the First Amendment.

A Constitutional Revolution

In 1915, at the time of the Ohio movie case, the Supreme Court was still of the opinion that the Bill of Rights limited only the power of Congress, not that of the states, to censor the expression of ideas. It was clear that censorship was originally one of the powers reserved to the states, and the states had exercised it for more than a century. Ten of the fourteen states that had ratified the Constitution by 1792 (Vermont had joined the original thirteen) did not give absolute freedom to every utterance. Thirteen of them provided for prosecutions for libel, blasphemy or profanity, or both, were crimes in all fourteen. Therefore it was natural that when state obscenity laws were passed there was no lawsuit in the Federal courts to set them aside as violating the First Amendment.

That situation was altered by one of the great revolutions in the area of judge-made law. In 1925 the Supreme Court decided that the prohibitions on government action contained in the First Amendment applied to states and cities as well as to the Federal government. The case did not involve obscenity, blasphemy, profanity, or libel. The issue came before the Court in the area of revolutionary writing. A man named Gitlow had been convicted in New York State under a *state* law forbidding such expression. The Supreme Court in reversing Gitlow's conviction decided that the Fourteenth Amendment to the Constitution incorporates the First Amendment. The Fifth Amendment, part of the original Bill of Rights, made sure Congress could not take away life, liberty, or property without due process of law, which means without a fair trial in all its important aspects. The Fourteenth Amendment, adopted in 1868, applied these same protections for the people against the actions of *any state*. In setting aside the conviction of Mr. Gitlow, the Supreme Court decided that the Fourteenth Amendment also meant that the First Amendment protection of freedom of expression was sacred and immune from abridgements by *states* as well as by the *Federal* government.

Keep this date, 1925, in mind. It is the turning point in this field. The new mass media, and especially the movies, were most particularly affected by the Gitlow decision, since up to 1925 the Supreme Court had held that the separate states could legally censor or even precensor films without any limits except those imposed by the state's own constitution as interpreted by its highest court.

The very next year, 1926, an event occurred that had important consequences, although outside the law. Talking pictures were produced for the first time, and Hollywood was not so easily analogized to the flea circus or mere entertainments. The realities of life created new judicial attitudes and hence new legal rules. The greatness of the law appeared—as it so often does—unashamed to admit prior error.

Precensorship as a Remedy

Increasingly after the Gitlow decision, attempts were made in various state courts to cut down some of the extreme absurdities of state movie precensorship boards. In 1948, in a movie case involving combinations in restraint of trade by the giant movie companies (*U.S.* v. *Paramount Pictures, Inc.*), the Supreme Court tangentially declared, "We have no doubt that moving pictures like newspapers and radio are included in the press whose freedom is guaranteed by the First Amendment."

But a case arose in the United States Supreme Court in 1952 to present another hurdle for the law. The case was *Joseph Burstyn* v. *Wilson,* and it involved the old area of blasphemy—only, in the law the word was "sacrilege." The picture in the case was *The Miracle,* which had been refused a license by the New York Film Censorship Board. Although, strictly speaking, obscenity was not the issue, the Court's decision is of historic importance because for the first time it applied the strict standards of the First Amendment to state precensorship of movies.

Three illuminating opinions were handed down. Justice Tom Clark wrote: "We hold only that under the Constitution and Amendments thereto a state may not ban a film on the basis of a censor's conclusion that it is sacrilegious."

Justice Stanley Reed agreed with Judge Clark but wrote separately: "Assuming that a state may establish a system for the licensing of motion pictures our duty requires us to examine the facts of the refusal in *each* case to determine whether the principles of the First Amendment have been honored. This film does not seem to me to be of a character that the First Amendment permits a state to exclude from the public view." Thus Justice Reed admitted that our highest Court would, he thought, become the final board of censorship review for the nation.

Justice Felix Frankfurter with Justice Burton wrote a third opinion:

> Prohibition through laws that fail to convey what is permitted and what is prohibited for want of objective standards offends the Constitution in two ways:
>
> First, it does not sufficiently apprise those bent on obedience of law of what may reasonably be foreseen to be found illicit by the law-enforcing authority, whether court or jury or administrative agency. Secondly, where licensing is rested, in the first instance, in an administrative agency, the available judicial review is in effect rendered inoperative. On the basis of such a portmanteau word as "sacrilegious" the judiciary has no standards with which to judge the validity of administrative action which necessarily involves, at least in large measure, subjective determinations. Thus, the administrative first step becomes the last step.

Justice Frankfurter, leaving the area of constitutional power, printed an appendix to his opinion, excerpting from dictionaries, printed from 1951 to date, definitions of "blasphemy," "sacrilege," and "profane." As we have seen, he could have gone back to 1605, when a law was enacted "to restrain abuses of Players."

Thus the Court in the movie field edged closer to the illegality of precensorship—a position long and stoutly held as to newspapers and books. But the vagueness of a word such as "sacrilege" evoked in 1952 a search for clarity of meaning that we are only now on the verge of undertaking as to words like "obscene," "prurient," and their other subjective synonyms—different in the mind of each jurist, and not nearly so obviously understood as Judge Wagner, long ago in the innocent days of the *Casanova's Homecoming* case, believed.

The *Miracle* case was only one of a number of movie cases involving the constitutionality of the standards used by local film-censorship authorities in determining whether or not a film might be exhibited.

Since 1952 the Supreme Court of the United States has decided that words like "sacrilegious," "immoral," "harmful," and "sexual immorality" are not capable of a meaning precise enough to give film makers a clear idea of what is prohibited. Precensorship ordinances containing these words were accordingly held unconstitutional. However, the question of whether the precensorship procedure itself violated the Constitution of the United States was not decided until 1961 in the now famous case of *Times Film Corp.* v. *Chicago.*

In an epic decision of 1931, the then Chief Justice of the United States, Charles Evans Hughes, had decided that precensorship ("prior restraint," as he called it) was unconstitutional as applied to newspapers. As we have seen, it was only in 1952 that the Court decided that movies were part of "freedom of the press." And yet it remained until 1961 before our highest Court was asked to decide on the constitutional right of a city or state to precensor a movie.

The facts in the *Times Film* case are simply stated. In order to test the constitutionality of the Chicago precensorship ordinance, an independent distributor refused to submit the sexually inoffensive movie *Don Juan* to the Chicago censor for a permit. The Chicago ordinance read, in part:

> Such permit shall be granted only after the motion picture film for which said permit is requested has been produced at the office of the commissioner of police for examination or censorship. . . .
>
> If a picture or series of pictures, for the showing or exhibition of which an application for a permit is made, is immoral or obscene, or portrays depravity, criminality, or lack of virtue of a class of citizens of any race, color, creed, or religion and exposes them to contempt, derision, or obloquy, or tends to produce a breach of the peace or riots, or purports to represent any hanging, lynching, or burning of a human being, it shall be the duty of the commissioner of police to refuse such permit; otherwise it shall be his duty to grant such permit.

Since the film itself was never seen by the precensor, who in this case was the Chicago police commissioner, whether *Don Juan* was or was not obscene was never an issue. The question presented to the Court was simply whether precensorship of movies was constitutional.

Before reading what the Court said, ask yourself how you would decide the issue. Do you think motion pictures are as important as books to our culture? Is the audience effect substantially different from that of a tabloid newspaper? Do you think any group of non-experts, such as policemen (or even experts), should be allowed to decide what films we shall see? There are, of course, many other questions to be asked. The issue is, like most legal (and human) issues, not a simple one.

The Supreme Court had its problems with the case. In fact the nine judges split 5 to 4 over it. The majority decided that precensorship of films in itself was not unconstitutional. The minority dissented vehemently.

Said Justice Clark for the majority:

> The movie company would have us hold that the public exhibition of motion pictures must be allowed under any circumstances. The State's sole remedy, it says, is the invocation of criminal process under the Illinois pornography statute, and then only after a transgression. But this position, as we have seen, is founded upon the claim of absolute privilege against prior restraint under the First Amendment—a claim without sanction in our cases. To illustrate its fallacy, we need only point to one of the "exceptional cases" which Chief Justice Hughes enumerated in 1931 in *Near* v. *Minnesota,* namely, "the primary requirements of decency (that) may be enforced against obscene publications." Moreover, we later held specifically "that obscenity is not within the area of constitutionally protected speech or press." Chicago emphasizes here its duty to protect its people against the dangers of obscenity in the public exhibition of motion pictures. To this argument the movie company's only answer is that regardless of the capacity for, or extent, of such an evil, *previous restraint* cannot be justified. With this we cannot agree. We recognized in *Burstyn* v. *Wilson* that "capacity for evil . . . may be relevant in determining the permissible scope of community control," and that motion pictures were not "necessarily subject to the precise rules governing any other particular method of expression. Each method," we said, "tends to present its own peculiar problems." Certainly the movie company's broadside attack does not warrant, nor could it justify on the record here, our saying that—aside from any consideration of the other "exceptional cases" mentioned in our decisions—the State is stripped of all constitutional power to prevent, in the most effective fashion, the utterance of this class of speech.

Thus, at least according to the majority, motion pictures, being of a greater "capacity for evil," are denied the protection against prior restraint granted to newspapers and books. Justice Clark was careful to point out, however, that his decision does not mean that each and every decision of a precensorship board will necessarily be constitutional. Indeed, he concluded his opinion on a note of caution:

> We, of course, are not holding that city officials may be granted the power to prevent the showing of any motion picture they deem unworthy of a license.
>
> As to what may be decided when a concrete case involving a specific standard provided by this ordinance is presented, we intimate no opinion.

Chief Justice Earl Warren and three of his brethren disagreed with this decision. Justice Warren's dissent was long, impassioned, and brilliant. We want to share most of it with you now:

> Mr. Chief Justice Warren, with whom Mr. Justice Black, Mr. Justice Douglas and Mr. Justice Brennan join, dissenting.
>
> I cannot agree either with the conclusion reached by the Court or with the reasons advanced for its support. To me, this case clearly presents the question of our approval of unlimited censorship of motion pictures *before* exhibition through a system of administrative licensing. Moreover, the decision presents a real danger of eventual censorship for every form of communication, be it newspapers, journals, books, magazines, television, radio or public speeches. The Court purports to leave these questions for another day, but I am aware of no constitutional principle which permits us to hold that the communication of ideas through one medium may be censored while other media are immune. Of course each medium presents its own peculiar problems, but they are not of the kind which would authorize the censorship of one form of communication and not the others. I submit that in arriving at its decision the majority has interpreted our cases contrary to the intention at the time of their rendition and, in exalting the censor of motion pictures, has endangered the First and Fourteenth Amendment rights of all others engaged in the dissemination of ideas.
>
> The vice of censorship through licensing and, more generally, the particular evil of previous restraint on the right of free speech have many times been recognized when this Court has carefully

distinguished between laws establishing sundry systems of previous restraint on the right of free speech and penal laws imposing subsequent punishment on utterances and activities not within the ambit of the First Amendment's protection.

Justice Warren now turns to what he considers to be the evil of the censor and of censorship, and gives his brethren of the majority (and us) a lesson in how the censors operate and what exactly some of them have done:

The Hand That Wields the Sword

It would seem idle to suppose that the Court today is unaware of the evils of the censor's basic authority, of the mischief of the system against which so many great men have waged stubborn and often precarious warfare for centuries, of the scheme that impedes all communication by hanging threateningly over creative thought. But the Court dismisses all of this simply by opining that "the phrase 'prior restraint' is not a self-wielding sword. Nor can it serve as a talismanic test." I must insist that a "pragmatic assessment of its operation," lucidly portrays that the system that the Court sanctions today is inherently bad. One need not disagree with the Court that Chicago has chosen the most effective means of suppressing obscenity. Censorship has been so recognized for centuries. But, this is not to say that the Chicago plan, the old, abhorrent English system of censorship through licensing, is a permissible form of prohibiting unprotected speech. The inquiry stated by the Court, but never resolved, is whether this form of prohibition results in "unreasonable strictures on individual liberty," whether licensing, as a prerequisite to exhibition, is barred by the First and Fourteenth Amendments.

There is no sign that Milton's fear of the censor would be dispelled in twentieth century America. The censor is beholden to those who sponsored the creation of his office, to those who are most radically preoccupied with the suppression of communication. The censor's function is to restrict and to restrain; his decisions are insulated from the pressures that might be brought to bear by public sentiment if the public were given an opportunity to see that which the censor has curbed.

The censor performs free from all of the procedural safeguards afforded litigants in a court of law. The likelihood of a fair and impartial trial disappears when the censor is both prosecutor and judge. There is a complete absence of rules of evidence; the fact is that there is usually no evidence at all as the system at bar vividly illustrates. How different from a judicial proceeding where a full case is presented by the litigants.

The Victims of Subjectivity

A revelation of the extent to which censorship has recently been used in this country is indeed astonishing. The Chicago licensors have banned newsreel films of Chicago policemen shooting at labor pickets and have ordered the deletion of a scene depicting the birth of a buffalo in Walt Disney's *Vanishing Prairie*. Before World War II, the Chicago censor denied licenses to a number of films portraying and criticizing life in Nazi Germany, including the March of Time's *Inside Nazi Germany*. Recently, Chicago refused to issue a permit for the exhibition of the motion picture *Anatomy of a Murder* based upon the best-selling novel of the same title, because it found the use of the words "rape" and "contraceptive" to be objectionable. The Chicago censor bureau excised a scene in *Street With No Name* in which a girl was slapped because this was thought to be a "too violent" episode. *It Happened in Europe* was severely cut by the Ohio censors who deleted scenes of war orphans resorting to violence. The moral theme of the picture was that such children could even then be saved by love, affection and satisfaction of their basic needs for food.

The Memphis censors banned *The Southerner* which dealt with poverty among tenant farmers because "it reflects on the south." *Brewster's Millions,* an innocuous comedy of fifty years ago, was recently forbidden in Memphis because the radio and film character Rochester, a Negro, was deemed "too familiar." Maryland censors restricted a Polish documentary film on the basis that it failed to present a true picture of modern Poland. *No Way Out,* the story of a Negro doctor's struggle against race prejudice, was banned by the Chicago censor on the ground that "there's a possibility it could cause trouble." The principal objection to the film was that the conclusion showed no reconciliation between blacks and whites. The ban was lifted after a storm of protest and later deletion of a scene showing Negroes and whites arming for a gang fight.

Memphis banned *Curley* because it contained scenes of white and Negro children in school together. Atlanta barred *Lost Boundaries,* the story of a Negro physician and his family who "passed" for white, on the ground that the exhibition of said picture "will adversely affect the peace, morals and good order" in the city. *Witchcraft,* a study of superstition through the ages, was suppressed for years because it depicted the devil as a genial rake with amorous leanings, and because it was feared that certain historical scenes, portraying the excesses of religious fanatics, might offend religion. *Scarface,* thought by some as the best of the gangster films, was held up for months; then it was so bady mutilated that retakes costing a hundred thousand dollars were required to preserve continuity. The New York censors banned *Damaged Lives,* a film dealing with venereal disease, although it treated a difficult theme with dignity and had the sponsorship of the American Social Hygiene Society. The picture of Lenin's tomb bearing the inscription "Religion is the opiate of the people" was excised from *Potemkin.* From *Joan of Arc* the Maryland board eliminated Joan's exclamation as she stood at the stake: "Oh, God, why hast thou forsaken me?" and from *Idiot's Delight,* the sentence: "We, the workers of the world, will take care of that." *Professor Mamlock* was produced in Russia and portrayed the persecution of the Jews by Nazis. The Ohio censors condemned it as "harmful" and calculated to "stir up hatred and ill will and gain nothing." It was released only after substantial deletions were made. The police refused to permit its showing in Providence, Rhode Island, on the ground that it was communistic propaganda. *Millions of Us,* a strong union propaganda film, encountered trouble in a number of jurisdictions. *Spanish Earth,* a pro-Loyalist documentary picture, was banned by the board in Pennsylvania.

During the year ending June 30, 1938, the New York board censored, in one way or another, over five percent of the moving pictures it reviewed. Charlie Chaplin's satire on Hitler, *The Great Dictator,* was banned in Chicago, apparently out of deference to its large German population. Ohio and Kansas banned newsreels considered pro labor. Kansas ordered a speech by Senator Wheeler opposing the bill for enlarging the Supreme Court to be cut from the March of Time as "partisan and biased." An early version of *Carmen* was condemned on several different grounds. The Ohio censor objected because cigarette-girls smoked cigarettes in public. The Pennsylvania censor disapproved the duration of a kiss. The

New York censors forbade the discussion in films of pregnancy, venereal disease, eugenics, birth control, abortion, illegitimacy, prostitution, miscegenation and divorce.

A member of the Chicago censor board explained that she rejected a film because "it was immoral, corrupt, indecent, against my . . . religious principles." A police sergeant attached to the censor board explained, "Coarse language or anything that would be derogatory to the government—propaganda" is ruled out of foreign films. Nothing pink or red is allowed," he added. The police sergeant in charge of the censor unit has said: "Children should be allowed to see any movie that plays in Chicago. If a picture is objectionable for a child, it is objectionable period." And this is but a smattering produced from limited research. Perhaps the most powerful indictment of Chicago's licensing device is found in the fact that between the Court's decision in 1952 in *Joseph Burstyn, Inc.* v. *Wilson,* and the present case, not once have the state courts upheld the censor when the exhibitor elected to appeal.

This is the regimen to which the Court holds that all films must be submitted. It officially unleashes the censor and permits him to roam at will, limited only by an ordinance which contains some standards that, although concededly not before us in this case, are patently imprecise. The Chicago ordinance commands the censor to reject films that are "immoral," or those that portray "depravity, criminality, or lack of virtue of a class of citizens of any race, color, creed, or religion and (expose) them to contempt, derision, or obloquy, or (tend) to produce a breach of the peace or riots, or (purport) to represent any hanging, lynching, or burning of a human being." May it not be said that almost every censored motion picture that was cited above could also be rejected, under the ordinance, by the Chicago censors? It does not require an active imagination to conceive of the quantum of ideas that will surely be suppressed.

After opening our eyes with his "parade of horribles," Justice Warren explains why, at least in the opinion of the minority, precensorship is so much worse than censorship through criminal action taken after the book or movie has been exhibited:

If the censor denies rights protected by the First and Fourteenth Amendments, the courts might be called upon to correct the abuse if the exhibitor decides to pursue judicial remedies. But, this is not a satisfactory answer as emphasized by this very case. The delays in adjudication may well result in irreparable damage, both to the litigants and to the public. Vindication by the courts of *The Miracle* was not had until five years after the Chicago censor refused to license it. And then the picture was never shown in Chicago. The present litigation has now consumed almost three years. This is the delay occasioned by the censor; this is the injury done to the free communication of ideas. This damage is not inflicted by the ordinary criminal penalties. The threat of these penalties, intelligently applied, will ordinarily be sufficient to deter the exhibition of obscenity. However, if the exhibitor believes that his film is constitutionally protected, he will show the film, and, if prosecuted under criminal statute, will have ready that defense. The perniciousness of a system of censorship is that the exhibitor's belief that his film is constitutionally protected is irrelevant. Once the censor has made his estimation that the film is "bad" and has refused to issue a permit, there is ordinarily no defense to a prosecution for showing the film without a license. Thus, the film is not shown, perhaps not for years and sometimes not ever. Simply a talismanic test or self-wielding sword? I think not.

Moreover, more likely than not, the exhibitor will not pursue judicial remedies. His inclination may well be simply to capitulate rather than initiate a lengthy and costly litigation. In such case, the liberty of speech and press, and the public, which benefits from the shielding of that liberty, are, in effect, at the mercy of the censor's whim. This powerful tendency to restrict the free-dissemination of ideas calls for reversal.

Freedom Endangered

Freedom of speech and freedom of the press are further endangered by this "most effective" means for confinement of ideas. It is axiomatic that the stroke of the censor's pen or the cut of his scissors will be a less contemplated decision than will be the prosecutor's determination to prepare a criminal indictment. The standards of proof, the judicial safeguards afforded a criminal defendant and the consequences of bringing such charges will all provoke the mature deliberation of the prosecutor. None of these hinder the quick judgment of the censor, the speedy determination to suppress. Finally, the fear of the censor by the composer of ideas acts as a substantial deterrent to the creation of new thoughts. This is especially true of motion pictures due to the large financial burden that must be assumed by their producers. The censor's sword pierces deeply into the heart of free expression.

The reader will recall that Justice Clark, speaking for the majority, maintained that motion pictures should be treated differently from other forms of communication. Justice Warren once again disagrees:

The Court, through Justice Clark, in no way explains why moving pictures should be treated differently than any other form of expression, why moving pictures should be denied the protection against censorship—"a form of infringement upon freedom of expression to be especially condemned." When pressed during oral argument, counsel for the city could make no meaningful distinction between the censorship of newspapers and motion pictures. In fact, the percentage of motion pictures dealing with social and political issues is steadily rising. The Chicago ordinance makes no exception for newsreels, documentaries, instructional and educational films or the like. All must undergo the censor's inquisition. Nor may it be suggested that motion pictures may be treated differently from newspapers because many movies are produced essentially for purposes of entertainment.

The contention may be advanced that the impact of motion pictures is such that a licensing system of prior censorship is permissible. There are several answers to this, the first of which I think is the Constitution itself. Although it is an open question whether the impact of motion pictures is greater or less than that of other media, there is not much doubt that the exposure of television far exceeds that of the motion picture. But, even if the impact of the motion picture is greater than that of some other media, that fact constitutes no basis for the argument that motion pictures should be subject to greater suppression. This is the traditional argument made in the censor's behalf; this is the argument advanced against newspapers at the time of the invention of the printing press. The argument was ultimately rejected in England, and has consistently been held to be contrary to our Constitution. No compelling reason has been predicated for accepting the contention now.

Judges, of course, do not always agree, and often, as here, their disagreements are passionate. But a court of law, and especially the Supreme Court, is more than a tilting ground for lawyers and judges. In it, policies are made that govern society. It is good that judges on our highest Court are sensitive to governmental encroachments on our liberties—sensitive not only intellectually but also emotionally. Of course, the emotions, as well as the logic, run on both sides. Where, as in law, there is no absolute certainty, there must be, as Judge Hand has said, "a passable compromise."

In the *Times Film* case precensorship won—and remains with us today in a few states. But the dissenters had their say too—and, to us at least, a persuasive one. However, even the minority had differing degrees of emphasis. Indeed, Justice Douglas took an even broader position than did Justice Warren, and concluded that:

> The First Amendment was designed to enlarge, not to limit, freedom in literature and in the arts as well as in politics, economics, law, and other fields. Its aim was to unlock all ideas for argument, debate, and dissemination. No more potent force in defeat of that freedom could be designed than censorship. It is a weapon that no minority or majority group, acting through government, should be allowed to wield over any of us.

However, Justices Warren, Douglas and their confreres to the contrary notwithstanding, the majority, as is proper, made the law of that day.

Thus at this moment of history a city may license and may *precensor* motion pictures provided only that there be no "unreasonable strictures" on individual liberties resulting from precensorship "in particular circumstances"—at least as far as the Federal Constitution is concerned.

It is well to remember, however, that we are a Federal system with fifty separate state constitutions—and what the Federal government might permit by way of censorship may be held unconstitutional by a particular state under its constitution. For example, the Sovereign State of Georgia had a precensorship ordinance much like the Chicago one. In 1962 the Georgia Supreme Court held *pre*censorship unconstitutional, saying in essence that the Georgia constitution is more protective of free speech than is the United States Constitution. Or was it saying that the Georgia judges were more protective than the

Federal ones? At any rate—who says that Georgia is always back-
ward? Not movie people, and others who view precensorship with
Justice Warren's eye.

One final irony (and confusion) to this precensorship debate is
worth noting. One of the briefs in the *Times Film* case pointed out
that since television channels are owned and controlled solely by the
Federal government, which has no system of precensorship, a motion
picture denied access to the theaters of a state because of state precensorship may nevertheless be seen in the home on television. Why,
asks the brief, should precensorship be denied to films on television
but not to films in theaters?

> Ideas on celluloid to be presented in theaters by separate oper-
> ators in each theater are subject to burdens of pre-treatment and
> pre-controls by the sovereign—in this case a city. But the identical
> ideas on identical types of film or equivalent tape may now in fact
> flow free of any pre-control or prior restraint if transmitted by T.V.
> into a saloon, a home or a church. In fact, the present state of the
> law declares for unequal treatment between: (*a*) pre-censorship
> in Chicago of a piece of film shown to the public from a single
> machine run in a theater by an operator and (*b*) the identical
> piece of film shown in the same theater to the same audience free
> of pre-control, if and only if the mechanical process of diffusion is
> over the ether. Surely this obvious discrimination casts grave doubt
> upon the constitutionality of the Chicago ordinance.
>
> In addition, under the present system of the transmission by
> television of motion pictures previously exhibited in theaters, mo-
> tion pictures which may be denied clearance by the Chicago licens-
> ing law may nevertheless be shown to people of all ages in all
> homes throughout the Chicago area by means of television. More-
> over, with regard to certain special films, there exists the practice
> of exhibiting these films on television prior to exhibition in motion
> picture theaters. This was the case, for example, with the film
> "Richard III" produced and directed by Sir Laurence Olivier. It
> is submitted that deep thought by even the most imaginative
> among us would fail to disclose what possible benefit the applica-
> tion of the Chicago licensing law would have had upon the citizens
> of the City of Chicago in relation to the exhibition of "Richard III"
> in theaters since it had already been shown to millions in Chicago
> and elsewhere on non-precensored television. Nor need one be a
> prophet to state with some assurance that the growing use of so-

called subscription or pay television will increase drastically the number of films which are shown on television prior to exhibition in motion picture theaters.

Thus, the considerations proliferate, as they are bound to do in this most subjective field of law. Just for fun, won't you now review the *Times Film* case and decide it anew for *yourself?* See how your new verdict, as well as your reasons for it, compares with your old one. Would that more judges (and lawyers) played this game—for law grows best when nurtured by those intelligent and brave enough to change their minds when the evidence warrants it.

23

The Book's the Thing

$\mathbf{A}$lthough most books have historically been outside the grasp of the precensor in this country, such has not been the fate of all. It had long been in the power of Congress and Congress alone to pass laws to prevent the prosecution of someone who received an "obscene book" from *abroad* under the Customs Law, and, after conviction, to destroy the book itself, thus presumably prohibiting foreign "evils" from corrupting our pure land. Although not technically precensorship, the effect was the same, since foreign books declared obscene could not gain access to the American mind.

Those Obscene People of Foreign Cultures!

However, in the late 1920's, Senator Bronson Cutting, of New Mexico—the only state still without a statewide obscenity law—became convinced that the Federal government was confused in its techniques for keeping the so-called "obscene" out of our country.

A rare event took place in the United States Senate. The doors of that great chamber were locked, and the senators—with what range of personal titillation we dare not imagine—read aloud portions of books excluded from the United States mails by the Post Office officials on grounds of obscenity and compared them with others barred from our shores by officials of the Customs Bureau of the Treasury Department on the same grounds. It was soon obvious that, though the words of the postal and customs laws were the same, they were interpreted so differently that what was legal for entrance into the country was often illegal for insertion in the mailbags, and vice versa.

Thus we got a dramatic demonstration of the uttter subjectivity of the Law of Obscenity. Out of this confusion a new approach to the problem was incorporated into a new law that, in effect, was a far-reaching extension of the old 1842 Customs Law (see Chapter 3). Instead of proceeding against the seller-exporter, usually unreachable by the arm of the law, or the importer-buyer, it was proposed that the power of the United States should be directed against the book itself! Obviously, when we deal with imports it seemed quite unfair and unworkable for a law to attack with criminal sanctions the persons to whom the supposed pornography was addressed from foreign shores. It was not always easy to prove who ordered the volume. Perhaps it was even ordered sight unseen or shipped to a person innocent of the content.

The procedure itself was not new. We had long ago adopted the theory of condemning food that was below standard. Many cases bear titles such as *U.S.* v. *30 Firkins of Butter, U.S.* v. *10 Crates of Tomatoes,* or *U.S.* v. *One Japanese Contraceptive.* In the area of tangible goods—physical commodities—standards by weight, ingredient, or size may and do raise problems, but man has developed able scales, rulers, test tubes, meters, and other instruments for measuring and gauging in order to meet agreed-upon standards. If the standards are not met, the goods are not allowed admission to our markets.

Despite the fact that sex, to most of us, is not in the category of rotten tomatoes and that there isn't as yet a sex-titillation meter or scientific slide rule for appraising degrees of shock or romantic effect to be derived from reading certain kinds of literature, the congressmen passed a new law. Henceforth books, like butter or tomatoes, were to be judged before entrance to our shores—and excluded if "below standard." The penalty was not individual—jails and fines were not used—rather, the book was merely to be destroyed. From the United States publishers' point of view this approach looked like, and was, in many situations a great relief. It took little courage to fight the good fight for freedom of press if the worst that could happen would be an order destroying the volume shipped in from abroad. The combatants would be a Customs official who refused to deliver a book and the person to whom it was addressed.

But all new techniques of the law invite activities good and bad. Surely the local official in charge of banning books acted with less caution if all he did was to advise by letter that "this volume will be destroyed unless you claim it and are willing to test the issue in a court" than if his only recommendation were for an indictment by a grand jury for a crime carrying a possible long jail sentence or heavy fine on some individual or company.

Many who favored what is called this innovation of an *in rem* (against the thing) procedure in 1930 concluded in later years that it had the disadvantage of reducing the courage of United States publishers and, of course, setting up some Customs official as a precensor of foreign books.

Many cases were soon to be brought into court under the new Customs process. At this point we include two companion cases that, as indicated by Judge Woolsey (of *Ulysses* fame, and the judge in both cases), raise several issues in the development of our still highly confused Law of the Obscene.

Marie Stopes had been a controversial and prolific author in England for many years. The chapter headings of her book *Married Love* tell much of her motivation: "The Heart's Desire," "The Broken Joy," "Woman's Contrariness," "The Fundamental Pulse," "Marital Adjustment," "Sleep, Modesty and Romance," "Abstinence," "Children," "Society," and as a finale, "The Glorious Unfolding."

The title of the case in brief is called *U.S. v. . . . "Married Love."* It was argued that the new Customs Law was unconstitutional, since the First Amendment states absolutely that Congress shall pass no law to abridge the freedom of the press. Though Judge Woolsey makes short shrift of this point, he nevertheless decides in favor of the book.

The reader will note that the attorneys for Putnam, the importing United States publisher, urged that another judge in another Federal court had decided the book was not illegally obscene. How many times must a book be defended?

The opinion by Judge Woolsey was arrived at without a jury. No issue of fact was involved. Putnam did not dispute that it ordered the volume and that the pages before the judge were the ones so ordered. There was no need for a trial and in fact there was no trial. The book was put in evidence, and the Court was asked to hear argument and read briefs. The case was passed on after Putnam made a motion to overrule the Customs censor and allow the book to be delivered as the address on the envelope directed.

UNITED STATES V. ONE OBSCENE BOOK ENTITLED "MARRIED LOVE" *April 6, 1931*

WOOLSEY, District Judge.

The first point with which I shall deal is as to the contention that the section of the Tariff Act under this case was brought, is unconstitutional as impinging on the right of the freedom of the press. I think there is nothing in this contention. The section does not involve the suppression of a book before it is published, but the exclusion of an already published book which is sought to be brought into the United States.

After a book is published, its lot in the world is like that of anything else. It must conform to the law and, if it does not, must be subject to the penalties involved in its failure to do so. Laws which are thus disciplinary of publications, whether involving exclusion from the mails or from this country do not interfere with freedom of the press.

At this point the reader may well ask whether Judge Woolsey is not being just a bit cavalier in his disposal of the precensorship argument. Surely there is a difference between a book published in this country and sold here before being censored and a book published in another country and censored before it has had a chance to be exposed to the American market. No matter how absolute Judge Woolsey sounds, behind his point lies a discrimination between "American" and "foreign" books—one which was, and is, generally held by judges and laymen less friendly to literature than the late Judge.

Perhaps because it may be dangerous for one to dally too long over absolutes (lest they prove less absolute after examination), Judge Woolsey moves quickly on to the main point of his opinion. First he gives us a description of the new law:

The statute reads in part as follows:

"All persons are prohibited from importing into the United States from any foreign country * * * any obscene book, pamphlet, paper, writing, advertisement, circular, print, pictures, drawing, or other representation, figure, or image on or of paper or other material, or any cast, instrument, or other article which is obscene or immoral, or any drug or medicine or any article whatever for the prevention of conception or for causing unlawful abortion. * * * No such articles, whether imported separately or contained in packages with other goods entitled to enter, shall be admitted to entry; and all such articles * * * shall be subject to seizure and forfeiture as hereinafter provided. * * * *Provided further,* that the Secretary of the Treasury may, in his discretion, admit the so-called classics or books of recognized and established literary or scientific merit, but may, in his discretion, admit such classics or books only when imported for noncommercial purposes.

Procedure Written into the Statute

"Upon the appearance of any such book or matter at any customs office, the same shall be seized and held by the collector to await the judgment of the district court. * * * Upon the seizure of such book or matter the district attorney shall institute proceedings in the district court for the forfeiture, confiscation, and destruction of the book or matter seized. Upon the adjudication that such book or matter thus seized is of the character the entry of which is by this section prohibited, it shall be ordered destroyed and shall be destroyed. Upon adjudication that such book or matter thus seized is not of the character the entry of which is by this section prohibited, it shall not be excluded from entry under the provisions of this section.

"In any such proceeding any party in interest may upon demand have the facts at issue determined by a jury and any party may have an appeal or the right of review as in the case of ordinary actions or suits."

As we have said, *Married Love* had been tried once before, and acquitted. Woolsey thinks a book, like a person, should not be subject to more than one court action for the same "crime."

Another copy of this same book was before Judge Kirkpatrick, United States District Judge for the Eastern District of Pennsylvania, and he ruled that the book was not obscene or immoral.

The only difference between the Philadelphia case and this case is that another copy of the same book has been here seized.

I think that the proper view of the meaning of the word "book" is not merely a few sheets of paper bound together in cloth or otherwise, but that a book means an assembly or concourse of ideas expressed in words, the subject-matter which is embodied in the book, which is sought to be excluded, and not merely the physical object called a book which can be held in one's hands.

Assuming it is proper so to view the meaning of the word "book" in the statute under consideration, Judge Kirkpatrick's decision at Philadelphia in a proceeding against this book is a bar to another similar proceeding such as this in this district.

I hold that Judge Kirkpatrick's decision established the book "Married Love" as having an admissible status at any point around the customs' barriers of the United States.

Analogy to Vessels of the Sea

It is perfectly obvious, I think, that, if a vessel had been tried for forfeiture at Philadelphia, and there acquitted of liability to forfeiture, on her coming around to New York she could not properly be tried again on the same count. That is the real situation in the present case.

A lower-court judge, whether Federal or state, is put in the insecure position of possibly having his opinions reviewed by a higher court. The right of appeal is, of course, one of the great safeguards in our judicial system, but it does tend to make a lower-court judge, even one as esteemed as Judge Woolsey, spend considerable time trying to second-guess the objections of his "board of review." Woolsey, for example, feels a decision "on the merits" might also be necessary in this case. With only a slight apology for digressing from the procedural aspects of the case, we bring you Judge Woolsey on *Married Love:*

Obscenity and Immorality

However, in case the Circuit Court of Appeals, to which I presume this case will eventually be taken, should disagree with my construction of the word "book," and should consider that it was a copy of the book that was subject to exclusion, and not merely the book regarded as an embodiment of ideas, or should disagree with my application of the admiralty law to a situation of this kind, I will now deal with the case on the merits.

The book "Married Love" does not, in my opinion, fall within the definitions of the words "obscene" or "immoral" in any respect.

Dennett for Children—Stopes for Adults

Dr. Stopes treats quite as decently and with as much restraint of the sex relations as did Mrs. Mary Ware Dennett in "The Sex Side of Life, An Explanation for Young People," which was held not to be obscene by the Circuit Court of Appeals for this circuit in *United States* v. *Dennett*.

The present book may fairly be said to do for adults what Mrs. Dennett's book does for adolescents.

The Dennett Case, as I read it, teaches that this court must determine whether the book alleged to be obscene falls in any sense within the definition of that word.

"Married Love" is a considered attempt to explain to married people how their mutual sex life may be made happier.

To one who had read Havelock Ellis, as I have, the subject-matter of Dr. Stope's book is not wholly new, but it emphasizes the woman's side of sex questions. It makes also some apparently justified criticisms of the inopportune exercise by the man in the marriage relation of what are often referred to as his conjugal or marital rights, and it pleads with seriousness and not without some eloquence, for a better understanding by husbands of the physical and emotional side of the sex life of their wives.

I do not find anything objectionable anywhere in the book, and I cannot imagine a normal mind to which this book would seem to be obscene or immoral within the proper definition of these words or whose sex impulses would be stirred by reading it.

Whether or not the book is scientific in some of its theses is unimportant. It is informative and instructive, and I think that any married folk who read it cannot fail to be benefitted by its counsels of perfection and its frank discussion of the frequent difficulties which necessarily arise in the more intimate aspects of married life, for as Professor William G. Sumner used aptly to say in his lectures on the Science of Society at Yale, marriage, in its essence, is a status of antagonistic co-operation.

In such a status, necessarily, centripetal and centrifugal forces are continuously at work, and the measure of its success obviously depends on the extent to which the centripetal forces are predominant.

The book before me here has as its whole thesis the strengthening of the centripetal forces in marriage, and instead of being inhospitably received, it should, I think, be welcomed within our borders.

This opinion was rendered on April 6, 1931. About three months later a book by the same author, entitled *Contraception,* came to our shores. This was one of the early cases where the courts had to decide whether any discussion of birth control was in itself obscene. Although the judge says this volume was written primarily for the medical profession, he does not legalize its distribution for doctors only. This even though law books contain rape and seduction cases that under the law may be deemed corrupting if sold to nonlawyers; but for some undetermined reasons lawyers have been granted the privileged status of being incorruptible. Likewise doctors!

UNITED STATES v. ONE BOOK, ENTITLED
"CONTRACEPTION," BY MARIE C. STOPES

July 16, 1931

WOOLSEY, District Judge.

Birth Control and Obscenity

I have read "Contraception," and I find that it does not fall, in any respect, within the definitions of the words "obscene" or "immoral."

"Contraception" is written primarily for the medical profession. It is stated, in an introduction written by an eminent English doctor, to be the first book dealing fully with its subject-matter—the theory, history, and practice of birth control. It is a scientific book written with obvious seriousness and with great decency, and it gives information to the medical profession regarding the operation of birth control clinics and the instruction necessary to be given at such clinics to women who resort thereto. It tells of the devices used now and in the past, to prevent conception, and expresses opinions as to those which are preferable from the point of view of efficiency and of the health of the user.

Such a book, although it may run counter to the views of many persons who disagree entirely with the theory underlying birth control, certainly does not fall within the test of obscenity or immorality laid down by me in the case of *United States* v. *Married Love,* for the reading of it would not stir the sex impulses of any person with a normal mind.

Actually the emotions aroused by the book are merely feelings of sympathy and pity, evoked by the many cases instanced in it of the sufferings of married women due to ignorance of its teachings. This, I believe, will be the inevitable effect of reading it on all persons of sensibility unless by their prejudices the information it contains is tabooed.

24

The
Other
Side of Life

Birth and death are and ever have been the prime curiosity of man. Between birth and death man has a chance of exploring for truth. But what could be more fascinating than the beginning and end of anything—particularly of life itself? Such fascination is the fulcrum of censorship—birth being spelled out as romance, love, lovemaking, all matters sexual, copulation and procreation. The entire bundle creates the target known as obscenity in the eyes of the law. The end called death in most cultures appears in the public marketplace of thought as a form of cruelty—pain, knives, guns, sadism, and murder.

Throughout the ages solons have appreciated that love and hate are often two sides of the same medallion. Thus, obscenity and sadism are symbolized by the fact that man often does kill the thing he loves, and it is not surprising, therefore, that so-called anti-obscenity statutes often link obscenity and sadism together. In the eyes of the law (and psychiatry) the state of "antagonistic co-opera-tion," the phrase Judge Woolsey used in the *Married Love* case to describe marriage, is not entirely unrelated to the more blatant aggressiveness involved in the perverted violence of sadism.

The proportionate doses of obscenity and sadism vary from culture to culture—nudity in the African tribes living in warm climates is proper, while in our culture we note long-skirted high-collared dresses of the woman of 1776. Our history is dotted with Mrs. Bloomer, nudist camps, stripteasers, women in men's slacks, tight-corseted girls of 1910, flat-chested ones of 1920, and the protruding earth-mother women of 1960. Such are the oddities of the convention of sexual manifestation and provocation—naturally and unavoidably related in the mind of the censor to the law of the obscene.

Sadism follows less conventional lines and is naturally less acceptable to society but is just as much a part of our folkway. Physical cruelty was in fact the core of the early pages of the Old Testament. Amos first taught the Jews that a God could have love and compassion, although gods of vengeance do not surrender easily. No one who views our present world situation, or lives in a society that practices capital punishment, can say that modern man has put violence and cruelty behind him. He is trying, however. For one thing, he has turned with anger upon certain kinds of cruelty that, in older times, were considered an accepted and acceptable part of human nature. Thus societies fearful of the cruder aspects of man's lovemaking also have become hostile to certain aspects of his hate. The censor's cry of "Keep sex clean" has been joined with "Keep hate nonsadistic." And the trials and tribulations and dangers of sex censorship have now, in some places, become also the burden of expressions and descriptions of crime and bloodshed. All of which leads us to our one "sadism" case—*Winters* v. *New York,* decided first in 1943.

In 1884 the State of New York, after a campaign by the Society for the Suppression of Vice, created a new crime. Certain ideas were to be restricted in the marketplace of thought if presented to children. In a few years—that is, in 1887—the limitation of the statute to sales, and so on, to children was removed. *All* human beings were to be immunized from certain ideas in print. By the early 1940's a score of states had laws similar to the New York one, but most were never used. The New York law read in part as follows:

> A person . . . who prints, utters, publishes, sells, lends, gives away, distributes or shows, or has in his possession with intent to sell, lend, give away, distribute or show, or otherwise offers for sale, loan, gift or distribution, any book, pamphlet, magazine, newspaper or other printed paper devoted to the publication, and

principally made up of criminal news, police reports, or accounts of criminal deeds, or pictures or stories of deeds of *bloodshed, lust* or *crime;* . . . is guilty of a misdemeanor. . . .

Not surprisingly, this so-called Antisadism Law was made a part of the state's antiobscenity statute.

For those who read the usual front pages of the big-city daily press of our nation, the words of the statute may create more than a cynical smile. Except for a score of our remaining 1,800 daily newspapers, front pages have long been dedicated to blood, death, and crime. Good news occurring throughout our Republic is not considered news, and a juicy divorce, a bloody murder, or a shocking cruelty by gun or knife takes over the front pages. The theory behind such irresponsibility of the press is that, they say, our people prefer to buy news of crime rather than news of hope and progress. And why not "give the people what they want"?

In 1940 a certain Mr. Winters had in his bookshop for the purpose of sale a magazine entitled *Headquarters Detective: True Cases from the Police Blotter.* The publication was brought to the attention of an outraged district attorney—and resulted in the conviction of Winters under the Antisadism Law. Indeed, the state's sense of outrage fairly leaps out from the stilted legal language of the formal accusation filed by the able district attorney:

> And I, the District Attorney, by this information, further accuse the said defendant of the Crime of Unlawfully Possessing Obscene Prints, committed as follows:
> The said defendant, on the day and in the year aforesaid, at the city and in the county aforesaid, with intent to sell, lend, give away and show, unlawfully did offer for sale and distribution, and have in his possession with intent to sell, lend, give away and show, a certain obscene, lewd, lascivious, filthy, indecent and disgusting magazine entitled "Headquarters Detective, True Cases from the Police Blotter, June 1940," the same being devoted to the publica- tion and principally made up of criminal news, police reports, and accounts of criminal deeds, and pictures and stories of deeds of bloodshed, lust and crime.

The conviction of Winters was upheld, despite objections as to the constitutionality of the law, by the highest New York court. The vote was 6 to 1. Here are excerpts from the majority opinion:

After trial Winters was convicted upon charges that he had possessed certain printed materials with intent to sell them, contrary to the law. Numerous copies of magazines composed entirely of such pictures and stories were found on the occasion in question in Winters' bookshop.

Winters' counsel takes the text of the statute at its literal meaning. "The statute (he says) makes no distinction between truth, fiction, or statistics. All come within its condemnation equally, provided they consist of 'criminal news' or 'police reports' or 'accounts of criminal deeds.'" From his viewpoint the statute "condemns any publication devoted to and principally made up of criminal or police reports or accounts of criminal deeds, regardless of the manner of treatment." This conception—which would outlaw all commentaries on crime from detective tales to scientific treatises—may, we think, be dismissed at once on the short ground that its manifest injustice and absurdity were never intended by the legislature. On the other hand, we are to heed the rule which tells us to read a statutory text in accordance with the general subject matter of which it is a part.

Indecency or obscenity is an offense against the public order. Collections of pictures or stories of criminal deeds of bloodshed or lust unquestionably can be so massed as to become vehicles for inciting violent and depraved crimes against the person and in that case such publications are indecent or obscene in an admissible sense, though not necessarily in the sense of being calculated or intended to excite sexual passion. This idea, as it seems to us, was the principal reason for the enactment of the statute.

The judge then gives a more elaborate description of the material than is usually found in the opinion of jurists:

There is, as we are also persuaded, ample warrant in the evidence for the finding that the magazines which were taken from the defendant's premises were obnoxious to the statute. The two thousand copies he kept there were tied up in small bundles that were suitable for delivery to distributors. There is proof of an admission by the defendant of his readiness to sell single copies indiscriminately. The contents are nothing but stories and pictures of criminal deeds of bloodshed and lust. The Lower Court said: "The stories are embellished with pictures of fiendish and gruesome crimes, and are besprinkled with lurid photographs of victims and perpetrators. Featured articles bear such titles as 'Bargains in Bodies,' 'Girl Slave to a Love Cult,' and 'Girls' Reformatory.' " It is not suggested that any of the contributors was distinguished by his place in the literary world or by the quality of his style. In short, we have here before us accumulations of details of heinous wrongdoing which plainly carried an appeal to that portion of the public who (as many recent records remind us) are disposed to take to vice for its own sake. Whether the statute extends to accounts of criminal deeds not characterized by bloodshed or lust is a question that does not here arise.

Then the majority, six judges, agreed that the Antisadism Statute is precise enough even though the style of indecency changes—a fact to be determined by courts—from time to time:

> We now pass to Winters' contention that the statute is unconstitutional because the criterion of criminal liability thereunder is "a personal taste standard, uncertain, indefinite and ex post facto in its practical operation." In the nature of things there can be no more precise test of written indecency or obscenity than the continuing and changeable experience of the community as to what types of books are likely to bring about the corruption of public morals or other analogous injury to the public order. Consequently, a question as to whether a particular publication is indecent or obscene in that sense is a question of the times which must be determined as matter of fact, unless the appearances are thought to be necessarily harmless from the standpoint of public order or morality. Never has this perception been more forcefully expressed than in this sentence by CARDOZO, J.: "Law accepts as the pattern of its justice a morality of the community whose conduct it assumes to regulate." The constitutional validity of that standard has long been established.

The lone dissenter—Judge Lehman—dissented because the statute "is so vague and indefinite as to permit punishment of the fair use of freedom of speech." Winters appealed through counsel to the United States Supreme Court, which freed him on the Lehman theory—by a vote of 6 to 3.

The majority opinion in the United States Supreme Court runs for twelve pages, and the dissent of three judges covers twenty pages. It takes a lot of words to debate vague propositions of law and legal semantics. In fact in this, the *Winters* case, the Supreme Court heard arguments on March 27, 1946; it ordered a reargument on November 19, 1946; again it was reargued on November 10, 1947, and the troubled Court then at last rendered the decision to free Winters on March 29, 1948.

Winters was first arrested in 1943. So the law process is honorably careful. Under a dictator Winters might have been shot upon arrest or even before!

The decision in the Supreme Court was 6 to 3. The majority decided that the statute was unconstitutional, and therefore freed Winters. Speaking through Mr. Justice Reed, the Court explained its decision this way:

The validity of the statute was drawn in question in the state courts as repugnant to the Fourteenth Amendment to the Constitution of the United States in that it denied the accused the right of freedom of speech and press, protected against state interference by the Fourteenth Amendment.

It is settled that a statute so vague and indefinite, in form and as interpreted, as to permit within the scope of its language the punishment of incidents fairly within the protection of the guarantee of free speech is void, as contrary to the Constitution. A failure of a statute limiting freedom of expression to give fair notice of what acts will be punished and such a statute's inclusion of prohibitions against expressions, protected by the principles of the First Amendment, violates an accused's rights under procedural due process and freedom of speech or press.

We recognize the importance of the exercise of a state's police power to minimize all incentives to crime, particularly in the firls of sanguinary or salacious publications with their stimulation of juvenile delinquency. Although we are dealing with an aspect of a free press in its relation, to public morals, the principles of unrestricted distribution of publications admonish us of the particular importance of a maintenance of standards of certainty in the field of criminal prosecution for violation of statutory prohibitions against distribution. We do not accede to the suggestion that the constitutional protection for a free press applies only to the exposition of ideas. The line between the informing and the entertaining is too elusive for the protection of that basic right. Everyone is familiar with instances of propaganda through fiction. What is one man's amusement, teaches another's doctrine.

Though we can see nothing of any possible value to society in these magazines, they are as much entitled to the protection of free speech as the best of literature. They are equally subject to control if they are lewd, indecent, obscene or profane.

Acts of gross and open indecency or obscenity, injurious to public morals, are a crime at common law, as violative of the public policy that requires from the offender retribution for acts that flaunt accepted standards of conduct. When a legislative body concludes that the mores of the community call for an extension of the impermissible limits, an enactment aimed at the evil is plainly within its power, if it does not transgress the boundaries fixed by the Constitution for freedom of expression. The standards of certainty in statutes punishing for offenses is higher than in those depending primarily upon civil sanction for enforcement. The crime "must be defined with appropriate definiteness." There must be ascertainable standards of guilt. Men of common intelligence cannot be required to guess at the meaning of the enactment.

The subsection of the New York Penal Law, as now interpreted by the Court of Appeals, prohibits distribution of a magazine principally made up of criminal news or stories of deeds of bloodshed or lust, so massed as to become vehicles for inciting violent and depraved crimes against the person. But even considering the gloss put upon the literal meaning by the Court of Appeals' restriction of the statute to collections of stories "so massed as to become vehicles for inciting violent and depraved crimes against the person . . . not necessarily . . . sexual passions," we find the specification of publications, prohibited from distribution, too uncertain and indefinite to justify the conviction of this petitioner. Even though all detective tales and treatises on criminology are not forbidden, and though publications made up of criminal deeds not characterized by bloodshed or lust are omitted from the interpretation of the Court of Appeals, we think fair use of collections of pictures and stories would be prohibited because of the utter impossibility of the actor or the trier to know where this new standard of guilt would draw the line between the allowable and the forbidden publications. No intent or purpose is required— no indecency or obscenity in any sense heretofore known to the law. The statute as construed by the Court of Appeals does not limit punishment to the indecent and obscene, as formerly understood. When stories of deeds of bloodshed, such as many in the accused magazines, are massed so as to incite to violent crimes, the statute is violated. It does not seem to us that an honest distributor of publications could know when he might be held to have ignored such a prohibition. Collections of tales of war horrors, otherwise unexceptionable, might well be found to be "massed" so as to become "vehicles for inciting violent and depraved crimes." Where a statute is so vague as to make criminal an innocent act, a conviction under it cannot be sustained.

Thus the *Winters* standard, which was aimed at suppressing literature "so massed" as to incite violence and depravity, went the way of the "sacrilege" standard in the *Miracle* case.

For historical reasons certain words have remained immune from attacks of vagueness, and others have been struck down. The reader may well wonder why words like "obscene" or "immoral" are considered more specific as standards of conduct than those involved in the *Winters* case.

Although the *Winters* case does not strictly fall within the area of attempted legal remedies for alleged "obscenity," we did feel that it belonged after *Married Love* and *Contraception* in order to show the scope of the emotions with which courts must sometimes deal. We now turn back to our survey of remedies—to the year 1954 and an attempt by the State of New York to add a civil injunction remedy as an easy alternative to the criminal law and process.

25

Injunction
as a Remedy

The Legislature of the State of New York for many reasons, including no doubt the reluctance of juries to convict anyone for crossing the boundary line marked "obscene," decided in 1954 to attempt a civil as well as a criminal remedy for obscenity. It copied in some respects the 1930 Federal Customs Law that permitted legal action to be taken against either the allegedly obscene publication itself in a civil court or against the individual thought to be responsible for its importation in a criminal court. It was also in some respects similar to the noncriminal process used in Massachusetts in the case against *Forever Amber* in 1948.

The new law authorized the counsel of any city or village to ask a court for an injunction prohibiting the sale of any printed matter of an "obscene, lewd, lascivious, filthy, indecent or immoral nature." It had to be *existing* printed matter, not something anyone might be proposing to print.

Basically, the new law of New York allowed the local authorities to stop a publication immediately after it had been offered to the public without going through the strict formalities of a criminal indictment. However, if the local authorities were upheld by a judge, they could destroy all copies they had seized. And one such conviction in any part of New York State would conclusively condemn the book throughout the state.

The New York law set forth what appeared to many to be adequate procedural safeguards. The person owning the attacked material had the right to a trial in one day's time, and the judge had to render his decision within two days thereafter. This had the appearance of promptness and fair play except that, of course, a newspaper would be valueless if held up for even several hours. And some people are not so sure that justice is inevitably served by sheer speed.

The book publishers did not fight against the enactment of this law even though it could be (and was) used against them. The newspaper publishers also did not oppose the law, probably because they thought that no one would dare apply such a law against them. At any rate, both apparently felt that here was a safer remedy than criminal proceedings. Interestingly enough, the censorship groups also felt they were better off under this type of civil procedure because they so often risked defeat if a criminal charge was placed, since juries are reluctant to convict under obscenity charges.

The first case under the new civil-injunction law was brought against a firm called Kingsley Books, fourteen of whose booklets, appearing under the title "Nights of Horror," had been displayed for sale. The company waived a jury trial, and, oddly enough, conceded for the sake of this case that the material was in fact obscene. Kingsley wanted to confine its defense to the constitutional point of freedom of the press under the First Amendment.

Judge Matthew Levy heard the case in the New York Supreme Court and upheld the new law. He also added a new standard for the difficult definition of obscenity—the illegal sort, he said, is "dirt for dirt's sake." The Court of Appeals of New York (the highest court in the state) upheld Judge Levy. The case then went to the United States Supreme Court. By a vote of five Justices to four, the New York law was declared constitutional.

Justice Frankfurter, believing that the method of control of censorship was a matter for the states to determine, wrote this for the majority:

> If New York chooses to subject persons who disseminate obscene "literature" to criminal prosecution and also to deal with such books as deodands of old [so that they will be forfeit to the sovereign], or both, with due regard, or course, to appropriate

opportunities for the trial of the underlying issue, it is not for us to gainsay its selection of remedies.

Then, comparing this injunctive procedure to a criminal one, Frankfurter writes:

> Criminal enforcement and proceedings of this nature interfere with a book's solicitation of the public precisely at the same stage. In each situation the law moves after publication; the book need not in either case have yet passed into the hands of the public. In each case the bookseller is put on notice by the complaint that sale of the publication charged with obscenity in the period before trial may subject him to penal consequences. In the one case he may suffer fine and imprisonment for violation of the criminal law, for disobedience of the temporary prohibition of sale. The bookseller may, of course, stand his ground and confidently believe that in any judicial proceeding the book could not be condemned as obscene, but both modes of procedure provide an effective deterrent against distribution prior to adjudication of the book's content—the threat of subsequent punishment.

Since Kingsley had waived its right to a jury trial, Frankfurter did not believe that a jury trial should nevertheless be required, and said, "Of course the Constitution does not subject the States to the necessity of having trial by jury in minor cases—such as misdemeanors." Although it is certainly true that punishment under the new law was not of the "major crime" (or felony) category, one may certainly quarrel with the Justice's attempt to characterize the subject itself as "minor"—after all, it did involve the availability of reading matter to the public.

The dissenting opinions truly point up an honorable quandary of the Law of Obscenity:
Chief Justice Warren, disagreeing.

> This is not a criminal obscenity case. Nor is it a case ordering the destruction of materials disseminated by a person who has been convicted of an offense for doing so, as would be authorized under provisions in the laws of New York and other States. It is a case wherein the New York police, under a different state law, located books which, in their opinion, were unfit for public use

because of obscenity and then obtained a court order for their condemnation and destruction.

The majority opinion sanctions this proceeding. I would not. This New York law places the *book* on trial. There is totally lacking any standard in the statute for judging the book in context. The personal element basic to the criminal laws is entirely absent. In my judgment, the same object may have wholly different impact depending upon the setting in which it is placed. Under this statute, the setting is irrelevant.

It is the manner of use that should determine obscenity. It is the conduct of the individual that should be judged, not the quality of art or literature. To do otherwise is to impose a prior restraint and hence to violate the Constitution. Certainly in the absence of a prior judicial determination of illegal use, books, pictures and other objects of expression should not be destroyed. It savors too much of book burning.

I would reverse.

But other judicial minds placed different values on the protection of the printed word.

Justice Douglas, speaking also for Justices Brennan and Black, stated his position as follows:

There are two reasons why I think this restraining order against this printed material should be dissolved.

First, the provision for an injunction (before trial) gives the State the paralyzing power of a censor. A decree can be handed down without a hearing and without any ruling on the issue of obscenity. This provision is defended on the ground that it is only a little encroachment, that a hearing must be promptly given and a finding of obscenity promptly made. But every publisher knows what awful effect a decree issued in secret can have. We tread here on First Amendment ground. And nothing is more devastating to the rights that it guarantees than the power to restrain publication before even a hearing is held. This is prior restrain and censorship at its worst.

Second, the procedure for restraining the distribution of all the condemned literature does violence to the First Amendment. The judge or jury which finds the publisher guilty in New York City acts on evidence that may be quite different from evidence before the judge or jury that finds the publisher not guilty in

Rochester. In New York City the publisher may have been selling his tracts to juveniles, while in Rochester he may have sold to professional people. The nature of the group among whom the tracts are distributed may have an important bearing on the issue of guilt in any obscenity prosecution. Yet the present law makes one criminal conviction conclusive throughout the state. I think every publication is a separate offense which entitles the accused to a separate trial. Juries or judges may differ in their opinions, community by community, case by case. The publisher is entitled to that leeway under our constitutional system. One is entitled to defend every utterance on its merits and not to suffer today for what he uttered yesterday. Free speech is not to be regulated like diseased cattle and impure butter. The audience (in this case the judge or the jury) that hissed yesterday may applaud today, even for the same performance.

The regime approved by the Court goes far toward making the censor supreme. It also substitutes punishment by contempt for punishment by jury trial. In both respects it transgresses constitutional guarantees.

Justice Brennan, while agreeing with Justice Douglas, had something more to write:

I believe the absence in this New York obscenity law of a right to jury trial is a fatal defect.

The jury represents a cross-section of the community and has a special aptitude for reflecting the view of the average person. Jury trial of obscenity therefore provides a peculiarly competent application of the standard for judging obscenity which, by its definition, calls for an appraisal of material according to the average person's application of contemporary community standards. A statute which does not afford the defendant, *of right,* a jury determination of obscenity falls short, in my view, of giving proper effect to the standard fashion as the necessary safeguard demanded by the freedoms of speech and press for material which is not obscene. Of course, as with jury questions generally, the trial judge must initially determine that there is a jury question, i.e., that reasonable men may differ whether the material is obscene.

The judges in this case did not have to test the material they were judging on obscenity meters or weigh it on judicial pruriency scales.

The *Kingsley* case raised a question of procedure, and we can rest assured that a 5 to 4 decision in our great High Court leaves our culture and the law in relation thereto in a less than peaceful mood. Furthermore, there are some questions outstanding. The majority says a jury trial is not *required,* but suppose Kingsley had insisted upon a jury trial? What if the situation Justice Douglas envisages arose in two places simultaneously and the judge in Rochester found the book innocent and the judge in New York City said "Guilty"? Is the implication that community standards are best determined by juries in each community a good practical procedure? Do we want to encourage a situation in which a publisher is faced with the prospect of having to defend his imprint in countless state and local jurisdictions (as has been the unhappy case recently with Henry Miller's *Tropic of Cancer*)? However you answer any of these questions, you will find "wise and honorable" judges who agree with you—and others equally "wise and honorable" who disagree.

But the question of whose standards to apply is only one of many new kinds of problems with which our courts have had to deal in the field of censorship in recent years. As judges, especially Federal judges, have become more sophisticated in their approach to obscenity, they find the going a bit tougher and the subleties more frequent. This is in our view a good sign because it shows on their part an increased understanding of the patience and care needed before information (or entertainment) should be denied the mind of man.

Only as recently as 1959 the United States Supreme Court confronted another important, and previously undecided, question in the field of obscenity law—as reported in our next chapter.

26

The
Bookseller's
Responsibility

Even assuming that the law is capable of defining the vague concept of "obscenity," another important aspect of the administration of justice goes to the question of what lawyers call "scienter" and others "awareness" or "knowledge." When any action is made a crime, an element of the crime is the accused person's realization that what he did was criminal.

This problem is not novel nor is it unique to obscenity cases. Ignorance of the law, generally speaking, is no defense. This must be so, particularly in big cities, states, or nations. Within a single tribe or small hamlet in the days of oxcart or camel, everyone in fact knew all the traffic rules. But that is quite unlike similar knowledge of traffic laws in the world of the automobile and airplane. In the large, complex society each citizen must be presumed to know the limits of lawful behavior; he is subjected to the burden of finding out about the law that touches on his own actions. Laws about possession of dangerous drugs do not permit a shopkeeper to plead successfully for an acquittal after a violation because he did not know it was illegal to hold for sale heroin or marijuana, or tobacco on which no government stamp tax had been paid. (We refer to drug laws because many proponents of censorship urge the analogy of obscenity as poison for the mind.)

But are booksellers, printers, and publishers in the same position? Surely the publisher who selects a manuscript for publication stands in a different position from the retailer who buys hundreds of books from dozens of publishers or the newsdealer who handles all magazines dumped, on consignment, on his stand. Nevertheless, retailers had been arrested under a wide variety of state and local obscenity laws before 1959, when the Supreme Court decided to write some law on this problem of the awareness (or lack of it) of the bookstore owners of the contents of the material they sell. The case was called *Smith* v. *California.*

The *Smith* case came to the highest Court from California where the City of Los Angeles felt that the state law was not sufficient to prevent obscenity in print, photograph, film, or (if you please) "wire recording." The city therefore passed a local ordinance forbidding the mere possession of obscene material in or within three hundred yards of a school, park or playground, in candy store or bookstore, ice-cream or soft-drink parlor, food store, or any place where newspapers, magazines, or postcards are sold, in any public toilet or rest room, in bar, liquor store, poolroom or billiard parlor or in any place where records, photographs, motion pictures, or transcriptions of any kind are made, sold, used, or exhibited. This law did not concern itself with sales or intention to sell. A stroll past a school or the use of a toilet in any hotel would be sufficient for arrest if you were unfortunate to have in your pocket a book deemed indecent or obscene. You may have just received the item by mail with the package still unopened—but you still would be subject to conviction.

The facts in the case of Eleazer Smith, however, did not stretch the new law. Smith was the proprietor of a bookstore that contained some allegedly "obscene" publications. Although there was no proof that Smith knew, or had reason to know, what was in the books he sold, his mere possession of them was sufficient, under the new law, to put him behind bars.

Smith's case went through the California courts, where his conviction was upheld. He appealed, finally, to the United States Supreme Court, arguing that it violated the concept of a free press to hold him to the same responsibility proper for the seller of drugs or poisons.

Thanks to Eleazer Smith and his valiant advocate, the Supreme Court has further narrowed the law of obscenity. The nine judges agreed that Smith's conviction had to be upset. But not all reversed it for the same reasons.

Justice Brennan wrote the principal opinion, that of "the Court," speaking for himself and four others. He decided in essence that because the Los Angeles ordinance did not require some proof that the bookseller was aware that the book complained of was obscene, it was unconstitutional.

The four other judges, while agreeing with the conclusion reached by Justice Brennan, wrote separate opinions. Their views, briefly stated, are:

1. Justice Black takes an absolute position, reading the First Amendment literally. *No* abridgement of free speech or press is constitutional, whether Federal, state, or local. Hence Justice Brennan's point is irrelevant, although his conclusion is correct.

2. Justice Douglas would permit suppression only if the material is so closely connected to illegal action as to be an inseparable part of that action. Again, Brennan's point becomes irrelevant.

3. Justice Frankfurter is more concerned with another issue—the exclusion by the trial judge of expert testimony on community standards.

4. Justice Harlan suggests the case be sent back to Los Angeles to be tried again with instructions to accept evidence (not necessarily by experts), as offered by Smith's able attorney, on community standards.

Since the opinions of some of the Justices in this case are important and illustrative of the nuances that have emerged in this area of law, we present excerpts from them here:

Justice Brennan:

Smith's offense was defined by the lower courts as consisting *solely* of the possession, in Smith's bookstore, of a certain book found upon judicial investigation to be obscene. The definition included no element of scienter—knowledge by Smith of the contents of the book—and thus the ordinance was construed as imposing a "strict" or "absolute" criminal liability. Smith said that if the ordinance were so construed it would be in conflict with the Constitution of the United States.

Books in a Preferred Position

California here imposed a strict or absolute criminal responsibility on Smith not to have obscene books in his shop. It is doubtless competent for the States to create criminal liabilities by defining criminal offenses without any element of scienter—though even where no freedom-of-expression question is involved, there are decisions of this court which hold that this power is not without limitations. But the question here is as to the validity of this ordinance's elimination of the scienter or "knowledge" requirement—an elimination which may tend to work a substantial restriction on freedom of speech.

This Court has intimated that stricter standards of permissible vagueness may be applied to a law having a potentially inhibiting effect on speech; a man may the less be required to act at his peril here, because the free dissemination of ideas may be the loser.

The Danger of the Ordinance to Free Speech

These principles guide us to our decision here. The ordinance here in question, to be sure, only imposes criminal sanctions on a bookseller if there in fact is to be found in his shop an obscene book. But we have not recognized any state power to restrict the dissemination of books which are not obscene; and we think this ordinance's strict liability feature would tend seriously to have that effect, by penalizing booksellers, even though they had not the slightest notice of the character of the books they sold.

There is no specific constitutional inhibition against making the distributors of food the strictest censors of their merchandise, but the constitutional guarantees of the freedom of speech and of the press stand in the way of imposing a similar requirement on the bookseller. By dispensing with any requirement of knowledge of the contents of the book on the part of the seller, the ordinance tends to impose a sever limitation on the public's access to constitutionally protected matter. For if the bookseller is criminally liable without knowledge of the contents, and the ordinance fulfills its purpose, he will tend to restrict the books he sells to those he has inspected; and thus the State will have imposed a restriction upon the distribution of constitutionally protected as well as obscene literature: "Every bookseller would be placed under an obligation to make himself aware of the contents of every book in his shop. It would be altogether unreasonable to demand so near an approach to omniscience." And the bookseller's burden would become the public's burden, for by restricting him the public's access to reading matter would be restricted.

If the contents of bookshops and periodical stands were restricted to material of which their proprietors had made an inspection, they might be depleted indeed. The bookseller's limitation in the amount of reading material with which he could familiarize himself, and his timidity in the face of his absolute criminal liability, thus would tend to restrict the public's access to forms of the printed word which the State could not constitutionally suppress directly. The bookseller's self-censorship, compelled by the State, would be a censorship affecting the whole public, hardly less virulent for being privately administered. Through it, the distribution of all books, both obscene and not obscene, would be impeded.

Conclusion—the Statute Is Unconstitutional

It is plain to us that the ordinance in question, though aimed at obscene matter, has such a tendency to inhibit constitutionally protected expression that it cannot stand under the Constitution.

Justice Frankfurter, although agreeing with Justice Brennan's conclusion, is more worried about how we are to decide whether a bookseller or newsdealer either knew or should have known that a publication he was selling was "obscene." He gives us no standard, but predicts that judges and juries will have trouble fixing one in the future. And because he finds the requirements vague, the Justice feels that expert testimony to determine whether a work has literary or moral or psychological value for a particular community is even more essential than before. He then adds:

Freedom of expression can be suppressed if, and to the extent that, it is so closely brigaded with illegal action as to be an inseparable part of it. As a people, we cannot afford to relax that standard. For the test that suppresses a cheap tract today can suppress a literary gem tomorrow. All it need do is to incite a lascivious thought or arouse a lustful desire. The list of books that judges or juries can place in that category is endless.

This role of censor in which we find ourselves is not an edifying one. But since by the prevailing school of thought we must perform it, I see no harm, and perhaps some good, in the rule fashioned by the Court which requires a showing of "scienter." For it recognizes implicitly that these First Amendment rights, by reason of the strict command in that Amendment—a command that carries over to the States by reason of the Due Process Clause of the Fourteenth Amendment—are preferred rights. What the Court does today may possibly provide some small degree of safeguard to booksellers by making those who patrol bookstalls proceed less high-handedly than has been their customs.

Justice Harlan takes a different tack, and shows himself to be a true believer in our experiments in Federalism. In his view, our fifty experimental laboratories—called states—live, and should live, within limits, separate ways of law-life. He is concerned about the nationwide boiler-plating of the minds of our nearly 200 million people. He is more concerned, for example, about restrictions imposed by nationwide postal censorship than about a city ordinance or state law restricting free speech.

Although Justice Harlan is not convinced by the need for proof of knowledge of the contents of the allegedly obscene book, and would prefer to let the City in California experiment with its new law, he nevertheless agrees with the decision of the Court to reverse the Smith conviction on a different ground:

> In my opinion this conviction is fatally defective in that the trial judge, as I read the record, turned aside EVERY attempt by appellant to introduce evidence bearing on community standards. The exclusionary rulings were not limited to offered expert testimony. This had the effect of depriving appellant of the opportunity to offer any proof on a constitutionally relevant issue. On this ground I would reverse the judgment below, and remand the case for a new trial.

Justice Black not only does not agree with Justice Harlan's approach but thinks that all the opinions thus far are too narrow. Here, as he has done consistently in other "free speech" cases, Justice Black makes a plea for a literal reading of the First Amendment—and no government censorship:

> The majority invalidates the ordinance solely because it penalizes a bookseller for mere possession of an "obscene" book, even though he is unaware of its obscenity. The grounds on which the Court draws a constitutional distinction between a law that punishes possession of a book with knowledge of its "obscenity" and

a law that punishes without such knowledge are not persuasive to me. Those grounds are that conviction of a bookseller for possession of an "obscene" book when he is unaware of its obscenity "will tend to restrict the books he sells to those he has inspected," and therefore "may tend to work a substantial restriction on freedom of speech." The fact is, of course, that prison sentences for possession of "obscene" books will seriously burden freedom of the press whether punishment is imposed with or without knowledge of the obscenity. The Court's opinion correctly points out how little extra burden will be imposed on prosecutors by requiring proof that a bookseller was aware of a book's contents when he possessed it. And if the Constitution's requirement of knowledge is so easily met, the result of this case is that one particular bookseller gains his freedom, but the way is left open for state censorship and punishment of all other booksellers by merely adding a few new words to old censorship laws. Our constitutional safeguards for speech and press therefore gain little. Their victory, if any, is a Pyrrhic one.

Certainly the First Amendment's language leaves no room for inference that abridgments of speech and press can be made just because they are slight. That Amendment provides, in simple words, that "Congress shall make no law . . . abridging the freedom of speech, or of the press." I read "no law abridging" to mean "NO LAW ABRIDGING." The First Amendment, which is the supreme law of the land, has thus fixed its own value on freedom of speech and press by putting these freedoms wholly "beyond the reach of FEDERAL power to abridge." No other provision of the Constitution purports to dilute the scope of these unequivocal commands of the First Amendment. Consequently, I do not believe that any federal agencies, including Congress and this Court, have the power or authority to subordinate speech and press to what they think are "more important interests." The contrary notion is, in my judgment, court-made not Constitution-made.

Courts Should Not Be Censors

If, as it seems, we are on the way to national censorship, I think it timely to suggest again that there are grave doubts in my mind as to the desirability or constitutionality of this Court's becoming a Supreme Board of Censors—reading books and viewing television performances to determine whether, if permitted, they might adversely affect the morals of the people throughout the many diversified local communities in this vast country. It is true that the ordinance here is on its face only applicable to "obscene or indecent writing." It is also true that this particular kind of censorship is considered by many to be "the obnoxious thing in its mildest and least repulsive form. . . ." But "illegitimate and unconstitutional practices get their first footing in that way. . . . It is the duty of the courts to be watchful for the constitutional rights of the citizen, and against any stealthy encroachments thereon." While it is "obscenity and indecency" before us today, the experience of mankind—both ancient and modern—shows that this type of elastic phrase can, and most likely will, be synonymous with the political, and maybe with the religious unorthodoxy of tomorrow.

Censorship is the deadly enemy of freedom and progress. The plain language of the Constitution forbids it. I protest against the judiciary giving it a foothold here.

Justice Douglas, the last opinion writer, takes a position against censorship except where it can be directly connected with illegal action:

Neither this book nor its author or distributor can be punished under our Bill of Rights for publishing or distributing it. The notion that obscene publications or utterances were not included in free speech developed in this country much later than the adoption of the First Amendment, as the judicial and legislative developments in this country show. Our leading authorities on the subject have summarized the matter as follows:

"In the United States before the Civil War there were few reported decisions involving obscene literature. This of course is no indication that such literature was not in circulation at that time; the persistence of pornography is entirely too strong to warrant such an inference. Nor is it an indication that the people of the time were totally indifferent to the properties of the literature they read. In 1851 Nathaniel Hawthorne's THE SCARLET LETTER was bitterly attacked as an immoral book that degraded literature and encouraged social licentiousness. The lack of cases merely means that the problem of obscene literature was not thought to be of sufficient importance to justify arousing the forces of the state to

censorship." Lockhart and McClure, Literature, The Law of Obscenity, and the Constitution.

Neither we nor Legislatures have power, as I see it, to weigh the
values of speech or utterances against silence. The only grounds
for suppressing this book are very narrow. I have read it; and
while it is repulsive to me, its publication or distribution can be
constitutionally punished only on a showing not attempted here.

Thus Eleazer Smith was freed because he did not have knowledge,
nor could he be expected to, of all the books in his shop. And what
would unquestionably have become a crippling burden upon the
dissemination of knowledge in this country was demolished by an
archaic legal word called "scienter." At least, that's what the majority
of the Court managed to agree upon.

It is to be hoped that Mr. Smith, now that he is free to sell books
again, will stock Mr. Charles Lamb's "A Dissertation upon Roast
Pig." Mr. Justice Frankfurter has read it, as our next chapter will
show.

27

How Not
to Roast
a Pig

One remedy for the dilemma into which the law gets itself when it tries to deal with obscenity is to have different laws to apply to different sections or classes or groups of the population who, in the eyes of the lawmakers, need some special protection. So we have special laws to protect women in industry, to keep children in school, and to bar the sale of liquor to minors. In the field of obscenty, legislation tries to get at this in two ways. First, there are laws to forbid the sale or distribution of obscene prints and pictures and films directly to children. Second are laws forbidding the general sale or distribution of obscenity that "might corrupt children."

Laws banning sale to the young of material that would not be censored for the mature are fairly common. However, there is a strong feeling that these laws do not go far enough, that if adults are permitted to have obscenity around the house, children are going to see it. So there have also been laws to keep out of general circulation publications deemed unfit for youth. One of these was enacted by the State of Michigan, whereupon one Butler was arrested for selling to a policeman a book that the officer, and the trial judge in Detroit called "a book containing obscene, immoral, lewd, lascivious language

192

or descriptions, tending to incite minors to violent or depraved or immoral acts, manifestly tending to the corruption of the morals of youth." Mr. Butler was convicted by a Detroit court; the State Supreme Court refused to hear his appeal, and he took his case to the United States Supreme Court in 1956 on the ground that his rights under the Fourteenth Amendment had been violated by Michigan.

On February 25, 1957, a rare judicial event took place. All nine judges of our High Court agreed to reverse the conviction of Butler. Judge Frankfurter's opinion was brief and, except for some technical sentences, it is printed in full:

BUTLER V. MICHIGAN

Section 343 of the Michigan Penal Code, in effect, makes it a crime to sell or make available to the general reading public any book containing obscene language "tending to the corruption of the morals of youth." For selling to an adult police officer a book which the trial judge found to have such a potential effect on youth, Butler was convicted of a violation of this section.

This appeal from a judgment of conviction entered by the Recorder's Court of the City of Detroit, Michigan, challenges the constitutionality of this provision of the Michigan Penal Code:

Butler was charged with a violation for selling to a police officer what the trial judge characterized as "a book containing obscene, immoral, lewd, lascivious language, or descriptions, tending to incite minors to violent or depraved or immoral acts, manifestly tending to the corruption of the morals of youth." Butler moved to dismiss the proceeding on the claim that application of this law unduly restricted freedom of speech as protected by the Fourteenth Amendment (which incorporates the First Amendment) in that the statute (1) prohibited distribution of a book to the general public on the basis of the undesirable influence it may have upon youth; (2) damned a book and proscribed its sale merely because of some isolated passages that appeared objectionable when divorced from the book as a whole; (3) failed to provide a sufficiently definite standard of guilt. After hearing the evidence, the trial judge in an oral opinion held that ". . . Butler is guilty because he sold a book in the City of Detroit containing this language (the passages deemed offensive), and also because the Court feels that even viewing the book as a whole, it (the objectionable language) was not necessary to the proper development of the theme of the book nor of the conflict expressed therein." Butler was fined $100.

Butler's argument here took a wide sweep. We need not follow him. Thus, it is unnecessary to dissect the remarks of the trial judge in order to determine whether he construed the law to ban the distribution of books merely because certain of their passages, when viewed in isolation, were deemed objectionable. Likewise, we are free to put aside the claim that the Michigan law falls within the doctrine whereby a New York obscenity statute was found invalid in the Winters case.

It is clear on the record that Butler was convicted because Michigan made it an offense for him to make available for the general reading public (and he in fact sold to a police officer) a book that the trial judge found to have a potentially deleterious influence upon youth. The State insists that, by thus quarantining the general reading public against books not too rugged for grown men and women in order to shield juvenile innocence, it is exercising its power to promote the general welfare. Surely, this is to burn the house to roast the pig. Indeed, the Solicitor General of Michigan has, with characteristic candor, advised the Court that Michigan has a statute specifically designed to protect its children against obscene matter "tending to the corruption of the morals of youth." But Butler was not convicted for violating this statute.

We have before us legislation not reasonably restricted to the evil with which it is said to deal. The incidence of this enactment is to reduce the adult population of Michigan to reading only what is fit for children. It thereby arbitrarily curtails one of those liberties of the individual, now enshrined in the Fourteenth Amendment, that history has attested as the indispensable conditions for the maintenance and progress of a free society. We are constrained to reverse this conviction.

Mr. Justice Black concurs in the result.

But we ask the reader to note the last line above. This means that Mr. Justice Black agrees in the conclusion but not in the reasoning set forth in the opinion of Mr. Justice Frankfurter. As previously noted, Mr. Justice Black has increasingly objected to the High Court acting as final censor of movies, plays, books, and the printed word generally. He holds that the First Amendment of our Bill of Rights (and the Fourteenth Amendment, which incorporates it) means what it says—no abridgement of free speech and press, means *no*—none—never. In fact, he has recently gone further in his logic and indicated that even a suit for libel is perhaps prohibited by the Constitution. It seems he would prefer all of the dangers of an utterly free marketplace of thought to the use by the government of even the slightest controls and prohibitions.

But the law has not heard the last of a legal endeavor to protect the literary diet of children without reducing the adults to the mush of the child. Great legal stirrings are in the offing to protect children by new movie laws that would cause theater owners to grade pictures —Adults, Adults with Children, Children Alone. This may be only a short legal step from legislation that now provides in many states that children under certain ages may not enter theaters showing certain films—a legal process analogized to age limits for buying cigarettes, beer, or whiskey.

So in the field of obscenity it became unconstitutional to burn down the house to roast a pig. But perhaps the reader will have noted that in more than eighty years since the adoption of the first Comstock Law and 115 since the first Federal restriction on obscene material, the Supreme Court had not once ruled whether, when the First Amendment said Congress should make no law to abridge the freedom of the press, it meant precisely what it said or whether there was some implied reservation that permitted abridgment of these freedoms on grounds of obscenity. This question the Court was called upon to answer at the very same session that saw the reversal of Butler's conviction.

Obscenity and
the Constitution

part IV

Obscenity and
the Constitution

28

The
Constitutionality
of It All

In 1946 a volume of short stories entitled *Hecate County,* by Edmund Wilson, a distinguished man of letters, was published. It was attacked in New York courts, while in California it was found unobjectionable. Today it circulates freely, except in New York, and circulates there freely but not openly.

In the case of *Hecate County,* a distinguished lawyer endeavored to apply to obscenity one of the legal rules laid down as far back as 1919 in a sedition case. In that year, Justice Oliver Wendell Holmes, a great phrasemaker as well as a great judge, in order to resist further suppressions by the Supreme Court, invented the then new test for free speech: He asked, "Is there a clear and present danger that a particular writing or speech will result in the evil aimed at?" This approach was welcomed by those who were least afraid of truth winning out in the free arena of thought.

But to many, words such as "clear," "present," and "danger" were also too subjective. Some people frighten more easily than others. A danger in the mind of your neighbor may not panic you at all. To some who have no sense of history all dangers are always present. There is now, in psychological terms, proved to be a type of person who lives on and off dangers—always apparent, always immediate.

Others are so short of imagination as to appear to be full of courage and bravery when in fact they fail to hold visions of real dangers.

This plea was made in the Supreme Court in behalf of *Hecate County:* Did it create a clear and present danger of corrupting (whatever that may mean) those into whose hands it might fall? Or rather was there a clear and present danger that the book would corrupt what Judge Woolsey in the *Ulysses* case called the normal person— (for surely the audience tested should not be pegged at the level of the most feebleminded. Such a test audience would reduce all writing to the mentality of the least civilized in our culture).

One of those odd and rare mishaps occurred in our highest court. One judge felt disqualified, and refused to sit on the *Hecate County* case. That left a bench of only eight jurists. They divided equally 4 to 4 and, as was then the custom in such cases, wrote no opinions. Hence the verdict of the New York Court adjudging the book to be obscene stood unreversed and untouched, and we shall never know whether the division arose because of the attempt to create for obscenity the "Guiding Rule of Clear and Present Danger" then, and still applied to trials for seditious writings or speech, or whether the judges divided on some other legal theory.

Another Supreme Court Justice—Louis D. Brandeis—had rewritten the Holmes "Clear and Present Danger" rule and translated Justice Holmes's motive into more objective terms. He said that the test was: Is there time, after the speech, to make answer or, in the alternative, time to call the police?

Perhaps the reader can appreciate the difference between the Holmes and Brandeis theories by imagining some hypothetical situations. A man shouts fire in a theater—a stampede results, though there is no fire. Is he guilty? Clearly so, even under Justice Brandeis's theory, because there is no time for answer or police. But what if a group—such as Coxey's army—announces that it will march to Washington and break every window in the Capitol. Is there time to ridicule or, in the alternative, time to have the police on hand to arrest the first man who picks up a brick? Probably so—and therefore Brandeis would permit the speech. But if there had been no public announcement, there would not have been time to make answer or call the police. Thus Justice Brandeis implied a distinction between "public" and "secret" speech—between speech that permits debate and allows the government time to prevent criminal action, and secret conspiracy to perform an illegal act. The former, according to

Brandeis, was speech protected by the Constitution, while the latter was not.

At the time of the *Hecate County* case, almost a century had passed since the first antiobscenity law had been enacted in this country. And yet, despite the proliferation of such laws over the years and the myriad of convictions, the question of whether so-called "obscene" communications were within the constitutional protections for free speech and press had never been decided by the United States Supreme Court. It is expensive to fight a case up to the Supreme Court, and most people convicted on obscenity grounds just don't bother. Furthermore, the cases that had been brought to the Supreme Court, as we have seen, dealt primarily with specific standards in particular obscenity laws; they did not raise the basic constitutional question.

Since the court split 4 to 4 over Mr. Wilson's book, the basic constitutional issue remained unresolved. Finally, in 1957, after waiting 115 years to address itself to the constitutionality of the Federal and state obscenity laws under the First and the Fourteenth Amendments, the Court uttered opinions on both of them on the same day. "Opinions" is properly in the plural because when faced with the unavoidable necessity of determining whether Government could make obscenity a crime, the nine judges produced no fewer than five opinions and an overall count of six for the power to censor, three against; and no more than two men agreed fully on the reasons underlying the opinions.

One of the cases on which the Supreme Court ruled this day, April 22, 1957, was an appeal brought by Samuel Roth from a New York conviction in Federal Court for violating the postal laws against sending obscenity through the mails. In the other, a man named Alberts asked the court to upset his conviction in California for "lewdly keeping for sale obscene and indecent writings" on the ground that the Fourteenth Amendment extended to him, against the state, the protections of the First Amendment.

The *Roth* case, whether or not we agree with the decision, is a beautiful example of the way in which significant decisions of law are reached. It does not take litigants of fame or fortune but jurists of philosophical, inquiring minds. The defendant himself was a man who had been convicted previously on obscenity charges. But when his conviction this time was appealed to the Circuit Court of Appeals, one of the three judges who heard the case was a legal scholar with an original mind, Jerome Frank. He concurred in a unanimous affirmation of Roth's conviction, but he confessed that his studies lately had led him to harbor doubts that the First Amendment really did permit exceptions for the prosecution of obscenity in the absence of evidence that the objectionable writing actually had incited someone to some sort of antisocial or immoral behavior. He expressed doubt that there ever was such a connection, and he noted the Supreme Court's silence on this key issue. He made up a sort of scorecard of obscenity actions in that court during eighty years, and found fourteen of them. Eight of them did not involve the obscenity issue as such; two concerned the validity of a conviction or indictment; two, the validity of state laws; one, advertisements for solicitation; and one involved a defendant who wrote letters to people accusing them of sexual immorality. Judge Frank found that all the references to the constitutionality of the Federal obscenity laws in the Supreme Court were made during the discussion of other issues, and such offhand remarks are not considered to be binding precedents. They are called "dicta." So Judge Frank's concurring opinion was, in effect, an invitation to the Supreme Court to address itself directly to the Constitution of the United States. The Supreme Court responded to Judge Frank's request, although it came to a conclusion different from the one he generally favored.

Although the separate opinions in the Supreme Court discuss other aspects of the law of obscenity, we report here only such portions of the opinions as go to the constitutional questions.

Mr. Justice Brennan delivered the opinion of the Court:

> The constitutionality of a criminal obscenity statute is the question in each of these cases. In ROTH, the primary constitutional question is whether the federal obscenity statute violates the provision of the First Amendment that "Congress shall make no law . . . abridging the freedom of speech, or of the press. . . ." In ALBERTS, the primary constitutional question is whether the obscenity provisions of the California Penal Code invade the freedoms of speech as they may be incorporated in the liberty protected from state action by the Due Process Clause of the Fourteenth Amendment.

Mr. Justice Brennan refers then to obvious collateral constitutional questions—vagueness of definition, whether the Federal government has any right to enter this field of control at all—that is, whether the power is in the states alone or whether, since the Federal government has power over the postal system, the states might not be prohibited from exercising any power over obscenity. This question of "jurisdiction" constantly recurs under our Federal system. The lines between state and Federal action are not always clear, and even if clear, often create situations of unbearable duplication, so that the Court must often declare that the Federal government has preempted the field exclusively, or on the other hand that the Federal government may not tread upon legal pastures owned by the states alone.

Justice Brennan then points to the real question:

> The *dispositive* question is whether obscenity is utterance within the area of protected speech and press. Although this is the first time the question has been squarely presented to this Court, either under the First Amendment or under the Fourteenth Amendment, expressions found in numerous opinions indicate that this Court has always assumed that obscenity is not protected by the freedoms of speech and press.

He Does Not Take the First Amendment Literally

> In the light of this history, it is apparent that the unconditional phrasing of the First Amendment was not intended to protect every utterance. This phrasing did not prevent this Court from concluding that libelous utterances are not within the area of constitutionally protected speech. At the time of the adoption of the First Amendment, obscenity law was not as fully developed as libel law, but there is sufficiently contemporaneous evidence to show that obscenity too was outside the protection intended for speech and press.

The original purpose of free thought was for political and social change—but this was before Freud pointed out the relation of sex to social change, all of which goes through the mind of Mr. Justice Brennan, who writes—

> The protection given speech and press was fashioned to assure unfettered interchange of ideas for the bringing about of political and social changes desired by the people. This objective was made

explicit as early as 1774 in a letter of the Continental Congress to the inhabitants of Quebec:

"The last right we shall mention regards the freedom of the press. The importance of this consists, besides the advancement of truth, science, morality and arts in general, in its diffusion of liberal sentiments on the administration of Government, its ready communication of thoughts between subjects, and its consequential promotion of union among them, whereby oppressive officers are shamed or intimidated, into more honourable and just modes of conducting affairs."

1 Journal of the Continental Congress 108 (1774)

All ideas having even the slightest redeeming social importance— unorthodox ideas, controversial ideas, even ideas hateful to the prevailing climate of opinion—have the full protection of the guaranties, unless excludable because they encroach upon the limited area of more important interests. But implicit in the history of the First Amendment is the rejection of obscenity as utterly without redeeming social importance. This rejection for that reason is mirrored in the universal judgment that obscenity should be restrained, reflected in the international agreement of over 50 nations, in the obscenity laws of all the 48 states, and in the 20 obscenity laws enacted by the Congress from 1842 to 1956. We hold that obscenity is not within the area of constitutionally protected speech or press.

Justice Brennan's opinion is undoubtedly well-written. His premises, however, are not without their problems. As the lawyers for Roth and Alberts pointed out, the particular vice of both Federal and state obscenity laws is that they punish communications that incite impure sexual thoughts not shown to be related to any overt antisocial conduct. Thus, in *Roth,* the trial judge instructed the jury: "The words 'obscene, lewd and lascivious' as used in the law, signify that form of immorality which has relation to sexual impurity and has a tendency to excite lustful *thoughts.*" In *Alberts,* the trial judge applied the test of whether the material has "a substantial tendency to deprave or corrupt its readers by inciting lascivious *thoughts* or arousing lustful desires." [Italics ours.]

By agreeing with these charges, Justice Brennan and a majority of the Court decide that since obscenity is in some vague way inherently repulsive to society it may be prohibited even though there is no proof of any relation to actual antisocial conduct.

But, one might well ask, how can we judge thoughts? What may excite one may simply bore another. And, really, is it the legitimate function of government in a democracy to meddle with the thought processes of its citizens? The dangers to a society of such impertinences by government are unfortunately all too well documented in the history of other communities—not all of them in the distant past.

There remains something uncomfortably circular in Brennan's argument. If something is obscene, he says, it is not protected by the Constitution. And yet, in determining whether it is obscene we need not give it the benefit of the tests and standards that are required to be applied to other kinds of speech—Holmes's "clear and present danger" or the Brandeis variant—all of which require some proof of causal relation to antisocial behavior. In other words, we first decide whether some writing is obscene and then we say that because it is obscene it is not entitled to any of the tests used to judge whether other kinds of writings are entitled to the protection of the Constitution. And yet, these are perhaps the very tests that should be used in the first instance to decide whether something is legally obscene.

As we have suggested throughout this volume, questions of sex and sadism strike at the very heart of the moral taboos of a society—and the emotional, rather than strictly intellectual, reactions of judges and laymen alike seem to motivate decisions in this area. Some may argue that it is quite natural and proper for a society to enforce its taboos through law. But whenever law attempts to control "antisocial" thought, as well as behavior, it is gambling with our freedom. Where to strike the balance, where to draw the line are the primary concerns of jurists—and, given the nature of our legal system, they cannot avoid it. No wonder, then, that judges often disagree with one another—and so do the rest of us.

Let us not think, however, that Justice Brennan and his colleagues are priggish or narrow-minded. These are not fuddy-duddies, but modern thinkers. In the *Roth* case, Brennan goes out of his way to disengage sex from obscenity, and in so doing moves our society further toward liberality of constitutionally protected expression:

> However, sex and obscenity are not synonymous. Obscene material is material which deals with sex in a manner appealing to prurient interest. The portrayal of sex, e.g., in art, literature and

scientific works, is not itself sufficient reason to deny material the constitutional protection of freedom of speech and press. Sex, a great and mysterious motive force in human life, has indisputably been a subject of absorbing interest to mankind through the ages; it is one of the vital problems of human interest and public concern. As to all such problems this court said in *Thornhill* v. *Alabama* (1940):

"The freedom of speech and of the press guaranteed by the Constitution embraces at the least the liberty to discuss publicly and truthfully *all matters of public concern* without previous restraint or fear of subsequent punishment. The exigencies of the colonial period and the efforts to secure freedom from oppressive administration developed a broadened conception of these liberties as adequate to supply the public need for *information and education with respect to the significant issues of the times. . . .* Freedom of discussion, if it would fulfill its historic function in this nation, must embrace *all issues about which information is needed or appropriate to enable the members of society to cope with the exigencies of their period.*"

The fundamental freedoms of speech and press have contributed greatly to the development and well-being of our free society and are indispensable to its continued growth. Ceaseless vigilance is the watchword to prevent their erosion by Congress or by the States. The door barring federal and state intrusion into this area cannot be left ajar; it must be kept tightly closed and opened only the slightest crack necessary to prevent encroachment upon more important interests. It is therefore vital that the standards for judging obscenity safeguard the protection of freedom of speech and press for material which does not treat sex in a manner appealing to prurient interest.

The leading standard of obscenity allowed material to be judged merely by the effect of an isolated excerpt upon particularly susceptible persons. *Regina* v. *Hicklin* (1868). Some American courts adopted this standard but later decisions have rejected it and substituted this test: whether to the average person, applying contemporary community standards, the dominant theme of the material taken as a whole appears to prurient interest. The *Hicklin* test, judging obscenity by the effect of isolated passages upon the most susceptible persons, might well encompass material legitimately treating with sex, and so it must be rejected as unconstitutionally restrictive of the freedoms of speech and press.

It is argued that the statutes do not provide reasonably ascertainable standards of guilt and therefore violate the constitutional requirements of due process. The federal obscenity statute (in *Roth*) makes punishable the mailing of material that is "obscene, lewd, lascivious, or filthy . . . or other publication of an indecent character." The California statute (in *Alberts*) makes punishable, the keeping for sale or advertising material that is "obscene or indecent." The thrust of the argument is that these words are not sufficiently precise because they do not mean the same thing to all people, all the time, everywhere."

Many decisions have recognized that these terms of obscenity statutes are not precise. This Court, however, has consistently held that lack of precision is not itself offensive to the requirements of due process. . . . The Constitution does not require impossible standards; all that is required is that the language "conveys sufficiently definite warning as to the proscribed conduct when measured by common understanding and practices." . . . These words, applied according to the proper standard for judging obscenity, already discussed, give adequate warning of the conduct proscribed and mark . . . boundaries sufficiently distinct for judges and juries fairly to administer the law. . . . That there may be marginal cases in which it is difficult to determine the side of the line on which a particular fact situation falls is no sufficient reason to hold the language too ambiguous to define a criminal offense. . . .

Having decided both that the old Hicklin test is no good and that words like "obscene" or "indecent," although perhaps vague, are nevertheless precise enough, Brennan then gives us his, the Court's, new definition of obscenity:

Obscene material is material which deals with sex in a manner appealing to prurient interest, and the test of obscenity is whether to the average person, applying contemporary community standards, the dominant theme of the material appeals to prurient interest.

Our dictionary defines "prurient" as "having an uneasy or morbid desire or curiosity. Given to the indulgence of lewd ideas; impure-minded." One may well ask whether the Court still isn't playing the old censorship game of trading with synonyms.

Thus the convictions were affirmed in both cases. But there are other points of view: Chief Justice Warren agrees with the result but is quite worried about the danger to free expression inherent in obscenity laws. In his justly famous simplicity of phrase, he writes:

> I agree with the result reached by the Court in these cases, but, because we are operating in a field of expression and because broad language used here may eventually be applied to the arts and sciences and freedom of communication generally, I would limit our decision to the facts before us and to the validity of the statutes in question as applied.
>
> That there is a social problem presented by obscenity is attested by the expression of the legislatures of the forty-eight States as well as the Congress. To recognize the existence of a problem, however, does not require that we sustain any and all measures adopted to meet that problem. The history of the application of laws designed to suppress the obscene demonstrates convincingly that the power of government can be invoked under them against great art or literature, scientific treatises, or works exciting social controversy. Mistakes of the past prove that there is a strong countervailing interest to be considered in the freedoms guaranteed by the First and Fourteenth Amendments.
>
> The line dividing the salacious or pornographic from literature or science is not straight and unwavering. Present laws depend upon the effect that the materials may have upon those who receive them. It is manifest that the same object may have a different impact, varying according to the part of the community it reached. But there is more to these cases. It is not the book that is on trial; it is a person. The conduct of the defendant is the central issue, not the obscenity of a book or picture. The nature of the materials is, of course, relevant as an attribute of the defendant's conduct, but the materials are thus placed in context from which they draw color and character. A wholly different result might be reached in a different setting.

Before coming to the complete and outright dissents of Justices Black and Douglas, let's listen to Mr. Justice Harlan, whose grandfather, sitting on the same bench in 1896, wrote the prevailing opinion in the *Rosen* obscenity case mentioned previously in this book.

Mr. Justice Harlan agrees with the majority in the *Alberts* California state case but dissents in the *Roth* Federal mail case.

| Mr. Justice Harlan:

Obscenity Is Not an Abstraction

In the final analysis, the problem presented by these cases is how far, and on what terms, the state and federal governments have power to punish individuals for disseminating books considered to be undesirable because of their nature or supposed deleterious effect upon human conduct. Proceeding from the premise that "no issue is presented in either case, concerning the obscenity of the material involved," the Court finds the "dispositive question" to be "whether obscenity is utterance within the area of protected speech and press," and then holds that "obscenity" is not so protected because it is "utterly without redeeming social importance." This sweeping formula appears to me to beg the very question before us. The Court seems to assume that "obscenity" is a peculiar *genus* of "speech and press," which is as distinct, recognizable, and classifiable as poison ivy is among other plants. On this basis the *constitutional* question before us simply becomes, as the Court says, whether "obscenity," as an abstraction, is protected by the First and Fourteenth Amendments, and the question whether a *particular* book may be suppressed becomes a mere matter of classification of "fact" to be entrusted to a fact-finder and insulated from independent constitutional judgment. But surely the problem cannot be solved in such a generalized fashion. Every communication has an individuality and "value" of its own. The suppression of a particular writing or other tangible form of expression is, therefore, an *individual* matter, and in the nature of things every such suppression raises an individual constitutional problem, in which a reviewing court must determine for *itself* whether the attacked expression is suppressible within constitutional standards. Since those standards do not readily lend themselves to generalized definitions, the constitutional problem in the last analysis becomes one of particularized judgments which appellate courts must make for themselves.

I do not think that reviewing courts can escape this responsibility by saying that the trier of the facts, be it a jury or a judge, has labeled the questioned matter as "obscene," for, if "obscenity" is to be suppressed, the question whether a particular work is of that character involves not really an issue of fact but a question of constitutional *judgment* of the most sensitive and delicate kind. Many juries might find that Joyce's "Ulysses" or Boccaccio's "Decameron" was obscene, and yet the conviction of a defendant for selling either book would raise, for me, the gravest constitutional problems, for no such verdict could convince me, without more, that these books are "utterly without redeeming social importance." In short, I do not understand how the Court can resolve the constitutional problems now before it without making its own independent judgment upon the character of the material upon which these convictions were based. I am very much afraid that the broad manner in which the Court has decided these cases will tend to obscure the peculiar responsibilities resting on state and federal courts in this field and encourage them to rely on easy labeling and jury verdicts as a substitute for facing up to the tough individual problems of constitutional judgment involved in every obscenity case.

Justice Harlan, as we shall see, is quite concerned that the Court treats a state obscenity law (*Alberts*) and a Federal one (*Roth*) in the same way. If, as the majority says, a particular communication is to be judged by contemporary community standards, we must, says Harlan, decide which "community" standard is to apply. His belief, and one which deserves serious consideration, is that each state should be allowed to apply its own standard—and that, consequently, the Federal government has no place in the obscenity field:

> My second reason for dissatisfaction with the Court's opinion is that the broad strides with which the Court has proceeded has led it to brush aside with perfunctory ease the vital constitutional considerations which, in my opinion, differentiate these two cases. It does not seem to matter to the Court that in one case we balance the power of a State in this field against the restrictions of the Fourteenth Amendment, and in the other the power of the Federal Government against the limitations of the First Amendment.
>
> We are faced in the *Roth* case with the question whether the

Federal obscenity statute, as construed and applied in this case, violates the First Amendment to the Constitution. To me, this question is of quite a different order than one where we are dealing with state legislation under the Fourteenth Amendment. I do not think it follows that state and federal powers in this area are the same, and that just because the State may suppress a particular utterance, it is automatically permissible for the Federal Government to do the same.

The Harlan Constitutional Legal Philosophy of Varieties of Sexual Morality

The Constitution differentiates between those areas of human conduct subject to the regulation of the States and those subject to the powers of the Federal Government. The substantive powers of the two governments, in many instances, are distinct. And in every case where we are called upon to balance the interest in free expression against other interests, it seems to me important that we should keep in the forefront the question of whether those other interests are state or federal. Since under our constitutional scheme the two are not necessarily equivalent, the balancing process must needs often produce different results.

The Federal Government has, for example, power to restrict seditious speech directed against it, because that Government certainly has the substantive authority to protect itself against revolution. But in dealing with obscenity we are faced with the converse situation, for the interests which obscenity statutes purportedly protect are primarily entrusted to the care, not of the Federal Government, but of the States. Congress has no substantive power over sexual morality.

Not only is the federal interest in protecting the nation against pornography attenuated, but the dangers of federal censorship in this field are far greater than anything the States may do. It has often been said that one of the great strengths of our federal system is that we have, in the forty-eight States, experimental social laboratories. "State statutory law reflects predominantly this capacity of a legislature to introduce novel techniques of social control. The federal system has the immense advantage of providing forty-eight separate centers for such experimentation." Different States will have different attitudes toward the same work of literature.

The same book which is freely read in one State might be classed as obscene in another. And it seems to me that no overwhelming danger to our freedom to experiment and to gratify our tastes in literature is likely to result from the suppression of a borderline book in one of the States, so long as there is no uniform nationwide suppression of the book, and so long as other States are free to experiment with the same or bolder books.

Quite a different situation is presented, however, where the Federal Government imposes the ban. The danger is perhaps not great if the people of one State, through their legislature, decide that "Lady Chatterley's Lover" goes so far beyond the acceptable standards of candor that it will be deemed offensive and nonsellable, for the State next door is still free to make its own choice. At least we do not have one uniform standard. But the dangers to free thought and expression are truly great if the Federal Government imposes a blanket ban over the Nation on such a book. The prerogative of the States to differ on their ideas of morality will be destroyed, the ability of States to experiment will be stunted. The fact that the people of one State cannot read some of the works of D. H. Lawrence seems to me, if not wise or desirable, at least acceptable. But that no person in the United States should be allowed to do so seems to me to be intolerable, and violative of both the letter and spirit of the First Amendment.

I judge this case, then, in view of what I think is the attenuated federal interest in this field, in view of the very real danger of a deadening uniformity which can result from nationwide federal censorship, and in view of the fact that the constitutionality of this conviction must be weighed against the First and not the Fourteenth Amendment. So viewed, I do not think that this conviction of Roth can be upheld. The petitioner was convicted under a statute which, under the judge's charge, makes it criminal to sell books which "tend to stir sexual impulses and lead to sexually impure thoughts" necessarily is "utterly without redeeming social importance." Not only did this charge fail to measure up to the standards which I understand the Court to approve, but as far as I can see, much of the great literature of the world could lead to conviction under such a view of the statute. Moreover, in no event do I think that the limited federal interest in this area can extend to mere "thoughts." The Federal Government has no business, whether under the postal or commerce power, to bar the sale of books because they might lead to any kind of "thoughts."

Clearly, there is an appeal to logic in the view, as expressed by Justice Harlan, that state obscenity laws are more apt accurately to reflect the standards of various communities than is one over-all Federal law. However, this view also poses a danger to, and perhaps an intolerable burden upon, freedom of speech. If the states are to decide for themselves what is or is not obscene, a book or magazine could be prey to a multitude of obscenity actions, and an acquittal in one state, under one obscenity definition, would not necessarily mean acquittal in the others. One might well ask how a publisher or author is supposed to know the obscenity laws of all fifty states, and what assurance would a publisher have that he would not be subjected to a multitude of costly civil and criminal lawsuits. As the recent state attacks upon *Tropic of Cancer* have shown, the burden multistate prosecutions place upon a publication are so great as to reduce seriously the future likelihood that publishers, however brave, will present "controversial" books to our public. Federal censorship, at least, subjects a book to judgment only once. It assumes nationwide distribution. State censorship, although perhaps more representative of what some of "the people" feel in different places at different times, might perhaps kill by mere economic intimidation that which it has no power constitutionally to prevent the American people from reading.

Justice Douglas and Justice Black dissent from the majority opinion, and disagree with Justice Harlan. Their decision clearly emphasizes the problems and dangers inherent in any society which attempts to regulate thought rather than behavior:

Mr. Justice Douglas, with whom Mr. Justice Black concurs, writes:

> When we sustain these convictions, we make the legality of a publication turn on the purity of thought which a book or tract instills in the mind of the reader. I do not think we can approve that standard and be faithful to the command of the First Amendment, which by its terms is a restraint on Congress and which by the Fourteenth is a restraint on the States.
>
> In the *Roth* case the trial judge charged the jury that the statutory words "obscene, lewd and lascivious" describe "that form of immorality which has relation to sexual impurity and has a tendency to excite lustful thoughts." He stated that the term "filthy" in the statute pertains "to that sort of treatment of sexual matters in such a vulgar and indecent way, so that it tends to arouse a

feeling of disgust and revulsion." He went on to say that the material "must be calculated to corrupt and debauch the minds and morals" of "the average person in the community," not those of any particular class. "You judge the circulars, pictures and publications which have been put in evidence by present-day standards of the community. You may ask yourselves does it offend the common conscience of the community by present-day standards."

The trial judge who, sitting without a jury, heard the *Alberts* case and the Appellate Court that sustained the judgment of conviction, took California's definition of "obscenity" from a case that held that a book is obscene "if it has a substantial tendency to deprave or corrupt its readers by inciting lascivious thoughts or arousing lustful desire."

By these standards punishment is inflicted for thoughts provoked, not for overt acts nor anti-social conduct. This test cannot be squared with our decisions under the First Amendment. This issue cannot be avoided by saying that obscenity is not protected by the First Amendment. The question remains, what is the constitutional test of obscenity?

The tests by which these convictions were obtained require only the arousing of sexual thoughts. Yet the arousing of sexual thoughts and desires happens every day in normal life in dozens of ways. Nearly 30 years ago a questionnaire sent to college and normal school women asked what things were most stimulating sexually. Of the 409 replies, 9 said "music"; 18 said "pictures"; 29 said "dancing"; 40 said "drama"; 95 said "books"; and 218 said "man."

The test of obscenity the Court endorses today gives the censor free range over a vast domain. To allow the State to step in and punish mere speech or publication that the judge or the jury thinks has an UNDESIRABLE impact on thoughts but that is not shown to be a part of unlawful action is drastically to curtail the First Amendment. As recently stated by two of our outstanding authorities on obscenity, "The danger of influencing a change in the current moral standards of the community, or of shocking or offending readers, or of stimulating sex thoughts or desires apart from objective conduct, can never justify the losses to society that result from interference with literary freedom."

Justice Douglas is concerned with the Court's decision also because the factual evidence linking the reading or viewing of so-called obscene material with antisocial behavior is, to say the least, inconclusive:

> If we were certain that impurity of sexual thoughts impelled to action, we would be on less dangerous ground in punishing the distributors of this sex literature. But it is by no means clear that obscene literature, as so defined, is a significant factor in influencing substantial deviations from the community standards.
>
> There are a number of reasons for real and substantial doubts as to the soundness of that hypothesis. (1) Scientific studies of juvenile delinquency demonstrate that those who get into trouble, and are the greatest concern of the advocates of censorship, are far less inclined to read than those who do not become delinquents. The delinquents are generally the adventurous type, who have little use for reading and other non-active entertainment. Thus, even assuming that reading sometimes has an adverse effect upon moral conduct, the effect is not likely to be substantial, for those who are susceptible seldom read. (2) Sheldon and Eleanor Glueck, who are among the country's leading authorities on the treatment and causes of juvenile delinquency, have recently published the results of a ten-year study of its causes. They exhaustively studied approximately 90 factors and influences that might lead to or explain juvenile delinquency, but the Gluecks gave no consideration to the type of reading material, if any, read by the delinquents. This is, of course, consistent with their finding that delinquents read very little. When those who know so much about the problem of delinquency among youth—the very group about whom the advocates of censorship are most concerned—conclude that what delinquents read has so little effect upon their conduct that it is not worth investigating in an exhaustive study of causes, there is good reason for serious doubt concerning the basic hypothesis on which obscenity censorship is defended. (3) The many other influences in society that stimulate sexual desire are so much more frequent in their influence and so much more potent in their effect, that the influence of reading is likely, at most, to be relatively insignificant in the composite of forces that lead an individual into conduct deviating from the community sex standards. The Kinsey studies show the minor degree to which literature serves as a potent sexual stimulant. And the studies demonstrating that sex knowledge seldom results from reading indicates [*sic*] the relative

unimportance of literature in sex thoughts as compared with other factors in society.

The absence of dependable information on the effect of obscene literature on human conduct should make us wary. It should put us on the side of protecting society's interest in literature, except and unless it can be said that the particular publication has an impact on action that the government can control.

Justice Douglas, with Justice Black at his side, now turns to the "community conscience test" of the majority. In determining that such a test is inimical to the Constitution, he gives us a valuable and perhaps classic exposition of the proper role of the government in matters involving free speech and press:

Community Conscience Should Not Decide Free Speech

As noted, the trial judge in the *Roth* case charged the jury in the alternative that the Federal obscenity statute outlaws literature dealing with sex which offends "the common conscience of the community." That standard is, in my view, more inimical still to freedom of expression.

The standard of what offends "the common conscience of the community" conflicts, in my judgment, with the command of the First Amendment that "Congress shall make no law . . . abridging the freedom of speech, or of the press." Certainly that standard would not be an acceptable one if religion, economics, politics or philosophy were involved. How does it become a constitutional standard when literature treating with sex is concerned?

Any test that turns on what is offensive to the community's standard is too loose, too capricious, too destructive of freedom of expression to be squared with the First Amendment. Under that test, juries can censor, suppress, and punish what they don't like, provided the matter relates to "sexual impurity" or has a tendency "to excite lustful thoughts." This is community censorship in one of its worst forms. It creates a regime where in the battle between the literati and the Philistines, the Philistines are certain to win. If experience in this field teaches anything, it is that "censorship of obscenity has almost been both irrational and indiscriminate." The test adopted here accentuates that trend.

Leave Thoughts Alone

I assume there is nothing in the Constitution which forbids Congress from using its power over the mails to proscribe CONDUCT on the grounds of good morals. No one would suggest that the First Amendment permits nudity in public places, adultery, and other phases of sexual misconduct.

I can understand (and at times even sympathize) with programs of civic groups and church groups to protect and defend the existing moral standards of the community. I can understand the motives of the Anthony Comstocks who would impose Victorian standards on the community. When speech alone is involved, I do not think that Government, consistently with the First Amendment, can become the sponsor of any of these movements. I do not think that government, consistently with the First Amendment, can throw its weight behind one school or another. Government should be concerned with anti-social *conduct,* not with *utterances.* Thus, if the First Amendment guarantee of freedom of speech and press is to mean anything in this field, it must allow protests even against the moral code that the standard of the day sets for the community. In other words, literature should not be suppressed merely because it offends the moral code of the censor.

The legality of a publication in this country should never be allowed to turn on the purity of thought which it instills in the mind of the reader or on the degree to which it offends the community conscience. By either test the role of the censor is exalted, and society's values in literary freedom are sacrificed.

The Court today suggests a third standard. It defines obscene material as that "which deals with sex in a manner appealing to prurient interest." Like the standards applied by the trial judges below, that standard does not require any nexus between the literature which is prohibited and action which the legislature can regulate or prohibit. Under the First Amendment, that standard is no more valid than those which the courts below adopted.

I do not think that the problem can be resolved by the Court's statement that "obscenity is not expression protected by the First Amendment." There is no special historical evidence that literature dealing with sex was intended to be treated in a special manner by those who drafted the First Amendment. I reject too the implication that problems of freedom of speech and of the press are to be resolved by weighing against the values of free expression, the judgment of the Court that a particular form of that expression has "no redeeming social importance." The First Amendment, its prohibition in terms absolute, was designed to preclude courts as well as legislatures from weighing the values of speech against silence. The First Amendment puts free speech in the preferred position.

Freedom of expression can be suppressed if, and to the extent that it is so closely *brigaded* with illegal action as to be an inseparable part of it. As a people, we cannot afford to relax that standard. For the test that suppresses a cheap tract today can suppress a literary gem tomorrow. All it needs is to incite a lascivious thought or arouse a lustful desire. The list of books that judges or juries can place in that category is endless.

I would give the broad sweep of the First Amendment full support. I have the same confidence in the ability of our people to reject noxious literature as I have in their capacity to sort out the true from the false in theology, economics, politics, or any other field.

These full excerpts from the *Roth* and *Alberts* cases are worth rereading with care. The differences among the justices are honorable, thoughtful, and wide. There is no sense in asking where justice truly lies in these cases unless you are willing to try to separate fact from assumption, reason from emotion. It is a worthy effort, and we commend it to the reader. Ask yourself first whether society should have the power to prevent you, or anyone else, from reading something which might arouse certain "impure" thoughts in your mind. Or should its power be limited to the suppression of material which clearly is related to antisocial behavior? Ask yourself why you believe the way you do—reason or emotion? Or both? If your vote is for suppression only where antisocial behavior results, ask yourself whether we have now, or indeed can ever have, the proof. We shall have more to say about this in a concluding chapter, but don't wait for us—or for any judge: you decide. Surely your decision will not be any less controversial or subject to change than any of those we have read.

Thankfully, there is no "last word" in the law, just as there is no end to social or cultural change. It required from 1898 to 1954 for the Supreme Court to change its constitutional attitude on racial segregation. We venture to suggest that the Court's definition of obscenity as expressed in *Roth* and *Alberts* will not see out the decade. Indeed, as we shall see, modifications in favor of increasing liberality have already occurred.

29

Roth
and *Alberts*
Updated

In his dissent in the *Roth* case, Justice Harlan took issue with the majority's "pruriency" definition of obscenity:

> The point is that this statute, as here construed, defines obscenity so widely that it encompasses matters which might very well be protected speech. I do not think that the federal statute can be constitutionally construed to reach other than what the Government has termed as "hard-core" pornography. Nor do I think the statute can fairly be read as directed only at PERSONS who are engaged in the business of catering to the prurient minded, even though their wares fall short of hard-core pornography. Such a statute would raise constitutional questions of a different order. That being so, and since in my opinion the material here involved cannot be said to be hard-core pornography, I would reverse this case with instructions to dismiss the indictment.

In 1961 the highest court of New York State had occasion to pass on the proper interpretation of the New York obscenity law and, in so doing, adopted Harlan's "hard-core pornography" test rather than the Brennan "pruriency" one. The facts in the case are succinctly stated by the able judge who wrote the majority decision, Judge Stanley Fuld:

People v. Richmond County News, Inc.

The defendant is a wholesaler of magazines, paper-covered books and newspapers. Among the 700-odd items carried by the defendant, which it receives from national distributors, was the magazine "Gent," and it was the sale and distribution of its April, 1957, issue which occasioned the prosecution under obscenity law. The photocover of "Gent" is similar to that of numerous other magazines which loudly proclaim their dedication to coarse sensuality. The contents, like the cover, exhibit the same attempt to pander to and commercialize upon man's taste for the bawdy and the ribald behind a bare disguise of aesthetic respectability. Thus, together with short stories of apparent literary merit, reprinted with permission from standard editions of the authors' works, which are inoffensive under any standard of sexual sensitivity, there appear the usual staples of this form of sexual provocation, including "artistic" photographs, salacious cartoons and short stories of sexual seduction.

Judge Fuld then decides that the "prurient interest" test is too broad and might exclude material that a modern-day society should not keep from its people. He and a majority of the New York court prefer the hard-core pornography test. Here is how Fuld explains it:

To be sure, there are some in the community who regard any realistic portrayal of sexuality, any form of erotic realism, as an insupportable threat to the social order. And there are others who view any intrusion of the State's power in this area as unnecessary and improper. The "critical point in the compromise" lies between these extremes. "All that we can say is that the line (must) be higher than the lowest level of moral principle and practice, and lower than the highest."

Mindful of the constitutional necessity to open the door barring state intrusion into this area "only the slightest crack necessary" and desirous of erecting a standard which embodies the most universal moral sensibilities and may be applied objectively, we are of the opinion that the prohibitions of the Penal Law should apply only to what may properly be termed "hard-core pornography."

The mere undemonstrated possibility of harm to the community from realistic accounts of normal sexuality is not of sufficient moment to warrant the exercise of the public force in their suppression. And this is true whether the narratives concerned may be said to have artistic or scientific justification or whether they lack anything of "any possible value to society."

Under our statute the test of the obscene, of the pornography, is not in the tendency or appeal of the material, but rather in its content objectively appraised. It focuses predominantly upon what is sexually morbid, grossly perverse and bizarre, without any artistic or scientific purpose or justification. Recognizable "by the insult it offers, invariably, to sex, and to the human spirit," it is to be differentiated from the bawdy and the ribald. Depicting dirt for dirt's sake, the obscene is the vile, rather than the coarse, the blow to sense, not merely to sensibility. It smacks, at times, of fantasy and unreality, of sexual perversion and sickness and represents, according to one thoughtful scholar, "a debauchery of the sexual faculty."

Applying this standard to the issue of the magazine before us, it is plain that it does not fall within the proscribed area. This is so because no one of its stories or pictures is obscene within the meaning of the Penal Law. If any single item, considered as a whole, were pornographic, the circumstance that it was included in a collection otherwise without taint would not save it from criminal prosecution. The fact is, however, that, while the magazine contains many stories or pictures which are aesthetically tasteless and without any redeeming social worth, none of them is pornographic. Numerous pictures and cartoons of nude or semi-nude women and numerous descriptions and depictions of sexual arousal and satisfaction are to be found in "Gent", but it contains nothing which smacks of sick and blatantly perverse sexuality.

According to the New York Court of Appeals, then, "hard-core pornography" refers only to "dirt for dirt's sake . . . the blow to sense rather than to sensibility . . . a debauchery of the sexual faculty." Although these definitions are perhaps no less vague than any others in our passing parade, they would seem to limit the area of unprotected speech far more narrowly than did the Supreme Court in the *Roth* case.

But what is the Supreme Court's present position—vintage 1962? In an important recent case, *Manual Enterprises* v. *Day,* the Court had to decide whether certain homosexual magazines were "obscene" under the Federal postal censorship law, the same law under which Mr. Roth had been convicted in 1957. Although six members of the Court said the magazines were not legally obscene and only one member said they were (two Justices did not participate in the case), the majority could not agree upon an opinion. However, the original "hard-core pornography" man, Justice Harlan himself, delivered the decision of the Court and wrote an opinion joined by Justice Potter Stewart. Justice Harlan described the magazines in question as follows:

> The magazines consist largely of photographs of nude, or near-nude, male models and give the names of each model and the photographer, together with the address of the latter. They also contain a number of advertisements by independent photographers offering nudist photographs for sale.
>
> On the issue of obscenity, the case comes to us with the following administrative findings, which are supported by substantial evidence and which we, and indeed the parties, for the most part, themselves, accept: (1) the magazines are not physical culture or "body-building" publications, but are composed primarily, if not exclusively, for homosexuals, and have no literary, scientific merit; (2) they would appeal to the "prurient interest" of such sexual deviates, but would not have any interest for sexually normal individuals; and (3) the magazines are read almost entirely by homosexuals, and possibly a few adolescent males; the ordinary male adult would not normally buy them.

After stating these facts, Justice Harlan tells us that the magazines had been adjudged obscene because the lower courts and the Post Office Department thought, erroneously, that the *Roth* case laid down a single test of obscenity, namely, "whether to the average person, applying contemporary community standards, the dominant theme of the material as a whole appeals to prurient interest."

Not so, says Justice Harlan—in fact, what the Supreme Court in the *Roth* case really meant to do was to set down two tests, not one:

> We find lacking in these magazines an element which, no less than "prurient interest," is essential to a valid determination of obscenity to which neither the Post Office Department nor the Court of Appeals addressed itself at all. These magazines cannot be deemed so offensive on their face as to affront current com-

munity standards of decency—a quality that we shall hereafter refer to as "patent offensiveness" or "indecency." Lacking that quality, the magazines cannot be deemed legally "obscene," and we need not consider the question of the proper "audience" by which their "prurient interest" appeal should be judged.

Obscenity under the federal statute thus requires proof of two distinct elements: (1) *patent offensiveness;* and (2) "prurient interest" appeal. Both must conjoin before challenged material can be found "obscene." In most obscenity cases, to be sure, the two elements tend to coalesce, for that which is patently offensive will also usually carry the requisite "prurient interest" appeal. It is only in the unusual instance where, as here, the "prurient interest" appeal of the material is found limited to a particular class of persons that occasion arises for a truly independent inquiry into the question whether or not the material is patently offensive.

The Court of Appeals was mistaken in considering that *Roth* made "prurient interest" appeal the sole test of obscenity.

To consider that the "obscenity" exception in "the area of constitutionally protected speech or press," does not require any determination as to the patent offensiveness of the material itself might well put the American public in jeopardy of being denied access to many worthwhile works in literature, science, or art. For one would not have to travel far even among the acknowledged masterpieces in any of these fields to find works whose "dominant theme" might, not beyond reason, be aimed to appeal to the "prurient interest" of the reader or observer. We decline to attribute to Congress any such quixotic and deadening purpose as would bar from the mails all material, not patently offensive, which stimulates impure desires relating to sex. It is only material whose indecency is self-demonstrating and which, from the standpoint of its effect, may be said predominantly to appeal to the prurient interest that Congress has chosen to bar from the mails by the force of the statute.

Even the most casual reader cannot help reflecting that the "patent offensiveness" that Justice Harlan here sets up as a prerequisite to any obscenity conviction sounds very much like the "hard-core pornography" he and Judge Fuld talked about previously. And although the Justice goes out of his way to state that he is not saying whether he is limiting the Federal power to reach hard-core pornography only, it is indeed hard to draw any other conclusion. Applying the "patent offensiveness" test to the magazines in question, Justice Harlan states, "Our own independent examination of the magazines leads us to conclude that the most that can be said of them is that they are dismally unpleasant, uncouth and tawdry. But this is not enough to make them "obscene." Shades of Judge Fuld!

Since Justice Harlan's opinion was joined by only one other Justice, and since the other Justices agreed with the decision, but for other reasons, we do not know precisely how much support the "patent offensiveness" or "hard-core pornography" test now has on the Supreme Court. However, it is clear that the Court is continuing to move toward increased protection from government censorship for what we read and see. Perhaps we will soon see an end of the "synonym parade" and of concern by our government with "impure thoughts." Before that happens somebody will have to define (or try to) "patent offensiveness." How about you?

30

The
Post Office
as Censor

In the *Manual Enterprises* case, Justices Warren, Brennan, and Douglas agreed that the magazines were "not guilty," not for the reasons Harlan gave, but because they felt that the Post Office, which stopped the magazines in the first place, does not have the constitutional right to decide whether anything carried in the mails is obscene. Because this view is becoming increasingly prominent in judicial circles, it is well to consider it briefly.

The reader will recall that the first Federal Obscenity Law, in 1842, was based upon the congressional power over imports—a power obviously not suitable for separate city or state control. And then, beginning in 1857, the Federal government enacted further obscenity laws based upon its control over interstate commerce and its power over the mailbags.

For example, the *Ulysses* and *Stopes* arose under the import powers, while the *Dennett* and Roth cases were begun by the Post Office Department.

Because the Post Office has played a mighty role as censor of our literary diet, it might be helpful to take a quick look at its activity in this field.

In the early days mail was carried by private messengers and then

by private postal companies. Highjacking was so prevalent that much
of the mail was sent C.O.D.—for many would not venture expensive
stamps only to find that a letter was never delivered. Benjamin Franklin was the father of our postal service, and George Washington is
reported to have opposed the use of government stamps for fear that
a service charge might lead to control by the government over the
content of the mail pouches. In 1835 the great constitutional lawyers
in the Senate urged that any censorship of the mails would be unconstitutional and in contradiction of the great First Amendment.

But in 1857 all these advices of caution were forgotten, and from
1868, and during the Comstock era, the major controls over obscenity
were in the hands of the Postmasters, who could just refuse to deliver
a magazine or a book if they thought it obscene. Today, the Post Office
Department has the power to stop mail at the place of mailing and at
the place of receipt.

The debate about postal power over the obscene, which began with
much heat when the first postal censorship law was passed, has been
continuing much like a low-grade fever—not too noticeable, just
below the surface, and carrying with it the danger of unexpected
eruption into something big. Many judges and lawyers have felt that
the debates in Congress before passage of the Postal Obscenity Law
made it clear that a majority of the drafters of the law never intended
to give the Post Office power to stop mail if thought obscene. They
look on a person's use of the mails as a constitutional right and not
merely a privilege. If it is a right, they argue, before the Post Office
can stop your mail it has to get a *court* determination that the mail is
obscene.

This view, however, is contrary to the presently prevailing opinion
that use of the mails is merely a *privilege* granted to the public by
Congress. The "privilege" approach has permitted what is presently
the Post Office practice of stopping mail without a prior court order
and then putting the burden on the individual to adjudicate the matter in court if he wants the mail released.

Often, as in the *Lady Chatterley* and *Manual Enterprises* cases, the
courts have overthrown Post Office determinations of "obscenity"—
but these were decisions rendered after the mail had been stopped
—and mailing delays can be very costly, especially to those who do
most of their business by mail.

Although the Post Office can inspect other classes of mail, it may
not open first-class mail. This exemption is not helpful to book and
magazine publishers, however, since it is much too expensive to send

these items first class—and they are almost invariably sent second class, and are consequently subject to the prying eyes of the Post Office. Indeed, a requirement that magazines be sent first class would probably put all magazines out of business—and dangerously limit the people's right to information.

As we have said, the right of the Post Office to censor the mail has always been subject to question. In the *Manual Enterprises* case three Justices of the Supreme Court served notice that they thought that Congress had not granted the Post Office such power and that, if it had, such grant was probably unconstitutional. Perhaps Justice Brennan best summarized their position as follows:

> Questions of procedural safeguards loom large in the wake of an order such as the one before us. Among them are: (*a*) whether Congress can close the mails to obscenity by any means other than prosecution of its sender; (*b*) whether Congress, if it can authorize exclusion of mail, can provide that obscenity be determined in the first instance in any forum except a court, and (*c*) whether, even if Congress could so authorize administrative censorship, it has in fact conferred upon postal authorities any power to exclude matter from the mails upon their determination of its obscene character.
>
> Mr. Justice Holmes has said: "The United States may give up the Post Office when it sees fit, but while it carries it on the use of the mails is almost as much a part of free speech as the right to use our tongues, and it would take very strong language to convince me that Congress ever intended to give such a practically despotic power to any one man."
>
> Whether Congress has authorized the Postmaster General to censor obscenity, is our precise question.
>
> We have sustained the criminal sanctions against a challenge of unconstitutionality under the First Amendment. (*Roth* v. *United States*). We have emphasized, however, that the necessity for safeguarding First Amendment protections for nonobscene materials means that Government "is not free to adopt whatever procedures it pleases for dealing with obscenity . . . without regard to the possible consequences for constitutionally protected speech." I imply no doubt that Congress could constitutionally authorize a noncriminal process in the nature of a judicial proceeding under closely defined procedural safeguards. But the suggestion that Congress may constitutionally authorize any process other than a fully judicial one immediately raises the gravest doubts. How-

ever, it is enough to dispose of this case that Congress has not authorized the Postmaster General to employ any process of his own to close the mails to matter which, in his view, falls within the ban of that section. "The provisions . . . would have to be far more explicit for us to assume that Congress made such a radical departure from our traditions and undertook to clothe the Postmaster General with the power to supervise the tastes of the reading public of the country."

Clearly this view is gaining strength. Clearly, also, it has a sound base in fact. Since the *Manual Enterprises* case two new Justices have come to the Supreme Court. If these two, Justices White and Goldberg, join with the three dissenters in the next Post Office case, the censorship department of the Post Office may well be out of business.

At best, censorship is a tricky, uncertain, and vague business. If it has to be done by government, we suggest it had best be left to the courts. The delegation of such great power to nonjudicial bodies like the Post Office, if there really was such delegation in the first instance, is incompatible with a society that seeks to protect most fully the constitutional freedom of an individual to think for himself.

part V

The
Social
Problem

31

Cowboys
and
Indians

In the Old West, so we are told by motion pictures and television, people usually got to a place before law and order did. Many social groups were not content to allow crime to run roughshod over their community until the law caught up with their westward expansion. Consequently, the more "public-minded" of them formed so-called "vigilante" groups to act as a kind of *ad hoc* and informal police force. As the law moved into the frontier territory, very often it came into conflict with these vigilante groups who were unwilling to give up the power they had come to enjoy.

In the field of censorship, at least, the problems of the "new frontier" are not dissimilar from those of the old. In this book we have watched judges and lawyers groping for some satisfactory method, if there is one, of limiting the power of government in the field of censorship of obscenity. We have seen that, although much confusion still remains and the basic problem is perhaps unsolved, there nevertheless has been a narrowing of the areas of government action in this field and an increased awareness on the part of the courts that the citizenry is not so fragile a reed as Mr. Comstock might have thought.

The great irony, however, is that while courts are restricting the powers of government in the field of so-called obscenity, the "vigilantism" of private groups is on the increase. By "vigilantism," here, we are referring to all forms of essentially private pressure attempting to regulate what we read and see. In these times, vigilantes can be anyone from a little lady in the Midwest who takes a paperback book off a bookstore counter because she does not want other people to be corrupted by it, to an organized eastern committee which gives lists of "indecent literature" to the police department, which then practices a bit of extralegal intimidation on the booksellers.

Although this is primarily a casebook, the extent, and effect of private vigilantism on the reading habits and the available reading materials of the American people has been so great in recent years that we could not pass it by without at least some description and explanation. When you read the Supreme Court decisions and other cases in this volume, you might find it difficult to relate your reading habits directly to the things the judges talk about. While you can see what the judges are doing and saying, you might not feel that this somehow has an effect on you and your life. Nowhere is the direct and personal effect of censorship upon the citizen more obvious than in the field of vigilantism. Vigilante groups are interested in what you read, what your child reads, what your child's school has on its bookshelf, what motion pictures your family sees. Indeed, the whole course of education of your child might be changed by the elimination or addition to school library shelves of various books and periodicals, and also by the effect that private pressure groups have upon the mind and attitudes of your child's teacher.

Pressure groups in the field of obscenity take many forms. There are so-called strictly religious groups, such as the League of Decency and the Committee of the National Office for Decent Literature (NODL) of the Catholic Church, various other religious groups, citizens' committees in towns, cities, and villages, parent-teacher association committees all over the country, self-styled individual censors and local branches of organizations like the American Legion.

The examples of vigilantism are almost as numerous as there are towns, villages, and cities in this country. A few will suffice to give the reader some idea at least of what this vigilantism looks like.

A few years ago, the film *Baby Doll* was shown throughout the country. Not only did it fail to get the approval of the National Office for Decent Literature; it was also felt by the Archdiocese of New York to be so immoral that a picket line was thrown up around a theater that was showing the film in New Jersey, and the public was exhorted not to patronize that theater because it showed *Baby Doll*.

Recently a lady in the Midwest was accused of gluing up the pages of a paperback book found on a drugstore counter because, in her opinion, the book was "dirty."

Booksellers in many states have frequently complained of intimidation by police who, acting on the recommendation and perhaps direction of self-appointed citizens' clean-literature councils, "suggest" rather firmly to booksellers that certain books they carry should be removed from their shelves lest police action result. Of course, the books referred to have never been declared obscene by any court of law and probably wouldn't be declared obscene in today's judicial climate. Nevertheless, the booksellers have little choice if they want to remain on good terms with the police and with the community.

By far the most intensive, and perhaps effective, campaign has been waged by private pressure groups against books circulating freely in school libraries. The books considered by these groups to be unfit for reading by high school and other children vary greatly. However, it is perhaps astounding to note, for example, that in a high school library in Phoenix, Arizona, such works as *Brave New World, The Magic Mountain,* and *The Short Stories of Ernest Hemingway* have been placed on the restrictive list. In Little Rock, Arkansas, a private group of "laymen" protested against the inclusion of *Exodus* and a book called *Great American Negroes* on the library shelves. In California, a Protestant private pressure group attacked such library selections as Richard Wright's *Black Boy* and works by Carl Sandburg, John Steinbeck, Clifford Odets, and William Saroyan. One of their spokesmen said, "A common trait of atheistic totalitarians is an intense preoccupation with sex. . . ." Also in California, such works as *J.B.* by Archibald MacLeish, *Catcher in the Rye* by J. D. Salinger, and plays by George Bernard Shaw and Tennessee Williams have been attacked.

Perhaps the most humorous, and yet really not funny, example of private censorship in the year 1961 concerns a report from Los Angeles that Edgar Rice Burroughs's "Tarzan" books had been removed from elementary-school libraries because Tarzan and his mate, Jane, had never married.

In Michigan, parents of high school students objected to inclusion on the high school shelves of the following "pornographic and obscene" books assigned to the students: Hawthorne's *The Scarlet Let-*

ter, Pearl S. Buck's *The Good Earth,* and Walter Edmonds's *Drums Along the Mohawk.*

In Minnesota, *1984* came under attack from private pressure groups.

In New York, a Long Island schoolboard voted to ban *A History of the United States from the Age of Exploration to 1865* because it briefly reviewed the history of bundling and extolled its inherent chastity.

And so it goes. We have given only a few examples, but no state is immune from the activities of private pressure groups.

Where children are involved, most readers might agree that more care has to be used in choosing reading material, and yet the extreme inconsistencies shown by most private pressure groups do violence to any idea that their prime motive is intellectual rather than emotional. Recent studies indicate that books, as opposed to tabloid newspapers, movies, and television exert relatively little influence on children. A pity, perhaps, but it should make us investigate with somewhat more persistence where the "fire" really is. "Book burning" as practiced by many so-called "public-spirited citizens" creates little fire but much smoke, and the real areas of harm—tabloids and television emphasizing crimes of sex and sadism—remain obscured by the haze and substantially free from pressure.

And yet the school library situation is not uncomplicated. Most library budgets are small and necessitate a good deal of picking and choosing by committees composed of people with their own prejudices and views. Too often the standards by which they are to choose are ill defined or beclouded by personality clashes, and outrageous inconsistencies in judgment result.

Of course, some pressure groups, like some school library committees, are more organized and perhaps more thoughtful than others. Groups such as NODL, for example, appeal primarily to Catholics and do try, at least to some extent, to give lists of what should be read rather than lists of what should not be read. But it should not for a moment be thought that vigilantism is limited to religious groups, whether Catholic or otherwise. Indeed, nonreligious groups would seem today to be having more effect upon the reading habits of the young than do religious groups.

Since this is a casebook, and the reader has, by now, made friends with many judges, he may well ask whether this is a problem for the courts. The answer is not simple. Most of us favor and rely upon public criticism of mass media. If a movie critic pans a film and tries to persuade us not to see it, we are, indeed, grateful for his guidance. And yet certainly such criticism is a kind of private pressure itself. Where, then, should we (and the courts) draw the line? Should advice and persuasion be considered purely private affairs and not subject to judicial scrutiny? What about threats or even boycotts? Should they too be considered a permissible part of freedom of speech—or should they be regulated by court action? And take boycotts themselves: Should we allow the boycott of a particular film but call in the court to prevent a boycott of the theater where the film was previously shown?

Where should the line be drawn? As yet we cannot look to the courts for an answer because no clear pattern has emerged; therefore we are all allowed the luxury of consideration unfettered by much legal precedent. Certainly, to the extent that private pressure groups use, directly or indirectly, government enforcement agencies, such as police departments, to impose their particular reading taste upon the community, there is a serious question of illegality. To this extent, courts are an aid in protecting our freedom against encroachment by people who want us to read only what they read and to think only as they think.

Just recently the United States Supreme Court made it clear that certain activity by pressure groups is inimical to the Constitution. The case in the lawbooks is called *Bantam Books, Inc.* v. *Joseph A. Sullivan* and it was decided on February 18, 1963.

In 1956 the Rhode Island legislature created a commission to "Encourage Morality in Youth" whose members were given the duty to "educate" the public concerning "obscene" books, pamphlets, ballads, and so on, and to investigate and "recommend" the prosecution of violations of the Rhode Island obscenity laws. The ostensible purpose of this group of nine private citizens (all appointed by the governor for five-year terms) was to combat and reduce juvenile delinquency.

Unquestionably the commission went at its duties with vigor. In fact, Bantam and three other New York publishers of paperback books felt that too much vigor was used. It appears that these publishers used a Rhode Island wholesaler named Max Silverstein & Sons to distribute their books throughout most of the state. Mr. Silverstein was notified by the commission that certain of these paperbacks, including *Peyton Place* and *The Bramble Bush,* were considered objectionable for sale to youths under eighteen. At the time the case was brought, Silverstein had received thirty-five such notices.

The notices also pointed out that copies of the commission's lists of "objectionable" publications had been circulated to the local police departments.

Silverstein got the message. After receiving the notices, he took steps to pick up all unsold copies of the books, and returned them to the publishers. A policeman usually visited Silverstein after each notice was sent to learn what action he had taken, and Silverstein was usually able to give him evidence of his compliance with it. According to his testimony, Silverstein gave in "rather than face the possibility of some sort of court action."

The publishers of course objected. They were interested in selling books, not in having them returned, and they resented a procedure that, they felt, amounted to clear intimidation by the Rhode Island authorities, without any prior court decision that the "objectionable books" were obscene or even unfit for reading by youths under eighteen.

The highest court in Rhode Island *upheld* the commission's activities, and the publishers appealed to the United States Supreme Court. Here, speaking for a majority of the court, is Justice Brennan:

. . . It is true that the books have not been seized or banned by the State, and that no one has been prosecuted for their possession or sale. But though the Commission is limited to informal sanctions —the threat of invoking legal sanctions and other means of coercion, persuasion, and intimidation—the record amply demonstrates that the Commission deliberately set about to achieve suppression of publications deemed "objectionable" and succeeded in its aim. We are not the first court to look through forms to the substance and recognize that informal censorship may sufficiently inhibit the circulation of publications to warrant injunctive relief.

It is not as if this were not regulation by the State of Rhode Island. The acts and practices of the members and Executive Secretary of the Commission disclosed on this record were performed under color of state law and so constituted acts of the State within the meaning of the Fourteenth Amendment. It is true, as noted by the Supreme Court of Rhode Island, that Silverstein was "free" to ignore the Commission's notices, in the sense that his refusal to "cooperate" would have violated no law. But it was found as a fact —and the finding, being amply supported by the record, binds us —that Silverstein's compliance with the Commission's directives was not voluntary. People do not lightly disregard public officers' thinly veiled threats to institute criminal proceedings against them if they do not come around, and Silverstein's reaction, according to uncontroverted testimony, was no exception to this general rule. The Commission's notices, phrased virtually as orders, reasonably understood to be such by the distributor, invariably followed up by police visitations, in fact stopped the circulation of the listed publications ex proprio vigore. It would be naïve to credit the State's assertion that these blacklists are in the nature of mere legal advice, when they plainly serve as instruments of regulation independent of the laws against obscenity.

The Vice of the System

Herein lies the vice of the system. The Commission's operation is a form of effective state regulation superimposed upon the State's criminal regulation of obscenity and making such regulation largely unnecessary. In thus obviating the need to employ criminal sanctions, the State has at the same time eliminated the safeguards of the criminal process. Criminal sanctions may be applied only after a determination of obscenity has been made in a criminal trial hedged about with the procedural safeguards of the criminal process. The Commission's practice is in striking contrast, in that it provides no safeguards whatever against the suppression of non-obscene, and therefore constitutionally protected, matter. It is a form of regulation that creates hazards to protected freedoms markedly greater than those that attend reliance upon the criminal law.

The procedures of the Commission are radically deficient. They fall far short of the constitutional requirements of governmental regulation of obscenity. We hold that the system of informal censorship disclosed by this record violates the Fourteenth Amendment.

In holding that the activities disclosed on this record are constitutionally proscribed, we do not mean to suggest that private consultation between law enforcement officers and distributors prior to the institution of a judicial proceeding can never be constitutionally permissible. We do not hold that law enforcement officers must renounce all informal contacts with persons suspected of violating valid laws prohibiting obscenity. Where such consultation is genuinely undertaken with the purpose of aiding the distributor to comply with such laws and avoid prosecution under them, it need not retard the full enjoyment of First Amendment freedoms. But that is not this case. The appellees are not law enforcement officers; they do not pretend that they are qualified to give or that they attempt to give distributors only fair legal advice. Their conduct as disclosed by this record shows plainly that they went far beyond advising the distributors of their legal rights and liabilities. Their operation was in fact a scheme of state censorship effectuated by extra-legal sanctions; they acted as an agency not to advise but to suppress.

We note for the record that Justice Harlan disagreed with the majority—not because he is in favor of indiscriminate suppression but because he felt that Rhode Island had a right to use the procedures it did to attempt to reduce juvenile delinquency. Again we are aware of the balancing procedures which judges must use and how their scales come up with varied results. In this case, however, the preponderance of judicial weight went against the Commission's activities and, in one area at least, the Court has finally given us some standards by which to judge when "private" action really is "public" action.

But what of religious groups and private citizens' committees who exert purely private, nongovernmental pressure on libraries, bookstores, and publishers to ban certain books or to delete certain "objectionable and obscene" pages from them? We suggest that under our Constitution these are not matters for courts but for individuals. The First and Fourteenth Amendments to the Constitution prohibit invasions of free speech and press by the Federal and state governments; they do not prohibit countervailing private pressure. In a society such as ours, where ideas are supposed to prove their value by free and open conflict with other ideas, it is the duty and function of individuals, whether in groups or alone, to project their points of view so long as they act responsibly and with due regard for the rights of others.

Perhaps the strongest reason why private censorship groups have proliferated in recent years is that they have not been effectively opposed by countervailing private pressure groups. Certainly, nothing so widespread as today's vigilantism occurred even in the heyday of Comstockery. In those days Mencken would sell a copy of his magazine on the Boston Common, and later Roy Larsen was strong enough to stand behind "The Birth of a Baby." Today, only a few publishers dare (or can afford) to stand behind their books and to defend them in towns and villages where they are attacked.

Perhaps the most recent example is *Tropic of Cancer* by Henry Miller. In this case, a combination of government prosecution and private intimidation has wreaked havoc with ordinary peaceful publishing procedures. Of nearly two million copies of the book distributed recently, about three-quarters of a million were *returned* to the publisher. At least forty criminal cases were started against booksellers and wholesalers who handled the book. (Acquittals have occurred in several lower courts to date, and experts were not even allowed on the witness stand in other cases to testify about the literary merit of the book. All this after the Federal government refused to ban the book.) A number of civil suits to suppress the book were commenced. So-called "voluntary" bans came into being on intimidation by the police. This was the national pattern. Suits for damages running into millions of dollars were started by the publisher.

One should not, therefore, quickly condemn a publisher for not publishing controversial books some might think obscene. Grove Press, the publishers of *Tropic of Cancer,* were brave to publish the book and were brave to try to defend it in so many jurisdictions, but even they had to give way, and not long ago they issued a statement that they could not defend *Tropic of Capricorn,* another book by Henry Miller, on behalf of the booksellers. Governmental and private pressures have taken their toll.

Although we cannot condemn a publisher today for not personally defending every lawsuit, we can at least deplore the failure of those interested in the free dissemination of all literature (perhaps subject only to *judicial* censorship) from establishing a climate of opinion strong enough to counterbalance the activity of the censorious private pressure groups. True, there have been some, but they are too few and their voices weak.

Well-written protests and proclamations are, unfortunately, not enough. That they are not enough is proved by the recent great advance of the antibook crusaders. The librarian needs support, not so much on the issue of the removal of any book presently on his shelves but in order to counteract pressure on book committees not to purchase "objectionable" books for library shelves and in order to assure that the committees themselves are truly representative of the community's wishes.

Of course, the real danger of unimpeded private censorship is not the loss of certain books but rather the effect on publishers and authors who are printing and writing today. Regardless of where our courts go in this field, as long as the climate in the country is one of fear, intimidation, and narrowness, the present and future creativity of America, whether in books, movies, or plays, will be stunted.

The use of the courts to define the difference between persuasion and boycott has scarcely begun. On the whole, this is not a matter for the courts. It is, may we suggest, a matter for you. Perhaps an award should go to a librarian such as Harold W. Tucker of the Queens Borough (New York City) Public Library, who struck back at the American Legion when it attacked Henry Miller's *Tropic of Cancer* on the library shelf:

> Its controversial nature was fully recognized as well as opinions running the full range from condemnation to praise as a literary master-piece. Precisely because of this wide range of opinion, the book should be available in the public library. Our free society is based on the right of each individual to form his opinion, and I have faith in the ability of our people to think for themselves.
>
> The public library is one of the institutions responsible for the protection of these rights that are basic to our democratic way of life. There are many people in this community who would object strongly to removal of this book, just as you would protest pressures for removal of a book for which you see merit.

So long as courts are going to look at "community standards" in order to find their own meaning for obscenity, it is not only important but imperative that community standards in any given community be truly representative of that community. Unless citizens of all inclinations in this field make their opinions known clearly, there is great danger that courts, in applying community standards, will be applying standards of groups that may very well represent less than a majority of any particular community. Many liberals and intellectuals are quick to point fingers at private censorship groups like the NODL who pursue through nonlegal means perfectly legitimate methods of public persuasion. Pointing fingers, however, gets one nowhere. It is more important for the future of the reading and viewing public of this country that groups representing all sides of the question make themselves known, heard, and effective.

If, as our Founding Fathers hoped, truth is supposed to find its victory in the marketplace of ideas, the pressure groups, which are probably a very important aspect of human persuasion, cannot be allowed to impose, by any means other than persuasion, their ideas and thoughts on others. Persuasion cannot be conducted on a take-it-or-leave-it basis. There must be willingness on the part of all people with an ax to grind, or a message to give, to put their ideas and opinions up for discussion, consideration, and reconsideration. It may not be illegal, or even immoral, to condemn out of hand any particular anti- or pro-censorship group, but it is highly impractical; because without cross-discussion and cross-criticism based on goodwill, there is little hope that anything even resembling truth will come out of this clash over the "obscene." Society, like law, looks for a balance, but no proper balance can be achieved until all the elements are carefully weighed. Vigilante violence should, and must, be fought with democratic strength. Peaceful private pressures must also be answered with vigor, but not with pigheadedness, obstinacy, or ill will.

Perhaps the most ironic, and saddest, aspect of the "Cowboys and Indians" feuds so prevalent in our country today is that with so much energy expended on keeping out "bad" influences, there is little left to encourage a refinement of taste and sensitivity. The real danger in all this is not that some people will be exposed to pornographic vulgarity but that, by default, the rest of us will be exposed to very little that is much better. Certainly a civilization becomes more "civilized" by improving its prestige symbols, not by improving its methods of suppression. While we fight so strongly over what not to read and think and see, who is left to worry about the quality of what we are allowed to enjoy freely? And yet by that quality (or lack of it) will the heritage we leave be judged.

"Cowboys and Indians" may be a game, but the stakes are higher than we like to think, and "good" books may be the best antidote to so-called "bad" books.

32

Obscenity and the Law

Not all law is as untidy as the Law of the Obscene. Lawyers and jurists have always had trouble defining in a courtroom words such as "negligence" or "reckless," or drawing a picture of "The Reasonable Man." But even "reckless," for example, has some objective definable outlines. "Reckless" driving can be described in terms of the speedometer reading, condition of the road, density of population in the area and traffic on the road, infirmities of the driver, condition of the vehicle, and hundreds of factors on which factual testimony might be taken.

Not so with censorship of the obscene. When the men of the black robes review material aimed at the glands as well as at the mind, theirs is a subjective reaction in which their own sexual temperament, as well as eye and ear, may be involved. The same is true for most if not all of us. Where deep-seated taboos are involved—and sex is certainly enclosed within one—reactions will characteristically be emotional rather than rational, impetuous rather than considered.

Law is no more a science than any pursuit of man undertaken by group action. As the famous case of *Mankind* versus *Galileo* reminds us, law has rather consistently restrained science because of man's inherited deep emotional attachment to the taboos of his time and place.

Therefore, when man has had fears of such concepts as blasphemy, impiety, or obscenity, law attempts avoidance rather than solution, a relief by attempted sterilization instead of more scientific immunization.

Much of the early, and now curiously archaic-sounding, pronouncements on sex in this country can be traced to these fears. We have seen that in colonial days, and later, the fears were often muddled together: sex and sacrilege, imprudence and impiety, bawdiness and blasphemy. Laws were passed in haste, and enforced with that strange kind of intensity only the guilt-ridden have. Witness Comstock and Sumner. Witness some of our present-day vigilantes.

In view of these perhaps unavoidable emotional impediments, it is a tribute to all the participants in this field of law—judges, lawyers, and clients—that over the years, and as a result of countless legal battles, light has shown through, and thoughtful deliberation has taken place. And, if only by elimination, some progress toward the goal of a positive rather than a negative approach to censorship of obscenity has been made, although not always with consistency. (As this book is going to press we note that *Fanny Hill* has just been cleared in New York, while *Tropic of Cancer* has just been condemned as "obscene" by the New York Court of Appeals.) Nevertheless, the trend is toward freedom. We hope, and even dare to predict, that in the not too distant future the Supreme Court, and then other courts, will even stop juggling synonyms. Meanwhile, let us sum up some of the progress that has been made, and some of the areas of uncertainty that still remain:

a) As literacy increased and became general, the concept that freedom of speech was only for the speaker was ended, and the concern for the audience—reader or viewer or listener—became worthy of the law's attention.

b) Classics—that is, works of prestige that are mainly those of the past—seem to have gathered immunity from suppression, no matter how obscene by anyone's definition.

c) Literary works in general circulation will no longer be judged by their supposed effect on the young, the perverted, or the feeble-minded, but rather by their relation to that great American institution the "Average Man"—at least so far as the courts are concerned. But the activities of vigilantes have already caused a relapse in this area.

d) Scientists like the late Alfred Kinsey, and others with a purely professional concern with alleged pornography, are no longer hampered by the same stultifying legal restrictions that will weigh upon the rest of society.

e) Books must now be read as a whole (and the same provision will apply to movies if ever the association of moviemakers desires it enough to put the issue to a court test).

f) Anglo-Saxon words, usually of four letters, are not enough to ban a book any more.

g) If a book has "social value," it will be permitted to circulate. But there are few guidelines to define social purpose.

h) If the penalty for sinning is suffering—in print—this will usually help win clearance from the censors.

i) If the book has literary style or merit in the eyes of other writers, testimony to this effect will give a great boost toward freedom, no matter how provocative the sexual scenes may be. The recent victories of *Lady Chatterley's Lover* and *Fanny Hill* give evidence of this.

j) The motive of the author has not yet been sufficiently ambushed by judges for us to write a prescription as to this factor. But see *People* v. *Eastman* in Chapter 8 and *Gautier* in Chapter 10.

k) No book is to be banned merely because of its theme (*The Well of Loneliness* decision).

l) Sex education of youth is not to be suppressed by the law (decided in *U.S.* v. *Dennett*).

m) Words like "morality," "sacrilegious," "sadism" are far too vague to satisfy the judges, but "obscene," "indecent," "lewd," "lascivious," and now "prurient," apparently have a clarity that satisfies most of the Supreme Court judges, although their definitions of these words are usually muddled and conflicting.

n) The particular prurience that may be suppressed at a given time or place must conform to some extent to the prevalent attitudes of the community. (See the case in the appendix.) But will not present prurience, once popular and accepted, become imprurient, if not exactly pure? And, indeed, what community standards are we talking about—nation? state? town? yours? or ours?

And while law has been inching forward, thoughtful Catholic writers particularly have been asking our society to recognize the difference between a sin and a crime. The most important writing on this subject is *Catholic Viewpoint on Censorship* by Father Harold Gardiner, who states that his Church is not monolithic on the problem, that the Roman Catholic Index Expurgatorius is no longer of any value in these terms and that it should be repealed. He and others urge that the more people rely on the sovereign to curb sexual tawdriness in picture or print, the less the continuing pressure and duty on family, teacher, and cleric to educate the next generation to standards of subtlety, taste, and privacy on sex—the most private experience in our culture. A motion before the recent Ecumenical Congress in Rome to be considered by the bishops and cardinals suggesting the reconsideration of celibacy of Roman Catholic clerics was a telltale sign of change, and since the leaders of censorious vigilantism in our culture are often members of that faith, this and other debates at Rome may portend a real shift in Catholic logic in their attempts to reduce the sexually tawdry in our land.

But the forces for public "indecency"—if we may use that word in its vulgate sense—are, it seems to the authors, on the increase. The national TV networks may or may not supply a wasteland of entertainment, but no one can doubt the vast numbers of hours devoted to the gospel of violence and the portrayal of sexual relations as either exaggerated improbable romance or mere orgiastic gymnastics.

In England, too, some progress has been made. A new law of 1959 to replace the old statute of Lord Campbell gave some new protections that our practice already had included—that the book must be judged as a whole; that the bookseller who did not know what was in the volume could not be prosecuted; that author and publisher had a right to be heard in its defense.

But the English law added two other safeguards. One was that any material was immune to conviction "if it is proved that publication of the article in question is justified as being for the public good on the ground that it is in the interest of science, literature, art or learning, or of other objects of general concern." The second provided that either side could call experts "as to the literary, artistic or other merits of an article." So it could be argued that high literary quality will forgive obscenity. But the rationale for this view is unclear. Is good writing supposed to have less effect than badly or clumsily written prose? We doubt Parliament thought so. Then, is graceful writing itself supposed to reduce the potential peril or did Parliament mean that England could stand the corruption for the sake of the writing?

The first real test of this English law, in 1960, was made when the Crown tried to suppress an unexpurgated paperback edition of

Lady Chatterley's Lover, never before published openly in England. The defense put thirty-five witnesses on the stand—eminent authors, critics, and editors, high officials of the Church, educators, a psychologist, a lawyer, and a Member of Parliament (author of the law)—who spoke highly of Lawrence's novel for its art, moral values, philosophy, educational worth. The jury acquitted, and the case never got to the highest authority (the House of Lords), so that there is no way of knowing yet just how that authority would treat the law of 1959. The only judge who has spoken officially on it was the trial judge in this case, and he informed the jury that the law did not mean that any well-written obscenity was justified. It had to be not only artistic; the jury must also find that it was "for the public good."

On the basis of this law and this verdict, England may for a time reduce the severity of the drives against works censors do not like. But perhaps one reason for fewer cases will be that if a publisher can't get eminent authorities to testify in favor of a manuscript, that work may remain unprinted. This is in fact the situation with quite a few manuscripts today. Perhaps England has shifted in substance from verdicts by juries of our peers to reliance on juries of intellectuals and the literati. If this is true, then we may see some titanic battles between rival experts. It may be recalled that D. H. Lawrence himself urged the suppression of *Ulysses* by James Joyce as obscene. In the case of *Lady Chatterley's Lover* one wonders if all the eminent people called for the defense would have been on Lawrence's side when he was alive and the novel first was published, and whether the prosecution (which in 1960 called no experts) would have found some great names to support *its* contention had Lawrence been alive.

In the debate in the House of Commons that preceded the passage of the new English Obscene Publications Act, one Honourable Member explained the need for obscenity legislation by stating that it was the duty of the government to stamp out smut. Of course, many people agreed with him. And yet, even assuming smut can be defined, it seems reasonable to ask why a government should have such a duty. It is not enough, we suggest, to answer, "Because smut is bad," or, "Because smut has no redeeming social importance," or, "Because smut gives us impure thoughts."

Although we can probably say the same about seditious or other utterances that some might think harmful to the security and safety of our country, community, or persons, our courts have held that such an indictment is not enough to bar political or seditious speech. As Holmes and Brandeis pointed out, the Constitution requires some causal relationship between the utterance and antisocial or socially harmful *action* before the utterance can be banned. An evil effect on thoughts alone is not enough in these areas.

Why, then, should society have a different rule as to obscenity? Anyone who has read this book will realize that the answer is not a simple one—whatever else it may be. And yet perhaps the most appalling lack in this field of jurisprudence has been the failure of judges even to consider whether obscenity does in fact cause any demonstrable antisocial behavior. With very few exceptions, such as Judge Frank and Justice Douglas in the *Roth* case, judges have assumed, without proof, that obscenity produces "bad acts." Do we really know that?

The few psychological and sociological studies that do exist—and they are too few and too narrow as yet to be conclusive—point in other directions. Scientists have made lawyers and some judges involved in this field do some hard thinking. We hope they will do more. Modern developments in communication of expression and ideas do the same. We can only suggest some of the pertinent material thus far uncovered that is bound to have a wider impact upon the makers and the interpreters of our law as it progresses:

1. Despite assumptions to the contrary, women are not generally interested in nor do they buy obscene or pornographic material. Romance and romantic stories attract them, but obscenity, studies suggest, gets them not one inch nearer to a couch or bed. Male nudity is not so inviting to them as is female nudity to the American male.

This suggests we must discard one presumed motive for censorship. As often stated, this presumption is that pornography is all right for us men but we must stamp it out in order to protect our women. We may now ask: Protect them from what?

2. Children react, if at all, more keenly to nonfiction than to fiction. The fairy tales of our youth were replete with horrors—animals eating grandmas and all the rest—but we didn't believe them. In the newspapers we found reality, truth, and fact, often in the form of orgy and murder, cruelty and violence. The contrast is still true. Newspapers brought into the home by an adult, usually a parent, have a different and more effective impact on the young than do comic books or other fictional materials that for decades have borne the brunt of the censor's attacks.

3. In the field of sadism (note the *Winters* case opinions in Chapter 24) there is some evidence that specificity—to use the scientist's terminology—is more likely to incite to action than it is in the area of sexual titillation. Hence it is urged by some that the substantive danger of pornography is less than that of sadism. Since the *Winters* decision, which discussed the vagueness of a standard that could be used to put men in jail, much attention has been directed at the excessive volume of sadism in the daily press and on television —and much criticism too!

Perhaps it is ineluctably right that man should have his greatest curiosity in the areas of the beginning and end of all life. The beginning is birth—sex—"obscenity" to some. The end is death— pain—"sadism" to some. May we venture the guess that whenever a society disturbs the proper balance of curiosities between these two poles, the emotional and hence legal imbalance works out its own emphasis. During the last ninety years, in both England and the United States, the attempt to curtail the curiosity about birth may have led to the excessive desire for dealing with the other end, death. An attempted taboo on sex may be more than self-defeating; it may be responsible for the increasing emphasis on death and torture and sadism, subjects not unrelated to cynicism, despair, and a world without hope.

Censorship produces a technique for evasion and hypocrisy. There is no other simple way to explain the furious drive of Madison Avenue advertising gentry to seek with desperate zeal a sex aspect for so many commodities. On the other hand, the newspapers and TV believe their vast profits depend on satisfying the public demand for sadism on the ground that there is no other valid substitute for sex. The vagaries of censorship decree that in these media sex is often sug-gestive, while sadism is explicit to the last cry of anguish. In a general way both newspapers and broadcasters feed on those whose natural outlets for adventure are curbed. Law has proved inadequate to shame the networks, for example, into reducing the emphasis on material that will be likely to create impulses to punish, retaliate, and solve all problems of suppressed aggressiveness.

4. Studies have been made, and more are needed, to learn, if possible, the causal relationship, if any, between word or picture and human behavior. Courts increasingly allow testimony in such a direction to be heard by judge or jury, but this sector of science is of recent origin. However, one fact stands out: thus far to our knowledge not one of these studies has demonstrated the existence of such a

relationship in the field of obscenity! In fact, the indications seem to be to the contrary. One of the earliest studies originated in a Rockefeller benefaction, and one of the authors of this volume took over the questionnaires to analyze the answers of a thousand women. They represented a good cross section of their sex as to age, location, and education. When asked, "Where did you get your fist sexual knowledge?" the most frequent reply was the Bible and the Encyclopedia. When asked, "What sexually excites you most?" only 4 percent mentioned books, and among the books listed were again the Bible and "the Encyclopedia," as well as many books of highest esteem at the time.

In a report of the New York State Temporary Commission on Youth and Delinquency, the president of the National Probation and Parole Association submitted a list of twenty causes of delinquency. Reading material was not included, although "reading difficulty" ranks as Number 18. In Ramsey's "Sexual Development of Boys," sex stimuli noted include carnival rides, driving fast cars, playing a music solo, seeing a column of marching soldiers. Reading material is not mentioned Other authorities add such stimuli as sitting in hot sand or skiing or swimming. The late Judge Curtis Bok wrote in one of his obscenity opinions: "If a man reads the Mechanics Lien Act while his sensuality is high, things will stand between him and the printed page that have no business there."

Perhaps the prudish and censorious are themselves most affected by the material they think obscene. They, and not delinquents, respond most consistently to published erotica, although they may not be the most avid purchasers.

In view of all this, the law, we hope, will soon explore the question of what causal relationship, if any, there is between a particular work and antisocial human behavior, assuming lawyers can determine the evil to be aimed at. We do not suggest that for each book prosecuted a corrupted human being will be haled to court as an exhibit. But there should be some reasonably factual identification of the accused writing or picture with the unlawful evil behavior.

We are taught that when an effect is out of all proportion to its supposed cause, there must be other factors of greater force at work. So when we hear of vague dangers arising from reading, we must look for some forces other than books in most unlawful behavior, because books just do not have that kind of influence. We read, in fact, what accords with our preexisting interests. Sex maniacs, it often has been said, do not become maniacal from reading but read what they do because of their obsessive tendencies. A Senate Committee—Report Number 62, Eighty-fourth Congress, First Session—concluded that it is unlikely that the reading of crime and horror comics would lead to delinquency in a well-adjusted and normally law-abiding child.

But law and life are not related in such simple and absolute terms. Studies may, and do, differ. Judges, we know, do. The point is that in this field of law (and therefore human concern) we do not have all the facts. Perhaps not even most of them. What we, all of us, are just beginning to learn is that democratic society, if it is to survive, cannot afford to rule by taboo and temperament. It must rule by reason.

We have seen many judges take many winding roads in their search for the "obscene." They, and therefore all of us, are still wandering along those roads. With more thoughtfulness and less haste, we shall all finally find our way to something society can call "truth"—a relative truth, no doubt, but a democratic one. It is in this context and toward this end that the Law of Obscenity must be considered.

Appendix

Lagniappe–
A Case
in Full

Here is a modern law case in its pristine state—with all the citations, footnotes, and other assorted gobbledygook left *in*. We thought it might amuse you. If you will read it with care and patience, it will also instruct you.

This case is representative of important obscenity decisions in many ways. The material under attack also is described in enough detail so that you will be able to appreciate what it was, perhaps compare it with magazines you have bought or picked up in a waiting room or bus terminal.

You will read the footnotes—with zest, perhaps—and note the references by both sides to many of the opinions we have mentioned in previous chapters: *Roth* and *Kingsley, Butler* and *Winters, Kennerley* and *Smith, Times Film* and *Lady Chatterley's Lover,* and so on. You will note the entirely different interpretations that majority and minority put upon the Supreme Court's use of the word "prurient." Thus, and only thus, will you be able to make up your mind whether you agree with Judge Horney or Judge Hammond.

In either case, you may conclude, and with justice, that for a century the law of our land has been running very fast but not moving very far.

Harry MONFRED, James Spissler, Samuel Mendelson,
Sander A. Siegel, Benjamin M. Siegel and
Albert King

V

STATE of Maryland
No. 55. Sept. Term, 1961

Court of Appeals of Maryland
Aug. 9, 1961

Martin B. Greenfield, Baltimore (William Greenfield and Albert
B. Polovoy, Baltimore, on the brief), for appellants.

Clayton A. Dietrich, Asst. Atty. Gen. (Thomas B. Finan, Atty.
Gen., Saul A. Harris, State's Atty., and James W. Murphy, Asst.
State's Atty., Baltimore, on the brief), for appellee.

Before HENDERSON, HAMMOND, PRESCOTT, HORNEY and MAR-
BURY, JJ HORNEY, Judge.

The appellants, who engage in the retail sale of books, and magazines in Baltimore City, were convicted by the Criminal Court of
Baltimore of violating Code which makes it a misdemeanor for
any person to "knowingly * * * sell * * * any lewd, obscene
or indecent book, magazine * * * drawing or photograph." The
subject matter of the prosecutions was six magazines [1] commonly
known or described as "girlie" magazines, and a set of semi-nude
photographs portraying a sequential "striptease." [2]
The magazines and photographs were openly displayed and
offered for sale without overcharge along with other types of magazines on newsstands or in the establishments of the several appellants. The magazines which are the subject of this appeal were
purchased by members of the Baltimore City Police Department,
who were specifically instructed to make purchases of named or
similar magazines. The set of photographs was purchased by a

[1] The publication entitled *Candid* was introduced as evidence against Harry
Monfred; *Consort* against James Spissler; *Sextet* against Samuel Mendelson and
Albert King; *Cloud 9* against Mendelson; *Torrid* against Sander A. Siegel and
Benjamin M. Siegel; and *Black Garter* against Monfred, King and both Siegels.
[2] The set of fifteen photographs was introduced against the defendant King.

member of the Criminal Justice Commission. The record shows that publications of a similar type had been on display and sold in the city for at least five years prior to the arrest of the appellants. The trial court—applying the obscenity test set forth in Roth v. United States and (Alberts v. California), 1957, 354 U.S. 476, 77 S.Ct. 1304, 1 L.Ed.2d 1498—concluded that the magazines and photographs were "neither literary in nature, artful in presentation, nor innocent in purpose" and that the dominant theme of the magazines and photographs dealt "with sex in a manner appealing to prurient interest" in that they had a "tendency to excite lustful thoughts," and found that such materials were "lewd, obscene and indecent" and therefore violated the obscenity statute of this State. All the defendants were found guilty and all were sentenced to pay fines.

The appellants claim (i) that the magazines and photographs are not obscene within the meaning of the statute because such materials do not "as a matter of law" exceed contemporary community standards; and (ii) that if such materials are obscene under the statute, then the statute violated the First and Fourteenth Amendments to the Constitution of the United States. But the real contention is—inasmuch as it is claimed that the suspect material is not "hard-core pornography"—that the appellants were immune from prosecution under the statute.

Since these cases were tried by the court sitting without a jury, we have the right to review them on both the law and evidence to determine whether in law the evidence was sufficient to sustain the conviction in each case, though we may not set the verdict aside on the evidence unless it is clearly erroneous. Maryland Rule 741 c.

In cases such as these, where prosecution is based primarily on the exhibits introduced as evidence, oral evidence, as was the case here, is usually not abundant. The exhibits speak for themselves, but must be perused and examined with care. This has been done as to each of the seven exhibits—six magazines and one set of photographs.

[1] An examination of the set of photographs shows various poses of a woman in progressive stages of undress (though never quite naked), which to the normal person might be offensive or repulsive, but they are not necessarily obscene under the statute. And since mere nudity in and of itself is not obscene, we think the trial court in convicting King for selling the photographs was clearly in error as to the evidence.

[2] The same is true with respect to the magazine Black Garter. Most of the pictures in this magazine are of models who pose for "glamor" photography. They are portrayed scantily dressed either in black lingerie or white furs and other accessories in what might be described as coarsely offensive postures, but the pictures, even though obviously intended to arouse sex appeal, are not strictly obscene. And, which is more to the point with respect to the issue of obscenity, the textual matter accompanying the illustrations is in the main innocuous. Instead, it purports to discuss in detail the technique of using shadows and lights in photographing the nude. Therefore, since this magazine taken as a whole is not obscene, we think the trial court also erred in convicting Monfred, King and the Siegels for selling it.

[3] But when each of the other five so-called "girlie" magazines —Candid, Consort, Sextet, Cloud 9 and Torrid—is taken as a whole, that is, when the pictures reproduced therein are examined in conjunction with a perusal of the textual material, it is apparent that all of these publications are obscene within the meaning of the statute as well as under the obscenity test approved by the majority in the Roth-Alberts case, supra. All of them, without exception, present numerous pictures or drawings of nude or semi-nude women showing what the State characterized as "come hither" expressions and poses interspersed with pointedly suggestive sex stories so placed that a reader if he needs visual aid in following the story has only to glance at the opposite page for additional stimulation. All of these five publications were obviously calculated to excite lustful thoughts in the mind of the reader.[3] Thus, having

---

[3] Sextet (Vol. 1. No. 3), for example, in addition to showing more than fifty pictures and drawings of nude and semi-nude women on its forty-eight pages, also contains eleven articles indexed as "features," "fiction" and "pictorial." Four of such articles will suffice to demonstrate the intention to arouse prurient interest. Typical extracts from these include the following:
From "His Only Weakness" (a lewd narrative detailing the seduction of a hardened woman by a philanderer):
"That's my proposition * * *. If you want me in bed, now's your one and only chance. (p. 4)

*   *   *   *   *

"Now he was absolutely sure he was going to have [her]. And, if necessary, he would make it by force. Sort of an unlegalized rape. (p. 6)

*   *   *   *   *

"Suppose you let me feel you. (p. 40)

*   *   *   *   *

made a determination of our own that the findings of fact were correct, we are unable to say that the trial court was in error as to the evidence in convicting all of the defendants for selling one or more of these magazines; nor did the lower court reach the wrong conclusion as to the law.

In the Roth (Alberts) case, Roth, who was a "rare book" dealer,

---

"He could see her delicious breasts straining against the material of her smart black dress. (p. 40)

* * * * *

"He didn't say a word. He just nodded his head, leaped forward, grabbed her hand and dragged her into his bedroom.

"When it was over, they lay quietly on the bed * * * naked and exhausted." (p. 41)

From "The Paper Back Girls" (emphasizing the increase in the sexual aspect of cheap literature):

" * * * she is practically a virgin because she has only been to bed with eleven different men, not counting those before she was 13. [She] also confesses her fondness for dykes without giving any count in such regard. (p. 11)

* * * * *

" 'Kiss me * * * I haven't been laid in more than six months * * * she reached up and, with a terrific yank, ripped the front of her dress wide open, baring her breasts * * * rich, sexual woman was everywhere * * *.' (p. 12)

* * * * *

"The girls round robin it with the men and as circumstances permit they pair off and have an even more exciting time with each other." (p. 12)

From "The Cherry Orchard" (a story of a minor seduced by a prostitute):

"Larry's pants bulged with the thought. (p. 17)

* * * * *

"What a broad to pop with! He swallowed hard and crossed his legs. (p. 18)

* * * * *

"Her whisper was almost a sexual action. 'Your place or mine?' (p. 19)

* * * * *

"She moved her groin hard into his. (p. 19)

* * * * *

"He pulled her sweater from her shoulder, and she swung around. Nude, except for panties. * * * 'I told you gin makes me passionate.' She kicked off her shoes and flung herself on the bed. * * * 'I'll let you take the panties off. Guys like to do that.' (p. 19)

* * * * *

"Seconds later, he became a man." (p. 42)

From "A Date With Judy" (a fantasy of a partially nude woman inviting a man to her house):

" 'I'm so happy you could come,' she purrs with a sexy smile and a suggestive pose of welcome.

"Arm and arm they enter the semi-dark apartment." (p. 20)

was convicted of a violation of the Federal obscenity statute. Alberts, who was a distributor of photographs of nude and semi-nude women in various poses, was convicted under the California obscenity statute. In neither case was there any question as to whether or not the books sold by Roth and the photographs distributed by Alberts were obscene in fact. Thus, all that was decided was whether, on their faces, the federal and state statutes under consideration were violative of the First and Fourteenth Amendments respectively.

In speaking for the majority, Justice Brennan held that both statutes were valid, and, in the process, stated, 354 U.S. at page 489, 77 S.Ct. at page 1311, that the test of obscenity is "whether to the average person, applying contemporary community standards, the dominant theme of the material taken as a whole appeals to prurient interest." Material having such an interest was defined in a footnote as "material having a tendency to excite lustful thoughts." The Court also held that "obscenity is not within the area of constitutionally protected speech and press."

Chief Justice Warren concurred in the result reached in each case. His theory was—because it was not the material but a person that was on trial—that what is obscene should depend in the main on the reprehensible conduct of the seller in engaging in "the commercial exploitation of the morbid and shameful craving for materials with prurient effect" and not on the obscenity of the materials sold. Justice Harlan concurred in the result in Alberts and dissented in Roth. He was of the opinion that federal obscenity censorship should be limited to hard-core pornography and that the states should be allowed broader censorship powers. Justices Black and Douglas dissented. They were against all obscenity censorship except where it is shown that "the particular publication has an impact on action that the government can control."

In the next term after the Roth-Alberts decision, the Supreme Court disposed of several other obscenity cases by short per curiams. In three of them, the Court, by reversing federal courts of appeal—without any explanation for the reversals other than the citation of the Roth (and Alberts) case—gave final protection to the materials in question. In one, Times Film Corp. v. City of Chicago, 1957, 355 U.S. 35, 78 S.Ct. 115, 2 L.Ed.2d 72, which involved prior censorship of a French cinema with English subtitles based on a novel by Colette, the appellant attacked the Chicago censorship ordinance on the ground that it imposed an unconstitutional prior restraint. The appendix to the appellant's brief indicated that the censors had not taken any of the artistic merits of the film into account, and in fact four of the censors testified that the picture had not aroused their sexual desires, pruriently or otherwise. The appendix further indicated that there was no nudity, other than one short scene showing a boy's buttocks, and that the real reason a permit was denied was to prevent children from seeing the movie. The decision of the appellate court in this case had been handed down before the Supreme Court had decided Roth. In the second reversal, One, Inc. v. Olesen, 1958, 355 U.S. 371, 78 S.Ct. 364, 2 L.Ed.2d 352, which involved the right to send the magazine. One—a publication dealing with homosexuality—through the mails, officials of the Post Office Department had invoked the federal obscenity statute because the magazine was considered to be lewd and obscene. The petition for certiorari in this case had also been prepared before the decision in Roth. The government urged that the lower court had satisfied the Roth test, but the petitioner contended that the Supreme Court had not theretofore dealt with this specific question. A copy of the magazine was not included in the printed record; nor was it reproduced in either of the briefs, but, since the sole question was whether the magazine was obscene—a question of fact—the Court, by citing Roth, apparently applied the Roth test in determining that the publication was either not obscene or that taken as a whole it was not obscene. In the third reversal, Sunshine Book Co. v. Summerfield, 1958, 355 U.S. 372, 78 S.Ct. 365, 2 L.Ed.2d 352, another case involving the mailing of a magazine—Sunshine & Health—a copy of the publication was also not included in the printed record, but it is a "nudist" type magazine—a representative copy of which is included in the transcript in the instant case—in which, although the nudist way of life is advocated and the pictures show the genital areas of the body, there is nothing obscene in the text of the magazine. Thus, it appears that the reversal was based on the concept that mere nudity is not obscenity or the decision may have been based on the fact that the text was not in fact obscene. But in Adams Newark Theatre Co. v. City of Newark, 1957, 354 U.S. 931, 77 S.Ct. 1395, 1 L.Ed.2d 1533, involving the Newark city ordinances prohibiting lewd, obscene or indecent shows and performances, in which the petitioner had raised issues of vagueness and freedom of expression in a proceeding for a declaratory judgment before the city had attempted to enforce the ordinances, the

Supreme Court of the United States, in a brief per curiam, summarily affirmed the judgment of the New Jersey Supreme Court—which had upheld the constitutionality of the ordinances—by citing the Kingsley, Kingsley Books, Inc., v. Brown, 354 U.S. 436, 77 S. Ct. 1325, 1 L.Ed. 2d 1469, Roth and Alberts cases. And, in a fifth case, Mounce v. United States, 1957, 355 U.S. 180, 78 S.Ct. 267, 2 L.Ed.2d 187, the government having made a "confession of error" that the test used by the court of appeals was "materially different" from the Roth test, the judgment below was reversed and remanded to the district court for consideration in the light of Roth.

We think the Times Film case is fairly distinguishable from the instant case in that the censors not only made no effort to apply any sort of reasonable obscenity test, but principally because the main reliance of the appellant was on the "prior restraint" theory rather than the lack of an obscenity test. The Sunshine Book case is also easily distinguishable in that, unlike the instant case, there were no obscene stories in the nudist magazine. And, although the One, Inc. case is not as easy to distinguish as the other two, it is a fact that it, like the Sunshine Book case, also involved federal postal censorship, not a state criminal prosecution; besides, since the constitutional issue was not formally raised, it is possible that the decision may not have been based on the unconstitutionality of the statute.

Other recent federal obscenity cases also have no direct bearing on the cases before us. In Butler v. State of Michigan, 1957, 352 U.S. 380, 77 S.Ct. 524, 1 L.Ed.2d 412, decided prior to Roth, the Supreme Court merely condemned the Michigan obscenity statute by holding that it was violative of the First and Fourteenth Amendments—in that it prohibited the sale to an adult of a book unfit for a minor—without suggesting a constitutionally sanctioned alternative. In Kingsley Books, Inc. v. Brown, 1957, 354 U.S. 436, 77 S.Ct. 1325, 1 L.Ed.2d 1469, also decided before Roth, where the defendant was convicted under the New York obscenity statute, there was no question but that the material was obscene, and there was no intimation of what was soon to be stated in Roth. In Kingsley Intern. Pictures Corp. v. Regents of Univ. of N. Y., 1959, 360 U.S. 684, 79 S.Ct. 1362, 1363, 3 L.Ed.2d 1512, which involved the famous motion picture Lady Chatterley's Lover, the Supreme Court, without deciding whether or not the picture was obscene, declared that a part of the New York motion picture obscenity statute was unconstitutional in that it violated the basic "freedom to advocate ideas" guaranteed by the First Amendment. And in Smith v. State of California, 1959, 361 U.S. 147, 80 S.Ct. 215, 4 L.Ed.2d 205, in which the defendant was convicted of having obscene books in his possession, a Los Angeles city ordinance was declared unconstitutional in that it did not require proof of scienter on the part of the possessor, but again, the majority did not pass on the question of whether the books were actually obscene.

Thus, in the cases since Roth, the Supreme Court—at least in its majority opinions in the Kingsley Pictures and Smith cases— did not specifically apply the Roth test to the allegedly obscene materials before it in these cases. However, the test seems to have been applied in the per curiam reversals (Times Film, One, Inc., and Sunshine Book) and in the per curiam affirmance (Adams Newark Theatre), but we do not know for sure—other than that the Roth test of obscenity will be strictly construed—what the reasoning of the Court was in any of these per curiams.

It may well be that the Supreme Court will in time (assuming it has not already done so) declare that only "hardcore pornography" is not protected by the constitution, as a majority of four of the Court of Appeals of New York (in two opinions—the latter concurring in the result reached in the former—each of which was concurred in by one other judge) did recently in construing the meaning of the obscenity statute of that State in People v. Richmond County News, Inc., 1960, 9 N.Y.2d 578, 216 N.Y.S.2d 369, 175 N.E.2d 681, 686, involving the sale and distribution of the magazine Gent, when, in discarding the Roth test, it adopted an obscenity test of its own.[4] Or the Supreme Court might eventually accept the concept of "variable obscenity"[5] expressed by Chief Justice Warren in his concurring opinion in the Roth-Alberts case to the effect that the question of obscenity must turn, not on the material itself, but on the motives of the seller. In passing—since these sales were unquestionably commercial—we note that a vari-

[4] Judge Fuld in the opinion written by him stated that "the test of the obscene, of the pornographic, is not in the tendency or appeal of the material, but rather in its content objectively appraised" and then added that "it [the obscene] focuses predominantly upon what is sexually morbid, grossly perverse and bizarre, without any artistic or scientific purpose or justification."

[5] This concept seems to have been favored by Dean Lockhart and Professor McClure (of the University of Minnesota Law School) in their scholarly treatise on this area of the law entitled Censorship of Obscenity: The Developing Constitutional Standards published in 45 Minn.L.Rev. 5 (1960).

able obscenity test could have been applied in this case. But, until the Supreme Court specifically speaks further in this uncertain area, we think we are bound by what we understand the Roth test requires.

Applying the Roth test to the censorship power of the State under the provisions of our obscenity statute, as was done in these cases (although incorrectly with respect to two of the exhibits), it is, as we see it, evident that the conviction of King for selling the set of semi-nude photographs should be reversed; that the convictions of Monfred, King and both Siegels for selling the magazine Black Garter should also be reversed; and that the convictions of all of the appellants for selling one or more of the obscene magazines called Candid, Consort, Sextet, Cloud 9 and Torrid, should be affirmed, and we so hold.

Judgments against Albert King for selling the set of semi-nude photographs and against Harry Monfred, Albert King, Sander A. Siegel and Benjamin M. Siegel for selling the magazine Black Garter reversed; the Mayor and City Council of Baltimore to pay one-seventh of the costs.

Judgments against all appellants for selling one or more of the obscene magazines Candid, Consort, Sextet, Cloud 9 and Torrid affirmed; Apellants to pay six-sevenths of the costs.

HAMMOND, Judge (dissenting).

The opinion of the Court in this troublesome case is essentially syllogistic: the Maryland statute proscribing the sale of obscene books and magazines is to be construed as broadly as the Supreme Court will permit; the case of Roth v. United States, 354 U.S. 476, 77 S.Ct. 1304, 1311, 1 L.Ed.2d 1498, held that obscenity is not protected by the constitutional guarantees of freedom of speech and press, and said that material is obscene if, to the average person, applying contemporary community standards, "the dominant theme of the material taken as a whole appeals to prurient interest"; the trial judge found the magazines sold by the defendants appealed to "prurient interest" and, since this Court cannot say he was clearly wrong in his determination, the judgments and sentences of guilty must be affirmed. I find the premises and the deductive process unsound, and the conclusion therefore necessarily wrong and am constrained to dissent and express my reasons for disagreement.

The only testimony against each defendant was that he had sold the magazine or pictures introduced against him. There was no testimony as to contemporary community standards (except that the magazines had been sold openly in Baltimore for five years), or as to what comprises a community, or as to what effect the pictures and magazines would have on the average person. The Court held the separate group of pictures and those in the magazines not to be in themselves obscene (and with these holdings I agree), but decided that most of the texts, considered with the related pictures, justified Judge Sodaro in finding the magazines obscene under the Roth standards, as the Court understands them. Despite the Court's statement that its determinations were independent, this is no more in actuality than holding that "Judge Sodaro thought that most people would think the magazines obscene, we cannot say he was wrong and therefore, under the Maryland statute and the Constitutional tests, they are obscene."

In deciding the cast on this basis the Court, I think, failed to fulfill its obligatory duty to make a reflective independent appraisal of the controversial printings, for as Justice Harlan, concurring in Roth, said (as to the suppression of obscenity) at page 497–498 of 354 U.S., at page 1316 of 77 S.Ct.: "* * * the question [of] whether a particular work is of that character involves not really an issue of fact but a question of constitutional *judgment* of the most sensitive and delicate kind." A State appellate court, no less than the Supreme Court, has the same obligation. The People v. Richmond County News, Inc., 175 N.Y. 681, 216 N.Y.S.2d 369, 175 N.E.2d 681; Lockhart and McClure, Censorship of Obscenity: The Developing Constitutional Standards, 45 Minn.L.Rev. 114–120; 4 Davis, Administrative Law, 29.08; Niemotko v. State of Maryland, 340 U.S. 268, 271, 71 S.Ct. 325, 328, 95 L.Ed. 267; Feiner v. People of State of New York, 340 U.S. 315, 316, 71 S.Ct. 303, 95 L.Ed. 267; Napue v. Illinois, 360 U.S. 264, 271, 79 S.Ct. 1173, 3 L.Ed.2d 1217; Watts v. State of Indiana, 338 U.S. 49, 69 S.Ct. 1347, 93 L.Ed. 1801. Since Roth, cases that have recognized this obligation include United States v. Keller, 3 Cir., 259 F.2d 54; Capitol Enterprises, Inc. v. City of Chicago, 7 Cir., 260 F.2d 670; Commonwealth v. Moniz, 338 Mass. 442, 155 N.E.2d 762.

That the publications here involved are a form of vulgar and tawdry entertainment (for some part of the populace), lacking in all social value or artistic or scientific justification, does not deprive them of the constitutional protection of free speech and press. In Winters v. People of State of New York, 333 U.S. 507,

510, 68 S.Ct. 655, 667, 92 L.Ed. 840, the Court, noting its obligations as to an aspect of a free press (comic crime books) "in its relation to public morals" said: "We do not accede to appellee's suggestion that the constitutional protection for a free press applies only to the exposition of ideas. The line between the informing and the entertaining is too elusive for the protection of that basic right * * * What is one man's amusement, teaches another's doctrine. Though we can see nothing of any possible value to society in these magazines, they are as much entitled to the protection of free speech as the best of literature." Hannegan v. Esquire, Inc., 327 U.S. 146, 157, 66 S.Ct. 456, 462, 90 L.Ed. 586, said: "What seems to one to be trash may have for others fleeting or even enduring values."

The concept of obscenity in law is a complex and difficult one. I take it the Maryland Legislature intended by its use of "obscene" in the statute (Code (1960 Cum.Supp.), Art. 27, Sec. 418(a)) what the word meant in prevailing leading legal thought; otherwise it would be too vague to constitute a permissible standard in a criminal statute.

In People v. Richmond County News, Inc., supra, the Court of Appeals of New York, in holding a "girlie" magazine (indistinguishable from the worst of those in the case before us) not to be obscene, said of the New York statute (the equivalent of the Maryland section) at page 685 of 175 N.E.2d:

"In the Roth case (354 U.S. 476, 77 S.Ct. 1304, supra), the court did say that 'obscene material is material which deals with sex in a manner appealing to prurient interest' (at page 487 of 354 U.S., at page 1310 of 77 S.Ct.), and that the test was 'whether to the average person, applying contemporary community standards, the dominant theme of the material taken as a whole appeals to prurient interest' (at page 489 of 354 U.S., at page 1311 of 77 S.Ct.). These statements, however, can only indicate the broad boundaries of any permissible definition of obscenity under the United States Constitution; they do not pretend to, and cannot, give specific content to the meaning of 'obscene' as it appears in our statute."

In the Roth opinion the phrase "appeal to prurient interest" was lifted from a more comprehensive definition in the American Law

Institute's Model Penal Code, Tentative Draft No. 6, Sec. 207.10 (2) (a definition which the Court seemingly adopted as sound): "* * * A thing is obscene if, considered as a whole, its predominant appeal is to prurient interest, i.e., a shameful or morbid interest in nudity, sex or excretion and if it goes substantially beyond customary limits of candor in description or representation of such matters * * * ." The authors of Model Penal Code continue:

"We reject the prevailing test of tendency to arouse lustful thoughts or desires because it is unrealistically broad for a society that plainly tolerates a great deal of erotic interest in literature, advertising, and art, and because regulation of thought or desire, unconnected with overt misbehaviour, raises the most acute constitutional as well as practical difficulties. We likewise reject the common definition of obscene as that which 'tends to corrupt or debase.' If this means anything different from tendency to arouse lustful thought and desire, it suggests that change of character or actual misbehaviour follows from contact with obscenity. Evidence of such consequences is lacking * * *." [1]

[1] The Court of Appeals of New York comments on the last statements in The People v. Richmond County News, Inc., 9 N.Y.2d 579, 175 N.E.2d 681, 216 N.Y.S.2d 369, saying: "It is noteworthy that, despite the reams of material on the effect of books, magazines and other media of expression on sexual conduct, 'there is very little scientific evidence' on the subject. St. John-Stevas, Obscenity in the Law (1956), p. 196; see, also, Brown v. Kingsley Books, 1 N.Y.2d 177, 181, fn. 3, 151 N.Y.S.2d 639, 641, 134 N.E.2d 461, 463 * * *; United States v. Roth, 2 Cir., 237 F.2d 796, 812–817, per Frank, J., concurring, affirmed 354 U.S. 476, 77 S.Ct. 1304, 1 L.Ed.2d 1498, supra. Indeed, two authoritative writers in the field have concluded that, 'Although the whole subject of obscenity censorship hinges upon the unproved assumption that "obscene" literature is a significant factor in causing sexual deviation from the community standard, no report can be found of a single effort at genuine research to test this assumption by singling out as a factor for study the effect of sex literature upon sexual behavior.' (Lockhart and McClure, Obscenity and the Courts, 20 Law and Contemporary Problems, 587, 595; see, also, American Law Institute, Model Penal Code. Tentative Draft No. 6, § 207.10, p. 44). Some commentators have gone even further and suggested that 'for an undetermined number of individuals, the writing or reading of obscenity may be a substitute for rather than a stimulus to physical sexuality.' American Law Institute, Model Penal Code, Tentative Draft No. 6, § 207.10, p. 45." The suggestion in these writings is that there is no causal connection between what is regarded as "obscene" and antisocial conduct of a sexual nature.

The Supreme Court of Oregon in a careful opinion in State v. Jackson, Or., 356 P.2d 495, 507, adopted the Model Penal Code definition of obscenity as the meaning of the Oregon statute on the subject, and said:

"On the other hand, the Model Penal Code, by requiring that the material, to be obscene, must appeal to 'prurient interest' and go 'substantially beyond customary limits of candor in description or representation' emphasizes strongly that the manner of presentation must itself amount to shameful and disgusting conduct outside the pale of what is tolerable to the community at large. The majority opinion in the Roth case defines 'prurient' as 'having a tendency to excite lustful thoughts.' 354 U.S. 476, at page 486, note 20, 77 S.Ct. at page 1310. We think, however, that the court had in mind the narrower meaning used by the Model Penal Code or means to use the narrower meaning in cases following Roth."

The Roth case unquestionably established two constitutional tests of obscenity: (1) the material must be judged as a whole and (2) it must be judged under contemporary community standards by its impact upon average or normal persons, not the young, the weak, or the susceptible. There can be little doubt, I believe, that "community standards" means not state or local communities but rather the standards of society as a whole.[2] The phrase originated with Judge Learned Hand in his opinion in United States v. Kennerley,

[2] Manifestly local community standards as to what is or is not obscene vary to a considerable degree. What a jury in the more unsophisticated sections of Maryland—in some parts of the Eastern Shore and in more remote Southern and Western Maryland—might consider beyond the pale, a jury in Baltimore or the metropolitan counties of the State might find acceptable. Lockhart and McClure in their article in 45 Minn.L.Rev. 5 point out at page 36 that "In Los Angeles, New York, and perhaps also Chicago, the Post Office and Justice Departments had difficulty convicting persons for mailing obscene matter; courts and juries there were too sophisticated, their attitudes too liberal * * * the two departments supported the enactment of legislation authorizing prosecution of a mailer at any place through which the mail passed, as well as at the place of receipt of the mail. It would be easier to obtain convictions and heavier sentences in the hinterland * * *." The authors add at page 109 that "At trials in more straight-laced communities, the government could make particular effective use of such trial tactics as refusing to consent to waivers of jury trials; and then, having insisted on jury trials, it could peremptorily challenge the most literate and best educated jurors. If 'contemporary community

D.C., 209 F. 119, 121: "* * * should not the word 'obscene' be
allowed to indicate the present critical point in the compromise
between candor and shame at which the community may have
arrived here and now? * * * To put thought in leash to the
average conscience of the time is perhaps tolerable, but to fetter it
by the necessities of the lowest and least capable seems a fatal
policy." It seems plain Judge Hand was referring not to the standards of states or local communities, but rather to the contemporary
standards of society as a whole, and that the Supreme Court had
in mind that same standard in adopting the phrase. Messrs. Lockhart and McClure so interpret the Roth opinion. They say in their
article Censorship of Obscenity at p. 111 of 45 Minn.L.Rev.:

"* * * We believe the Supreme Court did not, as some of
the proponents of censorship hopefully thought, approve of the
application of state or local community standards in obscenity
cases. Indeed, in one of its per curiam decisions after the Roth-
Alberts opinion, the Court indicated that it would not tolerate
the application of restrictive local standards in obscenity censorship."

The error into which the trial judge and majority of this Court
fell, in my view, was to confuse and equate sex (and vulgarity,
crudeness and cheap, poor taste) with obscenity. They are not
synonymous and society as a whole and the courts recognize this.
The subject matter, the descriptions and references found in the
magazines held obscene in this case can be found in much the same
form in literally hundreds of novels and stories which have either
been accepted as not obscene or have been found not to be. The
Supreme Court in Roth emphasized the necessity of differentiating
between sex and lewdness:

"However, sex and obscenity are not synonymous. * * *
The portrayal of sex, e.g., in art, literature and scientific works,
is not * * * sufficient reason to deny material the constitutional protection of freedom of speech and press. Sex, a great
and mysterious motive force in human life, has indisputably

standards' has reference to the standards of state or local communities, and if
those standards are to be applied by a jury, then these tactics will enable the
government to secure convictions which heretofore would have been difficult or
impossible to obtain."

been a subject of absorbing interest to mankind through the ages; it is one of the vital problems of human interest and public concern." Page 487 of 354 U.S., page 1310 of 77 S.Ct., page 1508 of 1 L.Ed.2d.

I do not believe the trial judge permissibly could have been convinced beyond a reasonable doubt that the contents of the magazines, judged by the contemporary standards of our society as a whole, both appealed to "a shameful or morbid interest" in nudity or sex and at the same time went *"substantially* beyond customary limits of candor in description or representation of such matters." [3] As the American Law Institute said, we live today in "a society that plainly tolerates a great deal of erotic interest in literature, advertising and art." Judge Bryan made the same point in finding "Lady Chatterley's Lover" not obscene in Grove Press, Inc. v. Christenberry, D.C., 175 F.Supp. 488:

> "The tests of obscenity are not whether the book or passages from it are in bad taste or shock or offend the sensibilities of an individual, or even of a substantial segment of the community. * * * 175 F.Supp. at page 501.
> "* * * the broadening of freedom of expression and of the frankness with which sex and sex relations are dealt with at the present time require no discussion. In one best selling novel after another frank descriptions of the sex act and 'four-letter' words appear with frequency. These trends appear in all media of public expression, in the kind of language used and the subjects discussed in polite society, in pictures, advertisements and dress, and in other ways familiar to all. Much of what is now accepted would have shocked the community to the core a generation ago. Today such things are generally tolerated whether we approve or not." 175 F.Supp. at page 502.

I agree with the conclusion of the Court of Appeals of New York in its holding that the "realistic accounts of normal sexuality" in the magazine "Gent" (in which, as Judge Froessel makes plain in his dissenting opinion by extensive quotations and description,

[3] The Court found "Black Garter" not to be obscene. "Consort" and "Torrid" would not seem to be any more so under any reasonable test of obscenity. "Candid" and "Sextet" have one or two stories approaching the obscene and almost all of "Cloud Nine" is on the borderline.

LAGNIAPPE—A CASE IN FULL 269

the language and pictures were as direct and crude and vulgar as any in the magazines before us) were not obscene. Judge Fuld said for the Court at page 686 of 175 N.E.2d:

> "The fact is, however, that while the magazine contains many stories or pictures which are aesthetically tasteless and without any redeeming social worth, none of them is pornographic. Numerous pictures and cartoons of nude or semi-nude women and numerous descriptions and depictions of sexual arousal and satisfaction are to be found in 'Gent' but it contains nothing which smacks of sick and blatantly perverse sexuality."

Chief Judge Desmond, concurring, said at page 687:

> "This collection of sexy fiction and illustrations has little of literary merit or artistry and yet it is not in the First Amendment sense filthy or disgusting or deliberately corruptive or offensive to common decency under prevailing standards of taste. Virtuous adults will reject it (as all of us Judges would were we not restrained by the Roth-Alberts legal test). Adolescents may be hurt by it. But our prepossessions are not the law and the reactions of children are not valid tests (Roth v. United States, 354 U.S. 476, 489, 490, 77 S.Ct. 1304, supra)."

Whether the Court's reading of the Maryland statute, or mine, is correct as a matter of interpretation may well be immaterial. I am convinced that the Supreme Court has left no constitutional leeway to make the interpretation the majority makes and that its result violates the constitutional rights of the defendants and the publishers of free speech and free press.

In seeking to go to the Supreme Court, Roth raised four issues of substance—whether (a) the federal statute violated first amendment guarantees; (b) was too vague; (c) invaded the reserved powers of the States and the people; and, finally, (d) whether the publications were obscene. Roth seriously pressed only the first three; his argument on the fourth was so perfunctory the government did not reply. The Court limited the certiorari granted to the first three issues. The Alberts case, decided with Roth, ended in the Supreme Court in the same posture as Roth— at a level of abstraction so rarefied that the facts had become immaterial.

The Solicitor General brought the case to a more earthy level. In his brief he pointed out that the violations of the Federal obscenity statute fell into three categories. The first, some two per cent, comprised "novels of apparently serious literary intent" challenged because "they concentrate on explicit discussion of sex conduct in a vocabulary based on four letter words." The second category, less than ten per cent, he said was border line material, mainly photographic. The final group, ninety per cent of the whole, comprised what the Solicitor General described as "black market" or "hard-core" pornography. To make sure the Court knew what he meant by "hard-core pornography" he sent to the Court a carton containing numerous samples concededly in that category.[4]

[4] The Solicitor General described "hard-core" pornography as follows:
"This is commercially-produced material in obvious violation of present law * * * This material is manufactured clandestinely in this country or abroad and smuggled in. There is no desire to portray the material in pseudo-scientific or 'arty' terms. The production is plainly 'hard-core' pornography, of the most explicit variety, devoid of any disguise.
"Some of this pornography consists of erotic objects. There are also large numbers of black and white photographs, individually, in sets, and in booklet form, of men and women engaged in every conceivable form of normal and abnormal sexual relations and acts. There are small printed pamphlets or books, illustrated with such photographs, which consist of stories in simple, explicit, words of sexual excesses of every kind, over and over again. No one would suggest that they had the slightest literary merit or were intended to have any. There are also large numbers of 'comic books,' specially drawn for the pornographic trade, which are likewise devoted to explicitly illustrated incidents of sexual activity, normal or perverted * * * It may safely be said that most, if not all, of this type of booklets contain drawings not only of normal fornication but also of perversions of various kinds.
"The worst of the 'hard-core' pornographic materials now being circulated are the motion picture films. These films, sometimes of high technical quality, sometimes in color, show people of both sexes engaged in orgies which again include every form of sexual activity known, all of which are presented in a favorable light. The impact of these pictures on the viewer cannot easily be imagined. No form of incitement to action or to excitation could be more explicit or more effective.
"Brief for the United States, pp. 37–38, United States v. Roth, 354 U.S. 476 [77 S.Ct. 1304, 1 L.Ed.2d 1498] (1957).
"The Solicitor General also sought to distinguish hard-core pornography from material in 'the borderline entertainment area.' He said:
"The distinction between this [hard-core pornography] and the material produced by petitioner and others, as discussed above, is not based upon any difference in intent. Both seek to exploit the erotic market place. The difference is that the 'black-market' traffickers make no pretence about the quality and nature of the material they are producing and offering * * *."

The foregoing account of the Roth-Alberts case was taken from Lockhart and McClure, Censorship of Obscenity, 45 Minn.L.Rev. pp. 19–29. The authors later revert to the subject and conclude (p. 60):

"In voting to sustain the constitutionality of the obscenity statutes of California and of the United States, Justices Frankfurter, Burton, Clark, Brennan, and Whittaker must have had material of this kind in mind for hard-core pornography, particularly in pictorial form, is so blatantly shocking and revolting that it would have been impossible for the Justices to put it out of mind. Since the basic issue before the Court was only the constitutionality of the statutes on their faces and in a vacuum, without regard to their application in the two cases, it seems

---

D. H. Lawrence wrote in Pornography and Obscenity in Sex Literature and Censorship (1953):

"But even I would censor genuine pornography, rigorously. It would not be very difficult. In the first place, genuine pornography is almost always underworld, it doesn't come into the open. In the second, you can recognize it by the insult it offers, invariably, to sex, and to the human spirit.

"Pornography is the attempt to insult sex, to do dirt on it. This is unpardonable. Take the very lowest instance, the picture post-card sold underhand, by the underworld, in most cities. What I have seen of them have been of an ugliness to make you cry. The insult to the human body, the insult to a vital human relationship! Ugly and cheap they make the human nudity, ugly and degraded they make the sexual act, trivial and cheap and nasty.

"It is the same with the books they sell in the underworld. They are either so ugly they make you ill, or so fatuous you can't imagine anybody but a cretin or a moron reading them, or writing them."

The Kronhausens in Pornography and The Law 178–243 (1959) say pornographic books "are always made up of a succession of increasingly erotic scenes without distracting non-erotic passages. These erotic scenes are commonly scenes of willing, even anxious seduction, of sadistic defloration in mass orgies, of incestuous relations consummated with little or no sense of guilt, or superpermissive parent figures who initiate and participate in the sexual activities of their children, of profaning the sacred, of supersexed males and females, of Negroes and Asiatics as sex symbols, of male and particularly female homosexuality, and of flagellation, all described in taboo words. The sole purpose of pornographic books is to stimulate erotic response, never to describe or deal with the basic realities of life."

(As summarized by Lockhart and McClure, Censorship of Obscenity, 45 Minn.L.Rev. 63–64.)

See also the graphic description of the illicit traffic in "hard-core" pornography detailed in Chapter 1 of James Jackson Kilpatrick's "The Smut Peddlers" (1960).

likely that the Court upheld their constitutionality as imaginatively applied to hard-core pornography.

"We conclude, therefore, that the concept of obscenity held by most members of the Court is probably hard-core pornography, a conclusion consistent with the Court's 'rejection of obscenity as utterly without redeeming social importance.' "

This view is strongly confirmed by the per curiam decisions which followed Roth on distinctly mundane levels. In each on the citation of Roth the Court reversed United States Court of Appeals decisions that had upheld obscenity censorship, and demonstrated that in Roth it had placed really very tight restraints on what can constitutionally be censored as obscene.

The views of Messrs. Lockhart and McClure as to the meaning of Roth undoubtedly are shared by the Court of Appeals of New York which, in The People v. Richmond County News, Inc., supra, clearly indicated its interpretation of the New York statute as reaching only "hard-core" pornography was compelled by the Roth and the per curiam holdings. Chief Judge Desmond, concurring in the Richmond case, said so in so many words, and, concurring in Kingsley Intern. Pictures Corp. v. Regents of Univ. of N. Y., 4 N.Y.2d 349, 175 N.Y.S.2d 39, 151 N.E.2d 197, 207–208, observed that the Supreme Court in the per curiams must have looked at the challenged material and found it not obscene under Roth. Other cases which would seem to have shared the same views include those in the footnote below.[5]

One of the significant per curiams which followed Roth was Time Films Corporation v. City of Chicago, 355 U.S. 35, 78 S.Ct. 115, 2 L.Ed.2d 72. The Court of Appeals, 7 Cir., 244 F.2d 432, described the motion picture "The Game of Love," held obscene by it, as follows:

"We found that, from the beginning to end, the thread of the story is supercharged with a current of lewdness generated by a series of illicit sexual intimacies and acts. In the introductory scenes a flying start is made when a 16 year old boy is shown

[5] Excelsior Pictures Corp. v. City of Chicago, D.C.N.D.Ill., 182 F.Supp. 400; Commonwealth v. Moniz, 338 Mass. 442, 155 N.E.2d 762; City of Cincinnati v. Walton, Ohio Mun., 145 N.E.2d 407; United States v. Keller, 3 Cir., 259 F.2d 54; People ex rel. Burtman v. Silberglitt, 5 Misc.2d 847, 182 N.Y.S.2d 536.

completely nude on a bathing beach in the presence of a group of younger girls. On that plane the narrative proceeds to reveal the seduction of this boy by a physically attractive woman old enough to be his mother. Under the influence of this experience and an arrangement to repeat it, the boy thereupon engages in sexual relations with a girl of his own age. The erotic thread of the story is carried, without deviation toward any wholesome idea, through scene after scene. The narrative is graphically pictured with nothing omitted except those sexual consummations which are plainly suggested but meaningfully omitted and thus, by the very fact of omission, emphasized. * * *

"We do not hesitate to say that the calculated purpose of the producer of this film, and its dominant effect, are substantially to arouse sexual desires. We are of the opinion that the probability of this effect is so great as to outweigh whatever artistic or other merits the film may possess. We think these determinations are supported by the effect which this film would have upon the normal, average person." 244 F.2d 432, 436.

A second appeal, One Incorporated v. Olesen, 355 U.S. 371, 78 S.Ct. 364, 2 L.Ed.2d 352, was from the decision of the Court of Appeals of the Ninth Circuit, 241 F.2d 772, holding the magazine "One" and the advertisement in it of the magazine "Circle" which contained pictures and stories of homosexuality and lesbianism obscene. The Court of Appeals described its findings in this way:

"The article 'Sappho Remembered' is the story of a lesbian's influence on a young girl * * *. This article is nothing more than cheap pornography calculated to promote lesbianism. It falls far short of dealing with homosexuality from the scientific, historical and critical point of view.

"The poem 'Lord Samuel and Lord Montagu' is about the alleged homosexual activities of Lord Montagu and other British Peers and contains a warning to all males to avoid the public toilets while Lord Samuel is 'sniffing round the drains' of Piccadilly (London). The poem pertains to sexual matters of such a vulgar and indecent nature that it tends to arouse a feeling of disgust and revulsion. It is dirty, vulgar and offensive to the moral senses. * * *

"An examination of 'The Circle' clearly reveals that it contains obscene and filthy matter which is offensive to the moral senses, morally depraving and debasing, and that it is designed for persons who have lecherous and salacious proclivities.

"The picture and the sketches are obscene and filthy by prevailing standards. The stories 'All This and Heaven Too' and 'Not Til the End,' pages 32–36, are similar to the story 'Sappho Remembered,' except that they relate to the activities of the homosexuals rather than lesbians. Such stories are obscene, lewd and lascivious. They are offensive to the moral senses, morally depraving and debasing." 241 F.2d 772, 777, 778.

The third case, Sunshine Book Company v. Summerfield, 355 U.S. 372, 78 S.Ct. 365, 2 L.Ed.2d 352, involved a nudist magazine. The Court of Appeals, 101 U.S.App.D.C. 358, 249 F.2d 114, quoted with approval the language of Sunshine Book Company v. McCaffrey, 8 Misc.2d 327, 112 N.Y.S.2d 476, 483, that:

"Where the dominant purpose of nudity is to promote lust, it is obscene and indecent. The distribution and sale of the magazines in this case is a most objectionable example. The dominant purpose of the photographs in these magazines is to attract the attention of the public by an appeal to their sexual impulses.* * * Men, women, youths of both sexes, and even children, can purchase these magazines. They will have a libidinous effect upon most ordinary, normal, healthy individuals. Their effect upon the abnormal individual may be more disastrous." 249 F.2d 114, 118, 119.

The Supreme Court must have made an independent examination of the material in each case and found that censorship offended constitutional privileges, for the Court simply reversed on the citation of Roth, and so terminated the litigation and gave final protection to the material.

The material it protected had been thought obscene by the lower court judges, applying what they deemed to be the contemporary standards of the average or normal person. Yet the Supreme Court, as I interpret its actions, held the pictures and writings were not obscene under the Roth standards. I can only conclude that as of now the Supreme Court will permit the proscription only of hard-core pornography and I find nothing in the magazines before the Court coming within that category.

The Supreme Court in Roth, page 488 of 354 U.S., page 1311 of 77 S.Ct., page 1509 of 1 L.Ed.2d, said, speaking of "the fundamental freedoms of speech and press," that "Ceaseless vigilance is the watchword to prevent their erosion by Congress or by the States. The door barring federal and state intrusion into this area cannot be left ajar; it must be kept rightly closed and opened only the slightest crack necessary to prevent encroachment upon more important interests."

The background of Roth, and the three per curiams that followed, lead me to conclude that the door has been opened very slightly for the censors—not enough to permit them to get at the magazines in this case—and that the Roth standard, as understood and applied by the Supreme Court is a very tight standard, reaching only "hard-core" pornography. If I am right the application of the Maryland statute, applied as the majority has applied it in this case, was unconstitutional.

I would reverse the judgments appealed from.

Index

Dirty	Middle English *drit,* excrement
Filthy	Old Teutonic *foul.* At first, merely dirty in a physical sense. Now: morally foul or polluted; obscene.
Indecent	*In* = not + Latin *decere,* to become, to be fitting.
Lascivious	Latin *lascivus,* sportive; in bad sense: lustful, licentious.
Lewd	Old English *laewede,* of difficult etymology. Sense suggests formation on Roman *laicus,* lay. First meaning of lay: not clerical, not in holy orders. A lewd-frere was a lay-brother. Unlearned, unlettered. Rude, artless. Belonging to lower orders; common, low, vulgar. Ignorant, ill-bred. Bad, vile, evil, and so on. Finally: lascivious, unchaste.

Contributed by *The Oxford English Dictionary* via

87242